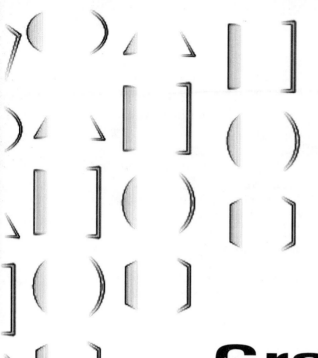

Graphics, Animation, and Multimedia

VOLUME **7** OF THE

Web Publishing Programming
Resource Kit

201 West 103rd Street
Indianapolis, IN 46290-1097
317-581-3500

To my parents, who don't have a computer-geek bone in their bodies. Thank you for that first computer (and the several purchases after that) and for continually encouraging, supporting, and nurturing me.

Copyright © 1997 by Sams.net Publishing

FIRST EDITION

International Standard Book Number: 1-57521-243-9

Library of Congress Catalog Card Number: 96-71698

2000 99 98 97   4 3 2 1

Interpretation of the printing code: the rightmost double-digit number is the year of the book's printing; the rightmost single-digit, the number of the book's printing. For example, a printing code of 97-1 shows that the first printing of the book occurred in 1997.

Composed in New Century Schoolbook and MCPdigital by Macmillan Computer Publishing

Printed in the United States of America

Trademarks

Publisher	Richard K. Swadley
Publishing Manager	Dean Miller
Director of Editorial Services	Cindy Morrow
Managing Editor	Mary Inderstrodt
Director of Marketing	Kelli S. Spencer
Assistant Marketing Managers	Kristina Perry
	Rachel Wolfe

Acquisitions Editor
Cari Skaggs

Development Editor
Brian-Kent Proffitt

Software Development Specialist
Patricia J. Brooks

Production Editor
Mary Inderstrodt

Copy Editor
Kris Simmons

Indexer
Erika Millen

Technical Reviewer
George Hoh

Technical Edit Coordinator
Lynette Quinn

Editorial Coordinator
Katie Wise

Editorial Assistants
Carol Ackerman, Andi Richter, Rhonda Tinch-Mize

Cover Designer
Jay Corpus

Book Designer
Louisa Klucznik

Copy Writer
Peter Fuller

Team Supervisors
Brad Chinn
Charlotte Clapp

Production
Sonja Hart, Mike Henry, Gene Redding, Shawn Ring

Overview

Part I   Graphics

   1   Graphic Design   3

   2   Color Theory and Color Models   27

   3   Typography   59

   4   Vector-Based Graphics   77

   5   Raster-Based Graphics   101

Part II   Animation

   6   Fundamentals of Animation   145

   7   2D Animation   161

   8   3D Animation   185

Part III   Multimedia

   9   Multimedia   229

   10   Interactive Multimedia Design Process   243

   11   Multimedia Fundamentals   273

   12   Interface Design and Metaphors   295

   13   Sound   317

   14   Video   341

   15   Immersive Environments: Virtual Reality   353

      Glossary   361

Appendix

   A   Graphics, Animation, and Multimedia Tools   377

      Index   385

Contents

PART I   Graphics

1   Graphic Design   **3**

    Eyeflow 5

        Positive and Negative Space 6

    Tone 9

        Balance and Layout 10

    Visual Appeal 13

    Consistency 15

    Communicative Power 17

    How the Browser Affects Layout 19

    Icons, Identities, and Abstractions 24

    Summary 25

2   Color Theory and Color Models   **27**

    The Occurrence of Color: Additive and Subtractive Colors 28

        Reflected Light 28

        Directed Light 31

    Attributes of Color 33

    Lighting Effect on Hues 34

    Interpretation of Color 41

        Visual Aspects 41

        Psychological Aspects 43

        Human Physiology 44

    Choosing Color Schemes 45

    The Negative Aspects of Color 48

    Theoretical Color Spaces 49

        Munsell 52

    Device-Dependent Color Models 53

        The CYM and RGB Color Models 53

    Browser Color 55

        Hexadecimal Color 56

        Calculating Hex 57

        Web Resources 58

    Summary 58

3   Typography   **59**

    Typefaces 65

    Characteristics 67

    Computer Fonts 70

        Vector Fonts 71

        Creating Fonts as Bitmaps 73

Styles 73

Choosing Fonts for Communication 75

Summary 75

4   Vector-Based Graphics   77

The Nature of PostScript 78

   Vector and Raster Images on the Web 80

Resolution 84

Device Independence 86

Advantages and Disadvantages of Vector Illustration 86

   The Nature of Vector Objects 88

   Closed Areas and Fills 89

   Grouping, Joining, and Boolean Operations 91

   Vector Elements and the Web 95

Rasterizing Vector Images 97

Summary 99

5   Raster-Based Graphics   101

The Nature of the Pixel 103

Device Dependency 104

Imaging Terms 105

   Image Resolution 105

   Image Size 109

   Image Bit Depth 111

   Browsers, Palettes, and Displays 125

   File Size 126

   Conclusions Concerning Raster Image Use 126

Layering and Sizing Images 127

   The Flatland Raster Environment 128

   The Layered Environment 129

Formats 135

   Graphics Interchange Format (GIF) 136

   Joint Picture Experts Group (JPEG) 136

   Other File Formats 138

   The Portable Network Graphics (PNG) Format 138

   Compression 139

Summary 142

PART II   Animation

6   Fundamentals of Animation   145

The Historical Perspective 147

Animation Fundamentals 148

   Methods of Integration 150

   Key Frames and In-Betweens 150

Frame Rate 152
Frame Size (Image Size) 152
Frame Bit Depth (Image Bit Depth) 154
Animation Software 155
2D Animations: Sprite, Vector, and Spline.............. 155
3D Animations: Motion Studies and Analysis........... 155
Limitations on the Web.. 157
Choosing Software and Hardware for Animation 158
Summary 159

7   2D Animation   161

Cel Contents 162
Static Frames 163
Raster Sprites.. 165
Vector Sprites.. 165
Paths of Motion 167
2D Animation Techniques 175
Onion-Skinning 176
Blending 177
Transparency 177
Source Images 178
2D Animation Effects 179
Color Cycling 179
Rotoscoping and Compositing 180
Chroma-Keying 180
Morphing 181
Filters 183
Summary 184

8   3D Animation   185

The Modeling Environment 187
Modeling Environment Variables 187
Types of 3D Models 191
Surface Modeling for Animation 194
Rendering Engines 199
Wireframe Rendering and Flat Shading 200
Gouroud 201
Phong 202
Radiosity and Ray-Tracing 203
The Rendering Environment 204
Cameras.. 206
Lighting 209

Object Textures and Characteristics 213
Procedural Mapping 219
The Animation Environment 220
Keyframe Animation 220
Paths, Translation, and Motion 221
3D Deformations 223
Kinematics, Inverse Kinematics, and Kinesiology 223
Particle Systems 224
Summary 225

PART III   Multimedia

9   Multimedia   **229**

Linearity 231
Linear Thinking: Inherent or Conditioned Behavior? 232
Linearity and Communication 233
Linearity and Learning 234
Linear Media 235
Non-Linear Media and Non-Linear Thinking 237
Hypermedia 238
Media That Support Non-Linear Communication 240
Summary 241

10   Interactive Multimedia Design Process   **243**

Planning 245
Nontransient Information 247
Transient Information 248
Content 249
Audience 254
Development 256
Delivery 258
Function 260
Design 263
Metaphor 264
Interface Design 266
Technical Design 268
Production 270
Implementation 271
Maintenance 271
Critical Points 272
Summary 272

11   Multimedia Fundamentals   **273**

The Multimedia Knowledge Base 274
The Development Team 276
    Developing the Content 277
    Developing Supporting Materials 277
    Networking Concerns 278
The Significance of the Browser 278
Browser Implications 279
How the Browser Functions 282
    Preferences 284
    The Cache 284
    Plug-Ins 285
    Scripting 286
    Embedded Programs 287
    Helper Applications 288
Other Internet Resources 289
    E-Mail 289
    News 289
    FTP 290
    Gopher 291
    Telnet 292
Summary 293

12   Interface Design and Metaphors   **295**

Interface Development 296
    Web Page Elements 298
Designing for Consistency 299
The Special Case: The Home Page 303
Designing for Efficiency 305
Designing for Control 307
Designing for Clarity 307
Designing for Practicality 310
Designing for Visual Appeal 310
Examples of Good Interface Design 311
Summary 316

13   Sound   **317**

Understanding the Two Types of Digital Audio 319
    Digital and MIDI: The Fundamental Difference 320
Advantages of a Digital World 322
Digital Audio: Is it Live or 324
    Sampling Rate 325
    Bit Depth 330

Channels: Monoaural and Stereo 331
File Sizes 333
Preparing to Sample Audio 334
MIDI Audio 336
Synthesized Sound 336
File Formats and Conversion 337
File Formats 337
Compression Technologies 338
Streaming 338
Comparison of Digitized and MIDI Sound 339
Summary 340

14   Video   341

Image Size, Frame Number, and Bit Depth 342
Animation Versus Video 345
Generating Video Clips 346
Compression Technologies 348
Video for Windows 349
QuickTime 350
MPEG 350
Streaming Versus Helper Applications 351
Summary 352

15   Immersive Environments: Virtual Reality   353

The Premise of Virtual Reality 354
Virtual Reality Systems 358
VRML and the Web 358
Other Implications 359
Summary 360

Glossary   361

A   Graphics, Animation, and Multimedia Tools   377

Graphics Tools 378
Other Graphics Tools 379
Animation Tools 380
Sound Tools 381
Video Tools 382
Authoring Tools 382
HTML Editors, Generators, and Site Management Tools 383
Browsers 384

Index   385

Acknowledgments

There are many people to thank for getting me involved in this project—first, the editors at Sams: Cari Skaggs and Brian Proffitt. In addition, I'd like to thank the others who have painstakingly worked on this book: Mary Inderstrodt, Lynette Quinn, and George Hoh.

Thanks also goes to the Department of Technical Graphics at Purdue University for giving me what I needed to write this book, as well as to all the students, to whom this book is written. Teaching you, teaches me. Go Purdue!

More than any other, I would like to thank my wife for the many hours she has sacrificed, allowing me to work on this project.

About the Author

James L. Mohler is Assistant Professor of Technical Graphics at Purdue University. He has produced interactive titles for national and international publishers, and provides technical training and media services to various industries through Sunrise Productions. James can be reached at jlmohler@tech.purdue.edu.

Technical Graphics at Purdue University prepares graphics managers and practitioners for careers in digital publication, illustration, modeling, animation, and engineering documentation specialties. You can visit the department at http://www.tech.purdue.edu/tg/.

Tell Us What You Think!

As a reader, you are the most important critic and commentator of our books. We value your opinion and want to know what we're doing right, what we could do better, what areas you'd like to see us publish in, and any other words of wisdom you're willing to pass our way. You can help us make strong books that meet your needs and give you the computer guidance you require.

Do you have access to CompuServe or the World Wide Web? Then check out our CompuServe forum by typing GO SAMS at any prompt. If you prefer the World Wide Web, check out our site at http://www.mcp.com.

> **note**
>
> If you have a technical question about this book, call the technical support line at 317-581-3833.

As the publishing manager of the group that created this book, I welcome your comments. You can fax, e-mail, or write me directly to let me know what you did or didn't like about this book—as well as what we can do to make our books stronger. Here's the information:

FAX: 317-581-4669

E-mail: opsys_mgr@sams.samspublishing.com

Mail: Dean Miller
            Sams.net Publishing
            201 W. 103rd Street
            Indianapolis, IN 46290

Conventions Used in This Book

The following conventions are used in this book.

> **note**
>
> A note box presents interesting pieces of information related to the surrounding discussion.

> **tip**
>
> A tip box offers advice or shows you an easier way to do something.

warning

A warning box advises you about potential problems and helps you steer clear of disaster.

HTML/path/
www.hrHTML/
path/www.hr
Chapter 8

This icon tells you where on the CD-ROM you can locate the file or code being discussed.

All code, filenames, and directory names appear in `monospace`. Placeholders (words that stand for what you actually type) in regular text appear in *`italic monospace`*.

When a line of code is too long to fit on only one line of this book, it is broken at a convenient place and continued to the next line. The continuation of the line is preceded by a code continuation character (➥). You should type a line of code that has this character as one long line, without breaking it.

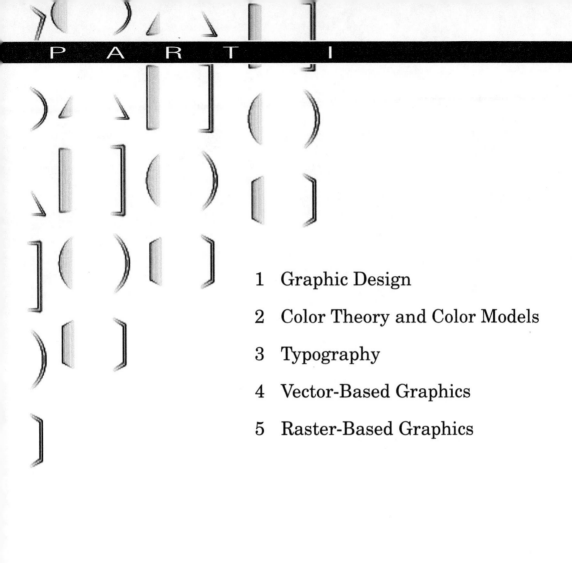

PART I

1   Graphic Design

2   Color Theory and Color Models

3   Typography

4   Vector-Based Graphics

5   Raster-Based Graphics

Graphic Design

When creating Web pages, one of your first concerns is the way the physical layout of the various elements appears. Graphic design is the way you lay out and present your pages—how the graphics, text, and other elements are arranged. The question for most developers is "How do you present your pages so that they are easily readable and visually stimulating?" Should you simply model your Web pages using traditional publications as your guide, or should you develop a unique Web page layout and design?

Much of what is currently being designed and delivered over the Web mimics the look of traditional publications; however, we must acknowledge that the Web is a completely unique medium when compared to traditional printed publications. The Web presents a nonlinear environment in which the user can choose what he or she wants to view. Because it is a nonlinear environment, the Web cannot be limited to a page-turning environment like that of a traditional publication. In addition, the Web allows you to use more than static text and graphics. With the variety of media elements that can be used, you should strive to make your Web site more than a traditional book or brochure in Web form. The Web is a unique medium that is slowly developing its look and feel.

Although the Web is a unique medium, many of the traditional graphic design principles still apply. In addition, many more are evolving, particularly ones that deal with the human-computer interface principles associated with graphic design. An important aspect of graphic design for the Web is that each page you create must be designed so that the audience can read it easily. Reading large segments of text can be laborious and not too stimulating when read from a computer monitor. There are other aspects that make designing for computer display different from designing for traditional publication. Arranging page elements a certain way can either hinder or enhance the communicability of your site's pages. The size of text, the arrangement of text, and the inclusion of graphics can all affect the audience's interpretation of your content. The layout of the elements that you use should not hinder the text information that is being presented; rather it should complement and complete it.

On your entire site, your page design should make the information readily available and easily accessible to your audience. One frustration for Web users is to have to spend a lot of time looking for the information or resources that they came to your site to find. The graphic design and layout of your site should not only be easy to read, but the graphic design should be such that navigating the information is not time-consuming. A very artistic-looking set of pages is good only if the information is easy to find as well as easy to read and digest. A page that is extreme or elaborately designed can often be difficult to navigate. Graphic design contributes in two significant ways to Web communication.

Graphic design is more than just making your pages look pretty. It strives to guide and direct the viewer's eye across a page. Using rules and other elements, you can draw attention to a specific area of a page or lead the user's eye away from a portion of the screen. Graphic design helps you control how the user digests your information, as in Figure 1.1, which shows a main graphic that is surrounded by a menubar. The surrounding elements help direct the audience's eyes to the center of the page. One of the most important things is to contain and direct the audience's eyes to the elements on the page. This helps to conduct the audience's attention by keeping their attention, not letting their eyes wander or be led off the page.

Graphics design affects delivery in these ways:

- By making each individual page easier to read, easier to interpret, and more aesthetically pleasing.
- By making the entire site easier to navigate so that the audience can readily find the information that they are looking for.

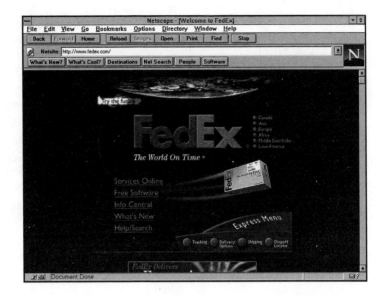

So what is it about the page layout that makes it effective? Is it simply the look? The content? Or is everything subjective? Well, when you browse the Web, you'll find that there are four main attributes on which most objective criticisms focus: eyeflow, tone, visual appeal, and consistency. These four areas create the legs for supporting communication and helping to enhance the content. Concerning page layout and design—the visual aspect—if any one of these items is weak, the overall impression of the page is that it has poor quality.

Eyeflow

The concept of eyeflow to some seems abstract, but it is simply the attempt of the developer to control the way the user views the page. It also helps make the information more digestible. Many items can be used to help corral the audience's eyes, but the most frequently used elements are simple rules created with the HTML <HR> tag. Using rules helps you break up information into blocks for the user.

Rules can be created using the HTML <HR> tag or inserted as inline images that are pictures, custom rules, or borders, as shown in Figure 1.2. In the figure is an inline image used as a border at the top of the page. The portion that says Digital Daily is an inline image that has been inserted into the page. Below this item are a couple of rules created with the <HR> tag. These surround miscellaneous information such as the date and other information.

Figure 1.2.
*Using HTML and
custom bitmap rules to
help format information
on a page.*

Most often you will want to create a custom border or rule as a bitmap and then insert it into your Web pages, rather than trying to utilize a vector element. Using bitmaps is the easiest and most visually pleasing method of inserting custom rules. Yet, no matter which method you choose, rules can be used to help guide the eyes of your audience and make your information easier to read.

Positive and Negative Space

Most well-designed Web pages not only use positive space effectively (spots with graphics and text), but they also use negative space effectively. It might seem absurd, but what you do with blank space is just as important as what you do with places in which you insert graphics.

Negative space (or white space) is an area on a page where no graphical or textural elements appear, as shown in Figure 1.3. In this figure, you see a considerable amount of negative space that contributes to the page's effectiveness. Alternatively, positive space is an area on a Web page that contains a media element such as text or a graphic. When you are creating pages, it is vitally important that you don't chock every nook and cranny with a visual element.

Have you ever tried to read a badly designed brochure? You know the kind I mean: horrendous brochures with graphics, lines, and text elements strewn all over the place—not to mention fonts that make your eyes sore. The same is true of many Web pages on the Internet. When you are designing, leave ample breathing room around the various text and graphic elements, as shown in Figure 1.4. Our eyes need the blank space around these elements to help us process the text and graphics. Concerning text, the white space helps us cognitively differentiate between paragraphs, columns, and text bodies. With graphics, the negative space aids us in visually interpreting the graphic being presented.

Figure 1.3.
Using negative space in design.

Figure 1.4.
Leaving ample space around text and graphics makes them easier to read and more visually appealing.

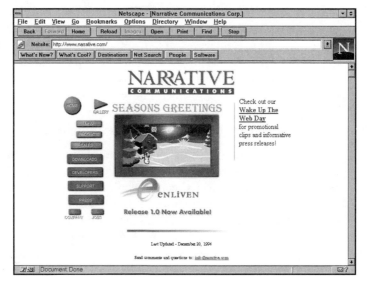

Figure 1.5 shows a well-designed Web page. In this figure, the negative space surrounding the graphic helps direct our eyes through the page. In design terms, this is called *eyeflow*. Eyeflow is the pattern or direction in which your eye flows across a page of information. Designers use text and graphics to direct the audience's eyes across the page and to draw attention to specific elements in the document.

Figure 1.5.
Directing the audience's eyes using positive and negative space.

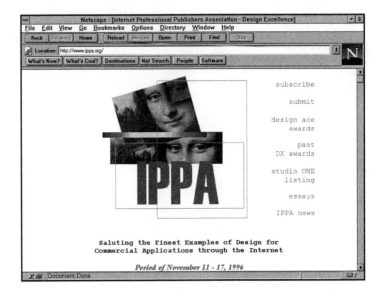

We are taught to read from left to right and top to bottom, so our eyes flow through a normal page of text. However, with a Web page composed of graphics and text, our eyes need to be directed in the way to read the page. Often Web pages are not designed like traditional documents. Whenever you use a nontraditional approach, you must help the reader by directing his or her attention. Using positive and negative space helps direct our eyes and focus our attention.

In Figure 1.5, the first thing that probably grabs your attention is the image in the middle of the screen, but then what do your eyes do? Note the white space on the left side of the screen, counterbalanced by the text on the right side. The absence of a balancing element on the left side (the negative space) causes our eyes to shift to the right side, drawing attention to the menu of text. In this way, the designer has indirectly pointed you to the navigational controls for the site. Hmm, quite clever, eh? But how many of us actually notice when this is happening? Well, to be honest, not very many. When you are developing the layout for your pages, however, focus on using your page elements to direct the audience's eyes.

Figure 1.5 shows one example of good graphic design in Web development. To design an effective page, you must control the audience's eyes. As is the case in the previous example, often you must start by getting the audience's attention (the center image in Figure 1.5). Then, using positive and negative space, you'll draw the audience's attention to a specific item. In our example, our eyes are drawn to the menu. In most Web pages, you eventually want to lead the audience's attention to your navigation items. In a scrolling environment, where pages extend beyond a single screen, this might be difficult to achieve at all times; however, you should try to present clearly the navigation items for your site.

As you are designing pages, be conscious of what the user's eyes will do as they view your page. On poorly designed pages, the user's eyes are often drawn off the page or left staring in one place. You really want to lead the audience's eyes, not just let them wander aimlessly until they figure out how to interpret your site. Use graphics, rules, and text elements to aid the user in finding his or her way around, by providing ample positive and negative space.

Tone

The second aspect of graphic design in Web pages is the way in which the pages themselves are presented to users. The *tone* of a site refers to the manner in which the Web document is presented to the audience. The tone of a Web site can be described as artistic, professional, avant-garde, and so on. Often the tone is focused on the intended audience for the site and is subjective, based on the audience's experience. A site might look artistic to one person but to another might not. Regardless, the tone of a site is affected by the layout of the pages and graphics. Let's take a closer look at how tone is created by the layout of the page. As we look at the overall layout of Web pages, keep in mind that there are several subordinate things that build toward this overall tone as well.

Figure 1.6 shows a Web page that presents a very professional tone; in other words, it looks like a formal business page. Let's examine why. First, notice the overall layout of the page. Notice how many of the elements are aligned and create a very formatted look. This is one way to create the tone of a site: through the balance of the items on the page.

Figure 1.6.
*Page layout contributes
to the tone of a Web site.*

Balance and Layout

Balance describes how the page elements are arranged visually, comparing one
half of a page to another. A page that has an equal number of elements on each
side of the page would have a *symmetrical balance*. A page with unequal elements
on each side would be said to have an *asymmetrical balance*, as shown in Figure
1.7. In general, a symmetrical balance presents a more professional, formalized
tone, whereas an asymmetrical balance is more informal and aesthetic.

Figure 1.7.
*Symmetrical and
asymmetrical balance.*

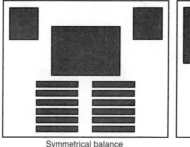
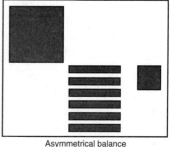

Symmetrical balance   Asymmetrical balance

As you'll remember from Figure 1.6, the page does not strictly adhere to a
completely formal balance definition, but it still presents the site with a professional tone. Overall, the page would be classified as formally balanced, but the
alignment of elements helps to create this formal look even though not explicitly
adhering to the definition.

Look at another site with a professional tone. Figure 1.8 follows the traditional idea of a formal balance. Notice all the elements are equally on either side of the screen. This presents a very formal presentation of the information. The highly structured and formal look is often required by professional organizations. A formal appearance, however, doesn't have to be aesthetically unappealing to the artistic crowd. As we'll see shortly, there is a middle ground that can be reached.

Figure 1.8.
Another site that uses formal balance.

In all of the preceding examples, you saw how the actual layout of the elements on the Web page contributes to the tone of the site. The tone is also formed by the look of the individual elements. Asymmetrical balance is generally used for aesthetic purposes, and symmetrical balance is used for a professional look. As you have seen, other elements also can contribute. For example, a specific typefont, graphic, or alignment of elements can aid in presenting the site professionally. In any site, the tone becomes stronger as more of the elements are presented in a similar manner. If all the elements on the page are presented the same way and with the same look and feel, the tone of the page becomes very strong and consistent. If there are conflicting elements—elements with varying styles—the page loses its tonal coherency.

Aside from formally balanced sites, you can also present an avant-garde, or nontraditional, look to your site by using more of an artistic flare in your pages. As discussed earlier, the whole idea of what tone is needed centers on your audience. What do they expect to see? How do they expect it to be presented? If your audience is made up of business professionals, use a symmetrical balance in your page. If flavoring your site for the artsy type, use an informal balance, as shown in Figure 1.9.

Figure 1.9.
Providing an artistic look through asymmetrical balance.

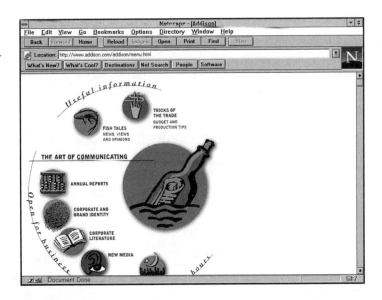

So what makes something look artistically designed? Notice in Figure 1.10 the asymmetrical look of the Web page. This is the first thing that contributes to the artistic look. Secondly, all the individual elements, such as text and graphics, provide a flare for the dramatic. The elements flow together and intersect, creating, as it were, a piece of art within the page itself. Lastly, the fonts that are used also contribute to make a piece that screams "I am avant-garde!"

Figure 1.10.
Aesthetic qualities presented in a Web page.

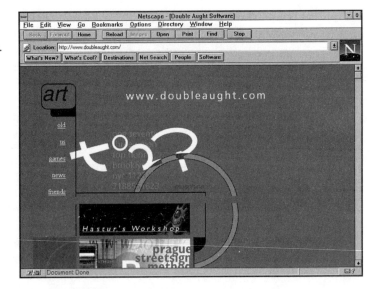

Much of what is presented on the Web, as well as the judgment of whether the pages are good and bad, is subjective. It is based on past experiences—what you are expecting versus what you have experienced in the past. Some sites might be avant-garde to you but not to me. Really, the term avant-garde describes a paradigm shift—a change from what we really expected. It is often used to describe something that is out of the ordinary. As you're surfing the Web, be conscience of things people incorporate into their Web pages that attract your attention. Also try to figure out why it attracts your attention in either a positive or negative way.

The previous figures showed opposing ends of the tonal spectrum. More than likely, most of your pages will be a combination of the aesthetic and professional, as shown in Figure 1.11. Carefully designed pages, centered around the audience, will increase the satisfaction of your audience and guarantee that return visit or the all-important bookmark.

Figure 1.11.
Combining the aesthetic
and the professional.

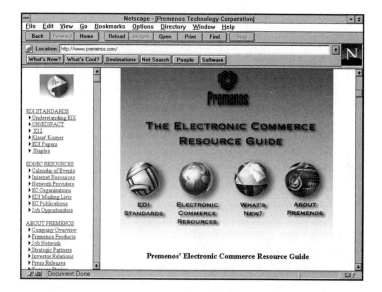

Visual Appeal

A third item that contributes to communication is visual appeal. Let's face it, this is what the Web is really about: allowing users to browse the myriad of information in a graphically pleasing way. Being able to look through the hundreds of pages of information without the graphics wouldn't be much more than a glorified Gopher menu. Strip a page of its graphics, and it will likely appear on Yahoo's Worst Top Ten list.

The visual appeal of a page is focused around several things. All the elements contribute to visual effectiveness, none more than graphics, as shown in Figure 1.12. Notice how the center graphic instantly grabs your attention, while also presenting what is at the site. A well-designed, sharp-looking graphic will always attract attention, but only when it is relevant to the content being provided and to the audience for whom the content is intended.

Figure 1.12.
Appealing to your audience through graphics.

The visual appeal of a page can be significantly hampered without design savvy. As you are designing, look for ways to intelligently incorporate graphics to enhance, support, or complement your site's content. You might want to use a graphic to show your site structure, as shown in Figure 1.13. The home page shown in Figure 1.13 is well-designed; its graphic quickly gives the reader an idea of what is at the site and where he or she can go. But what makes the graphic so sufficient by itself? Negative space, visual clarity of the buttons, and the typefont used all contribute to the effectiveness of this splash page graphic.

There are many different ways to effectively use graphics. Figure 1.14 shows a very artistic way to present the site's structure using graphics. Again, we see the same characteristics running through this graphic. It's well done because of the way negative space, visual clarity, and fonts all work together. The next couple of sections examine the common threads that can be found in all well-designed Web pages.

Figure 1.13.
A splash page graphic that shows the site's structure in an appealing way.

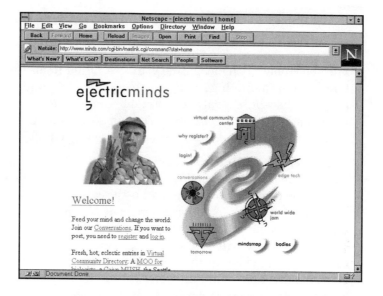

Figure 1.14.
An effective, yet artistic home page.

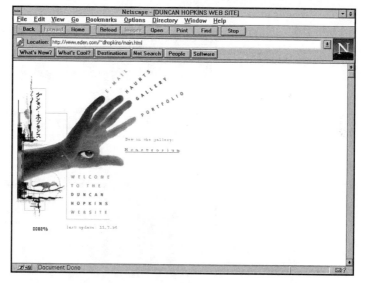

Consistency

The last item that contributes to well-designed communication is consistency. Consistency concerns navigation elements but can also relate to many other elements that occur throughout your Web site. A site in which navigation items shift from one location to another across pages frequently disorients the user. One of the characteristics of good site design is familiarizing your audience with how your pages work. Shifting navigation items around on the page will make the user uncomfortable when navigating your site. Other items that contribute to consistency include a running headline or logo, as well as multimedia elements used in the same place on several pages. Establishing conventions, you can make the user more comfortable with your site. You can also reduce the amount of time it takes for the user to download subsequent pages at your site.

You can create and maintain consistency at your site by using common elements on your pages, as shown in Figure 1.15. For example, you might use a title bar or navigation bar on all your pages, as is the case with this site's pages. As you read earlier, one of the main things you must do is familiarize your audience with your site's environment. If the audience has to continually search your pages for how to navigate, they will become disassociated with the content—and more concerned with navigation than acquiring information. Strive to create common elements that appear in the same location on every page. This will help to create consistency across your pages.

Figure 1.15.
Common elements across pages create consistency.

Often the elements that you use for navigation and eyeflow should be presented in the same place on every page. For example, a navigation bar at the side of the page (see Figure 1.16) tells the user that he or she can expect it to be there on every page. As you are surfing, notice how often you see an element on one page, such as a navigation bar, and then expect to see it in the same place on the other pages.

What happens if the location of the bar changes on another page? You have to search for the darn thing, right? Consequently, you become separated from the information—the thing you where focused on—to search for the silly navigation bar. Small things like this become significant hurdles for users. Some will exit stage left. As you are designing, design for consistency!

Figure 1.16.

Navigation and eyeflow elements are often prime choices to appear across pages.

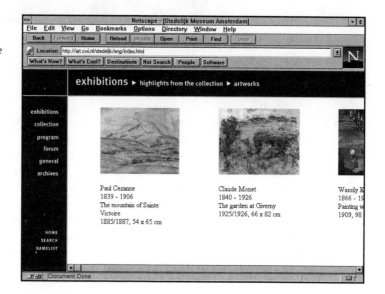

Communicative Power

As most developers know, rule number one in multimedia and hypermedia development is that content is king. Poorly designed content can never be masked. No matter the design or how many slick graphics, dancing bullets, or animated elements are added, if the content is poor, the site is poor. It's like dressing-up the exterior or interior of a house with a cracked foundation. It won't sell, because the footing on which everything else rests is unstable. The same is true of poor content. The content is the foundation from which communication occurs and which all supporting elements enhance and clarify.

Communication is a process that can be described graphically, as shown in Figure 1.17. For communication to occur, by definition, a sender must send a message, and a receiver must receive and comprehend the message. Also involved in the communication process is the issue of environmental noise.

Figure 1.17.
The communication model.

Sender   **Message**   **Receiver**

In Web communication, noise is something with which we are most concerned. As shown in Figure 1.18, noise disrupts communication. Noise distracts the receiver and inhibits reception of the message. Noise can, and most often does, occur from the sender in the form of poor content, graphics, or design. Many sites on the Web have things to say, but because of noise, their message does not get through. We must understand that today, people are inundated with information. When a message is blocked or surrounded with noise, it can be misunderstood, misinterpreted, or outright ignored. A site must communicate clearly, effectively, and precisely for maximum impact. For this to happen, the content, graphics, and design must be centered upon the needs of the audience.

Figure 1.18.
Noise disrupts communication.

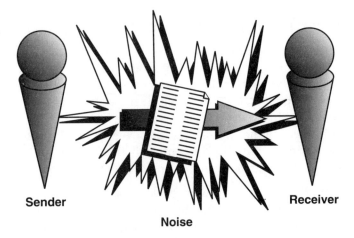

Sender   **Receiver**

Noise

In reality, creating a product that communicates effectively, whether it be a book, an article, a CD-ROM, or a Web site, requires the use of careful planning so that the product itself is successful. The success of such a product is determined by how well the message is conveyed and received by the audience. For the most part, creating a good Web site can be summed up in one word: *planning*—and design is largely involved with this. Most sites fail because issues arise that were not considered during the site's conception. People instantly jump behind a computer and start pushing pixels and spewing code, inevitably creating, in most cases, a horrid site. There is no replacement for time spent planning a site.

How the Browser Affects Layout

As you are working with Web documents, keep in mind that HTML is a semantic language. This means that the HTML code loosely defines the way elements on the screen—text and graphics—should be laid out. It is the browser, however, that actually composes the text and graphics after download. This means that each browser presents the contents of a Web page a little differently, as shown in Figures 1.19 and 1.20. This is due to differences in the way the HTML coding is interpreted by browsers, differences in the operating systems, and differences in the features the browser supports. Predominantly, the look of the page is affected by both the browser and platform on which the browser is running.

Figure 1.19.
Web page shown in Netscape.

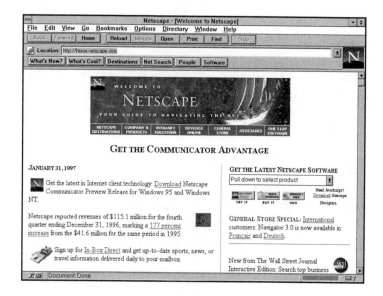

Because every Web page is composed on-the-fly, the browser can be thought of as a real-time HTML interpreter. It works similarly to interpreters that execute programming code a line at a time. The code itself, unlike an executable application, is read and executed on-the-fly. Problems or bugs don't appear when the user is entering code. Errors appear when the code is interpreted or executed.

With HTML, errors and undesirable formatting appear after the HTML code is loaded into the browser.

Figure 1.20.
Web page shown in NCSA Mosaic.

Another similarity between interpreted code and HTML is that both are nothing more than ASCII text, as shown in Figure 1.21. HTML code can be created in any text editor, as long as it stores the recorded file as simple or plain text. You can use a simple text editor such as WordPad (Windows 95), Notepad (Windows 3.x), or Simple Text (Macintosh) to create HTML files.

Figure 1.21.
HTML code is nothing more than a plain text file.

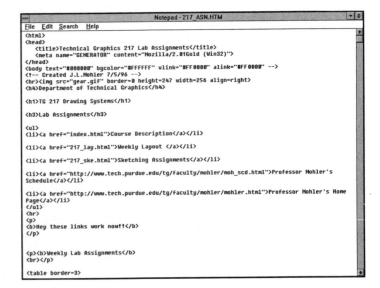

After HTML code is entered into a simple text file, the code can then be loaded into the interpreter (browser), and you see how the file works and how it is displayed. Because there are differences in the way different browsers interpret HTML code and because you can only see the differences in the browser, it is always a good idea to test your HTML code on various browsers to get a feel for how it displays when the user loads it.

Although browsers are a big part of the whole process that makes the Web function, to many they are a troublesome foe with which to work. Because of the wide variety of browsers used on the Net, it is difficult to code a Web page so that it looks exactly the same from every browser. Heck, it's nearly impossible to make a page look exactly the same across all browsers, as shown in Figures 1.22 and 1.23.

Figure 1.22.
Viewing a page in Netscape Navigator.

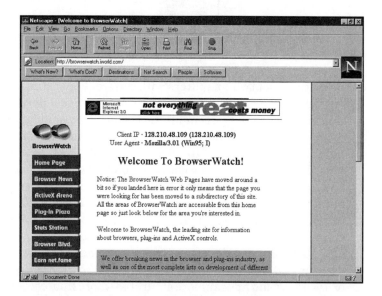

For the most part, the differences among browsers are subtle but noticeable, particularly if you are trying to get a specific formatted design every time. In many instances, it is important to get a relatively standard look across browsers. For now, realize that there are minor differences in the way HTML code is interpreted from browser to browser.

In addition to the browser, the operating system or platform can also affect the way in which the browser combines text and graphics. The operating system affects Web pages in two ways that include color and font issues.

Figure 1.23.
Viewing a page in
Microsoft Explorer.

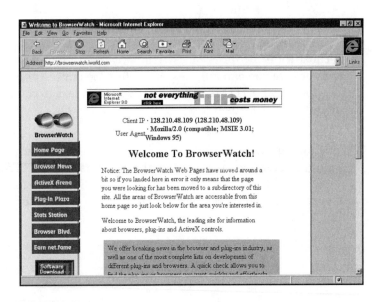

If you could set two computers with different operating systems side by side and view the same graphic image, you would notice a perceivable difference in the colors between the two computers. Generally speaking, colors from one platform to another appear different in value and saturation. The *value* of a color is the lightness or darkness of the particular color, such as a light blue versus a dark blue. The *saturation* of a color is the pureness of the color, such as a fluorescent blue compared to a subdued blue. Some of the apparent color shifting could be noticed just because of differences in the way computer hardware is manufactured. Variability and manufacturing errors are natural. But the way the operating system creates color is also a factor in this color shift. If you set a PC and Mac side by side, you would notice that the colors on the Macintosh are desaturated (not as pure) and lighter in value than the colors on a PC. The colors on the PC would appear more saturated (more fluorescent) and somewhat darker in value. If you threw in a UNIX box, the color change could be anywhere in between. In Chapter 2, "Color Theory and Color Models," you'll take a closer look at issues relative to colors and cross platform concerns.

The second operating system attribute that can affect the way a page is displayed is the typefont. A *typefont,* or font, is a set of characters with similar attributes, such as similar heights, widths, and spacing. Examples of typefonts include Arial,

Helvetica, and Times. Because of differences in the styles, widths, and heights of various typefaces, the text can shift significantly from platform to platform. This presents a problem if you are trying to tightly align text and graphics on a Web page. On one platform, the page might look good, but on another, the text might give you an undesirable appearance as it flows around graphics.

As you look at a typeface, the actual differences in size and spacing might not be perceivable, but additive differences cause the text and graphics to shift, as shown in Figure 1.24. Let's say the difference between text heights across platforms is approximately 1/8 of an inch and we have 64 lines of text flowing around some graphics. Multiplying the 1/8 inch by 64 lines would cause the text to shift by 1 inch at the end of the page. It would definitely be a noticeable shift, eh? Figures 1.24 and 1.25 show a comparison of a page shown in the same browser on different platforms. However, right now we're not going to worry about how to control this difference, but we do need to be aware of its overall effect. In Chapter 3, "Typography," you'll take a closer look at both the technical and design attributes of fonts in Web pages.

Figure 1.24.
Text appearance in Windows.

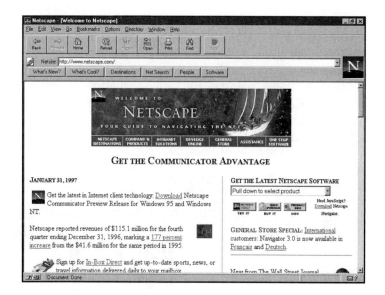

Figure 1.25.
Text appearance in Macintosh.

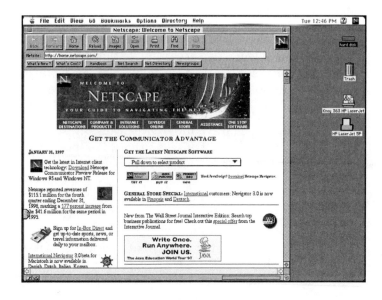

Icons, Identities, and Abstractions

Here is a final note before closing this chapter. As a designer, one of the most common things you do is create graphical abstractions or representations of clickable items, using icons, logos, and other graphics. An example would be a graphic that represents a portion of your site, as shown in Figure 1.26. Notice in the figure that the designer has created graphic representations that also incorporate text, making the areas of the Web site more apparent.

Figure 1.26.
Using graphic representations.

The way you design graphical icons, navigation buttons, and so on is based on assumptions you make concerning the audience. You must be very careful when using graphics in your designs. Because the Web is a global medium, some assumptions might not be apparent to your users. If you decide to use graphical icons, identities, or abstractions, make sure you use text with these items for more apparent relationships between what you intended and what the audience will interpret it as. In Chapter 10, "Interactive Multimedia Design Process," you'll take a closer look at designing around your audience and what safe assumptions you can make.

Summary

In this chapter you have seen the two main purposes of Web page design. The first is to make each individual page easier to read, easier to interpret, and more aesthetically pleasing. The second aim of Web page design is to make the entire site easier to navigate so that the audience can readily find the information that they are looking for. Designing effective Web pages requires careful planning for eyeflow, tone, visual appeal, and consistency. Almost all design criticisms focus on these four areas. Web pages should be easy to find, easy to read, easy to understand, and should present the readers what they need, when they need it. As you design Web pages, you'll find that a single Web page might look different if viewed from different browsers or on different platforms. The biggest differences are due to color discrepancy and font contrariety across platforms and browsers.

2

Color Theory and Color Models

When you are designing graphics, animations, and multimedia elements, there are several things that you should be aware of concerning color. When you see an effective media element, certainly the colors that were used in it are not by happenstance. Much planning goes into creating media elements, and color is one attribute that contributes to media element effectiveness. The interpretation and the communicative value of the media element can be either helped or hindered by the colors you choose. For example, the colors orange and yellow connote warning, at least in the U.S. Yet, not considering the color's perceived physiological attributes, which can vary, can be a hindrance in certain situations. As you are designing, you must be conscientious about both the psychological and visual aspects of the colors you use.

In addition, you must understand the ways in which colors are defined in the computer world. Colors associated with bitmap images are defined differently than those defined in the Web browser. In reality, there are a certain number of colors that can be viewed for any given device. Not every device can display, print, output, or receive every color that exists or that can be created.

In this chapter you will take a look at the various aspects of color and how they relate to Web design. You'll see how the human senses perceive color as well as how the brain interprets what it sees. This chapter doesn't go into the physiological aspects of this issue (entire books are devoted to that), but it does touch on how, often unknowingly, color connotes more than just what we see. In this chapter you'll see how colors are defined for the various media elements that are used on the Web. Let's begin this discussion by looking at what causes color.

The Occurrence of Color: Additive and Subtractive Colors

All color is the result of light, either reflected or direct. Colors we see in nature are the result of reflected pigments. Our eyes see only a portion of the actual colors that exist. There are actually millions of colors that exist, and even a trained eye can distinguish only around 50,000 of them.

The occurrence of color is actually an amazing phenomenon. By either reflecting or directing portions of the spectrum contained within visible light, color is created and perceived. *Reflected light* is what occurs naturally in our daily world. Everything you view in the real world is a result of reflected light. Following the discussion of reflected light, you will take a look at *directed light,* which is the man-made process used in computer monitors and other cathode ray tube devices to create color.

Reflected Light

Everything that our physical senses perceive is composed of analog data. *Analog data* is simply data that is composed of frequency variations. All the color that we see is composed of waves, which are frequency variations that belong to the electromagnetic spectrum. (See Figure 2.1.) Sound, too, is analog data. Pressure differences caused by speakers or other sound generating devices cause waves to occur, which our sense of hearing can perceive.

All light sources emit waves uniformly in all directions. Visible light is actually a very small portion of the electromagnetic spectrum. The portion of this spectrum that we can actually perceive as light and color is quite small, as shown in Figure 2.1.

Figure 2.1.
The electromagnetic
spectrum.

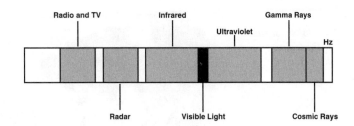

The portion of the spectrum that we see as visible light is actually composed of many waves that occur at different frequencies. Each frequency represents a different color. Visible light is composed of seven distinguishable colors from which all the other colors in nature are created. Figure 2.2 shows the band of the visible spectrum and how it is divided into colors. The seven naturally occurring colors are red, orange, yellow, green, blue, indigo, and violet (ROY G. BIV, for those who remember trying to memorize them in high school).

Figure 2.2.
The seven naturally
occurring colors of the
visible spectrum.

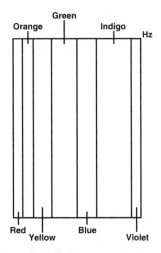

Any time light strikes an object, certain wavelengths (colors) are absorbed by the object that the light strikes. Alternatively, certain wavelengths (colors) are reflected back toward the eyes of the individual viewing the object. The reflected waves (colors) give the appearance that the object is a specific color. For example, in Figure 2.3, the object, a red block, absorbs all of colors except for the red wavelength. The red wavelength is not absorbed, so it is reflected back toward the eyes of the viewer, making the block appear red.

Figure 2.3.
A red block absorbs all wavelengths (colors) except the red wavelength.

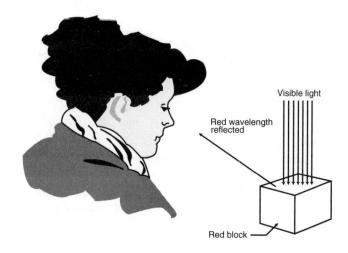

All colors that you see in the real world are the result of reflected wavelengths. When an object reflects all wavelengths (colors), it appears white. All color is reflected back toward your eyes. When an object absorbs all wavelengths (colors), it appears black, because no colors are being reflected back toward your eyes, as shown in Figure 2.4.

Figure 2.4.
Why black and white objects appear as they do.

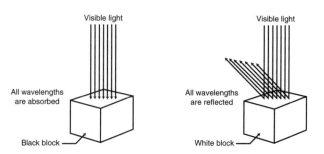

The theory of reflected colors is used daily in business and industry. For those of you who come from a publication background, you've probably been working with reflected color for a long time. However, when applied to print-based media reflected-color, this theory is called *subtractive color theory*. In essence, colors are subtracted from white paper, which, as you have seen, reflects all color. By adding pigments to white paper, colors are created by subtraction from a page that is already reflecting all colors toward the viewer. The primary colors, or colors from which all other colors are created, are cyan, yellow, and magenta. Figure 2.5 shows the subtractive primaries and the colors that can be created from them.

Notice the secondary primaries, or the colors created by mixing two primary colors. All colors that can be created on printed media are a result of cyan, yellow, and magenta.

Figure 2.5.
The subtractive primaries.

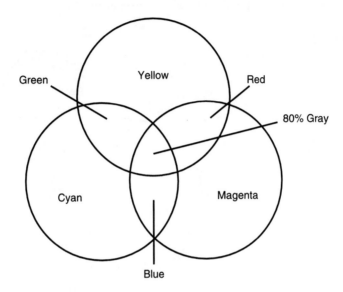

Note that the combination of cyan, yellow, and magenta should create a pure black, but it does not. It actually creates a dull 80 percent gray. In the print industry, four-color printing uses cyan, yellow, magenta, and black (CYMK) so that a true black can be obtained and so that shadows appear more photo-real. Printing with CYMK is called four-color process printing. Each color is printed over the other and creates a full-color image as a result.

Directed Light

When we are printing on paper, subtractive colors are used. This works only when the printing occurs on white paper, because the white paper is reflecting all colors back toward the viewer. But what happens when we want to create a projected image, such as for displaying color on a monitor or television screen? To display an image on these devices requires adding color to a black screen, rather than subtracting color from a white page.

To create color images on computer monitors requires the use of directed light, or additive colors. Additive colors add color to a black or dark screen. Rather than using CYMK as with subtractive colors, use the additive primaries—red, blue, and green (RGB), as shown in Figure 2.6. Notice the colors that are created from mixing any two additive primaries. These are the secondary primaries for additive colors: cyan, yellow, and magenta.

Figure 2.6.
The additive primaries.

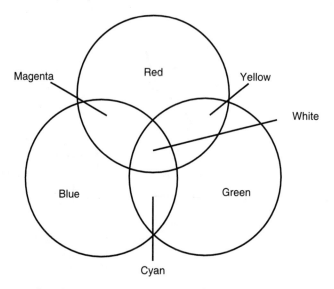

Note that with additive colors, the addition of all of the colors creates white. When no color is added, you have black. Let's take a closer look at this.

Additive colors are used with any directed light projection device, such as a television or computer monitor. Inside a computer monitor are three electron guns, which each direct a single primary color. (See Figure 2.7.) There is one gun for red, one for blue, and one for green. At the front of the monitor is a focusing screen that focuses on clustered dots of color. For any given pixel on the screen, there is a red, green, and blue portion. How much light is received by each portion—red, green, and blue—determines the color of the pixel. If all three parts are at maximum intensity, the pixel is white. If all three parts are at minimum intensity, no color is being projected; therefore, the pixel is black.

Figure 2.7.
*The phosphor guns in a
cathode ray tube use
additive color.*

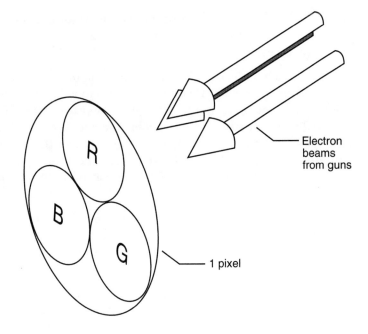

Electron
beams
from guns

1 pixel

Attributes of Color

All color that you can see can be described and defined by three primary
characteristics. You probably describe colors as, for example, a dark blue, a
fluorescent blue, a light blue, a bright blue, and so on. Every color, however, has
three dimensions: hue, value, and saturation. Much of what we perceive concerning a color is dependent upon these three characteristics.

The first of these characteristics is *hue*. Often we refer to a color by its name, such
as red, green, blue, and so on. The word "color" is synonymous with hue. A hue is
a property of the wavelengths of light.

The second characteristic is the *value* of the color. This refers to the amount of
white or black in the color. The difference between pink and red is an issue of
value. To create pink from red, you would add white to the hue. This creates a tint
of the red—pink. Alternatively, compare a dark red to the same red value. You
arrive at the dark red by adding black to the red hue. This creates a shade of the

red hue—a dark red. When you think of the value of a color, realize that the tints and shades of a color are created by adding *achromatic* colors (white, black, or gray) to the color.

When dealing with the value of a color, a common term that is used is *contrast*. Contrast is predominantly due to changes in value; however, saturation, which you'll read about in a minute, also contributes to contrast. Contrast describes the value differences between two or more adjacent colors. The higher the contrast, the greater the difference in values. The lower the contrast, the smaller the difference in values. One of the key characteristics of good graphics is the use of contrasting values or colors. Often, poor graphics have very little contrast and appear flat.

The final characteristic of color is *saturation*. The saturation of a color describes the purity of a hue. For example, red is more saturated than pink because pink has white added to red. Slate blue is less saturated than primary blue because it has black added to the hue.

Each color can be thought of as a mixture of a particular hue with either other hues or achromatic colors. The portion of the pure hue determines the saturation level. For example, to determine the level of saturation for a particular pink, you would determine how much red is in the hue. The pink might have a saturation of 45 percent, meaning that 45 percent of it is red, whereas the remaining 55 percent is white.

Every color can be measured or defined by its hue, value, and saturation. The same method, however, won't work for every device that exists, such as a computer monitor, application, and television screen. For each device, you must be able to define the number of colors that it can utilized. A little later in the chapter, in the section titled "Theoretical Color Spaces," you'll read about the methods of defining colors for various devices including those that actually exist.

Lighting Effect on Hues

Artists re-create what they see or imagine. How is it that we can all be in the same environment and see the same things, yet when it comes to creating a graphical representation of what we see, we all come up with different results? We all "see" the same things, but we perceive differently. Individual skill in re-creating what is perceived differs from person to person. But being really good at creating graphics depends upon perception.

Have you ever taken the time to look at a house or building on a bright and sunny day? In the Midwest, we haven't had many sunny days lately, but when it does happen, how often do we really look at how the light illuminates the house? How many of us notice the shadows and how they fall on the house, the landscape, and the surrounding area? In addition, how do the colors of light, shade, and shadow areas differ?

If you compare an average image and an exceptional image, what separates them? More than likely, the lighting has something to do with it. Textures, color, and geometry all contribute to overall effectiveness, but lighting inevitably separates the excellent from the average.

In most of the graphics you will deal with, the shadows and light areas are probably not as complex as those on a house, but they are equally important to the perception of the graphic. The hues of the light surfaces (those receiving direct light) should be lighter than those in shade (surfaces opposite the light source). In addition, there should be a difference in value of the hues between shade surfaces and shadow areas, areas where light is blocked by another object, as shown in Figure 2.8. The location of all these areas is determined by the source and direction of light. Where the light is positioned determines the saturation and value of the color appearing on the particular surface.

note

Because this book is in black and white, you will only be able to see the contrast. You can, however, see how the values differ from light, shade, and shadow areas.

Figure 2.8.
Light, shade, and shadow surfaces.

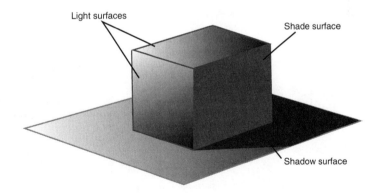

To create effective graphics, you must analyze anything you want to create in relationship to light sources. To get accurate representations requires looking at a source, such as a real object or a sample image, to determine how the lighting affects the colors and how the composition of the colors creates the image. In the previous chapter you saw how design affects the layout of your page. Here you will see how to create accurate and consistent lighting and color in your pages and graphics.

In the following example, you will see how shadows are cast on a 3D button. When you are designing Web pages, you don't actually see the button as presented here (in a three-dimensional view) but rather in a two-dimensional orientation. I'll use a 3D example for explanatory purposes.

Any time you are striving to achieve realistic lighting and color, you must first analyze what it is that you are drawing or creating. Often, a small sketch study is needed. Simply create a quick sketch and use it for analysis.

The first step in defining each of the surfaces is to determine the direction and elevation of a light source, as shown in Figure 2.9. A light source has both a direction and an elevation, which are used to determine each of the surface types, as well as to cast the shadows. When you begin planning your graphic, decide the direction of your light source. In areas where less light is being directed, the value of your hues will be darker. In areas receiving more light, your hue values will be lighter. You might also want to adjust the saturation levels of hues in these areas to get a more dramatic effect.

Figure 2.9.
Determining a light source direction and elevation.

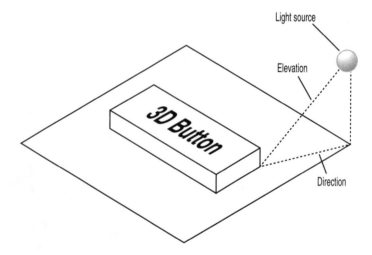

After you've assigned a theoretical light source, determine those surfaces that are directly receiving light, as shown in Figure 2.10. If you are using a sketch, label the light surfaces with a letter L. These are the surfaces that are directly hit by the light and will be the lightest in value.

Figure 2.10.
Determining light surfaces.

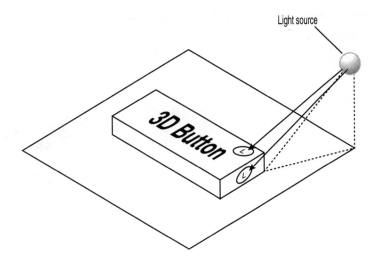

Next, determine which surfaces on the object will be opposite the light source, as shown in Figure 2.11. Label these surfaces S, for shade surfaces. These surfaces will be around a value of 50 percent on a hundred point scale from black to white and are receiving ambient light. *Ambient light* is the amount of light available without the light source.

Figure 2.11.
Determining shade surfaces.

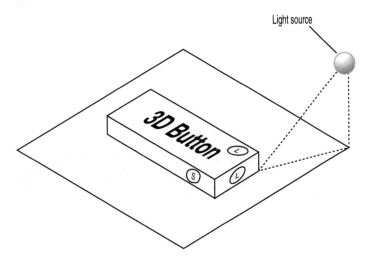

After you've determined the light and shade surfaces, find the intersection of these surfaces, as shown in Figure 2.12. The intersection clues you in to which surface edges will be casting shadows.

Figure 2.12.
*Determining lines that
are casting shadows.*

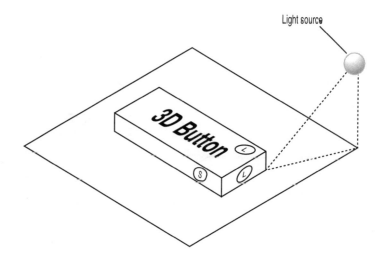

Now that you know what edges are casting shadows, you can use the direction and elevation of the light source to project the shadows of the object. Trace the connecting points on the shadow line to the plane the object is sitting on, as shown in Figure 2.13. Project away from the object using the direction vector (light ray) from your light source. Project down from the shadow line point to the direction line using the elevation vector. Play connect-the-dots to create the limits of the shadow.

Figure 2.13.
*Casting the shadows of
buttons.*

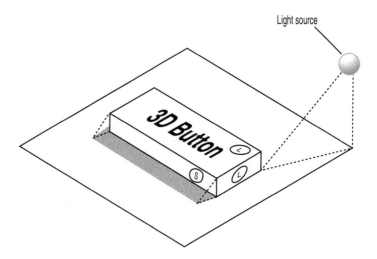

To finish the button you've been reading about requires colorizing and finishing the image, as shown in Figure 2.14. If you plan out your surface values as described, finishing the image is as easy as painting by the numbers. Realize that the procedure for determining light, shade, and shadow surfaces can be used any time you create graphics and need to make sure the lighting is correct. For most of your buttons, you can simply create them without casting the shadow because you might already know what they should look like. The technical phrase *fudge them in* applies here. Using this projection process every time you needed to create 3D objects with shadows would be absurd. But there might be times when you don't have a clue what the shadows should look like, let alone where they are.

Figure 2.14.
Finished view of the 3D button.

There are three general rules to follow when you are casting shadows using projection:

1. Any shadow can be found by projecting multiple points on the shadow line to the surface receiving the shadow and connecting the points, as shown in Figure 2.15.

2. If a line casting a shadow is parallel to the surface receiving the shadow, the shadow will be parallel to the line casting the shadow, as shown in Figure 2.16.

Figure 2.15.
Projecting points to find shadows.

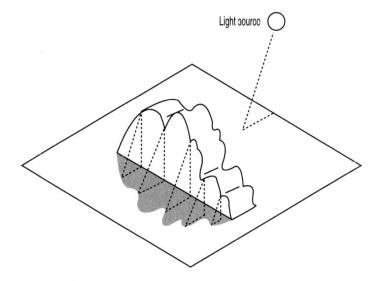

Figure 2.16.
Parallel relationship.

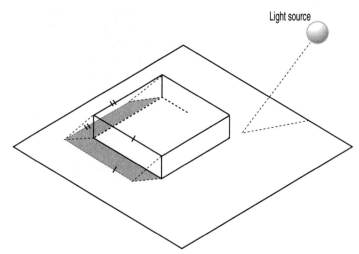

3. If a line casting a shadow is perpendicular to the surface receiving the shadow, the shadow will be parallel to the direction vector of the light source, as shown in Figure 2.17.

Figure 2.17.
*Perpendicular
relationship.*

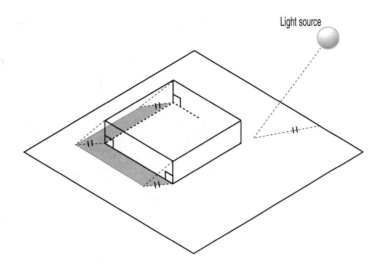

Interpretation of Color

As you have seen, colors vary in many different ways and are often dependent upon the intended use. Color also communicates to us in other ways. Color communicates not only in a visual aspect but also in a psychological one. The following subsections discuss color as it relates to the visual, psychological, and physiological domains.

Visual Aspects

Colors are known to have specific effects concerning the way we view them. Certain properties of colors are implicitly responsible for the way we see spatial relationships.

Colors can be divided into two major groups based upon the way that they affect us. Figure 2.18 shows various hues laid out in a circle. Notice the denotation of warm versus cool colors. In general, colors that are warm, such as red, orange, and yellow, appear to come toward us in graphic images. Colors that are cool, such as blue, violet, and green, appear to recede in graphic images.

Variations within a single color cause us to visually interpret many things from that color. For example, in nature, things closer to us seem to be darker in value and somewhat saturated (more pure). Colors toward the horizon appear to be desaturated and lighter. By lightening and darkening colors, you can create 3D effects. In addition, using cool versus warm colors can change your audience's depth perception.

Figure 2.18.
Warm and cool colors.

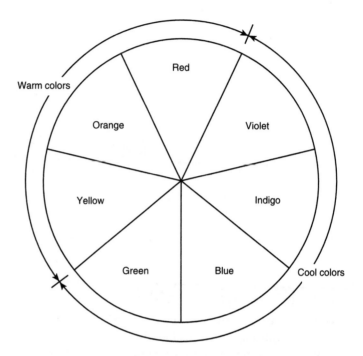

As you design Web pages, color can be a significant help or hindrance. Probably the most significant advantage of color is when you create photo-realistic images. As humans, we desire color, so images and other colored items will automatically please us if they are well-designed and adequately placed. There are, however, many other advantages to using color. Using color, you can do the following:

- Focus the attention of your audience on certain items. Color in Web pages, hotlinks, and text can be used to draw your audience's attention to specific parts of the page. In addition, you can use color in graphics such as buttons, button bars, and backgrounds to help guide your user to important parts of your page.

- Increase the spatial perception of your audience by using the principles of warm and cool colors. The wonderful part of Web development is that you can include graphic effects by using contrasting and similar colors.

- Increase learning, organization, and interpretation by using colors that contribute to the message being communicated. Educators have known for a long time that color can contribute to learning by helping the viewer organize and interpret a message. Using color coding schemes, you can represent items on your pages just as most browsers use specific colors for items such as visited and unvisited hotlinks.

- Increase the efficiency of decision-making and cognitive exercises by using color to help the user identify items on your pages. Again, color helps users distinguish and identify information more quickly and with greater accuracy.

Psychological Aspects

Much research has been done concerning colors and the actions and emotions they evoke in people. Specific colors elicit certain feelings, thoughts, and actions. For example, the color red often connotes danger or stop, whereas green can represent money or go. Table 2.1 shows some of the most common natural associations of colors.

Table 2.1. Color associations and meanings.

Color	Association	Meaning
Red	Blood	Danger
Orange	Fire	Heat
Yellow	Sun	Warmth
Green	Grass	Life
Blue	Water	Cool
Indigo	Ocean	Depth
Violet	Rainbow	Hope
White	Cloud	Purity
Black	Darkness	Death
Gray	Haze	Depression

The colors that we choose to use in our Web pages can be used to represent different things. For example, we might use green text for the financial section of a particular corporation's Web site or red to attract attention to information vital to the audience. Colors can be used representatively at a Web site to mean many different things. Table 2.2 shows colors as they relate to business. Notice how the association is dependent upon its relationship to the content.

Table 2.2. Business color associations.

Color	Association
Red	Loss
Green	Gain
Black	Gain

One thing for certain, however, is that color representation is culture- and experience-dependent. If you plan to use color association, you must be certain that your associations are consistent with those already accepted or used. Going against already established guidelines can be detrimental. For example, the reason we connote green with money, at least in the U.S., is because our money is green. In another culture, green might be a more negative color. All the research that has been done concerning colors does suggest that colors do evoke feelings, thoughts, and actions in people, but that these things are relative to the viewer's experience, background, and culture.

With Web pages, which are accessible worldwide, you need to also be conscious of the genre of the Web. On the Web, most links are displayed in blue, and other colors can represent other actions or things. When you're designing your page, be careful not to use strange colors with which people are unfamiliar. Particularly be aware of colors that are commonly used by browsers to represent certain things.

If your target audience crosses cultural boundaries, do some research on the cultural representations of colors and graphical elements. Don't assume that the audience will automatically know what something is by an abstraction based on your own experience.

Human Physiology

The process that enables vision is quite astounding. This phenomenon occurs as a result of rhodopsin in the rods of the human eye. However, you must always deal with concerns of those who cannot perceive color. Many individuals who are color blind would find most color-coded pages uninterpretable, or at least difficult to interpret.

One of the biggest things you can do to help alleviate some of the problems that the public at large has with colors is to always check your graphics and pages for color problems. Individuals who have any level of color blindness at all can still perceive contrast, because it is a function of the cones in the human eye rather than the rods. To check pages for color problems, convert the page to grayscale.

This is as simple as printing a black-and-white laser copy of the page. Look for places in the page where contrast is low, where loose edges or text becomes unreadable. This is what a color-blind person would see.

In addition to doing a grayscale check on your pages, you should also do the following:

- Avoid colors that are often difficult to discern. For example, approximately 10 percent of the population cannot discriminate between red and green when they are placed one upon another, such as red text on a green background. In addition, the combinations of blue and orange, and yellow and violet create problems. If you avoid these combinations, you'll find that you will eliminate a majority of color blindness problems.

- Make sure the colors you choose have an adequate amount of contrast. If you do the grayscale check as suggested, you'll find that many colors you choose might have little contrast between them. When you compare the grayscale of a red item to the grayscale of an orange item, you'll find little value differences between the two hues. Humans don't often perceive the value of a saturation. The only way to check this is through a grayscale comparison.

- Use color sparingly and for important purposes. Color is a great addition to a page, but you must consider the effect of its overuse. Using large blocks of colored text can be difficult to read. Also, pages with colored items all over the page can also be distracting. Consider using color, but in discretionary places on your page. In Chapter 3, "Typography," you'll read more about this.

Choosing Color Schemes

As you are working with color, you might wonder what colors you should use together. As with the production of any graphics-related product, you must choose your colors wisely.

When you are creating a graphic or other visual element, there are several ways that you can decide upon color. The research on the application of color shows that there are several color schemes to use. These color schemes are ones in which the colors work well together. Color schemes include monochromatic, complementary, and triad. These are most often used and create the most pleasing graphic representations.

The first of the color schemes, *monochromatic,* requires that the entire graphic or page be created from various values of the same hue. By adding black and white to the hue, the developer creates the graphic using one color (hue) and many different tints and shades of it. Often people interpret monochromatic as meaning composed of gray values. The gray scale is a monochromatic scale, but monochromatic can also include a page composed entirely of reds, blues, or any other hue.

On the Web, monochromatic color schemes are very effective. However, the biggest problem with monochromatic colors lies within the use of contrast. Often a monochromatic page will not contain enough contrast to adequately present the page. If you decide to use a monochromatic color scheme, make sure that the tints and shades of the hue are different enough for you to maintain contrast in your images and page.

The second type of color scheme is the *complementary* color scheme. This is the color scheme that causes the most problems, particularly when color blindness is an issue. Complementary colors are colors that lie directly across from one another on the color wheel, as shown in Figure 2.19.

Figure 2.19.
Complementary colors.

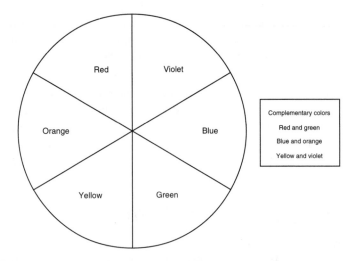

As you read earlier, complementary colors such as red and green, blue and orange, and violet and yellow cause problems for people who are color blind. It is recommended that you avoid complementary colors in your pages and graphics.

Probably the most effective color scheme to use on the Web is a *triad*. A triad uses three colors that are equally spaced on the color wheel. In the color wheel shown in Figure 2.20, there are six colors; red-yellow-blue creates one triad, whereas orange-green-violet creates another.

Figure 2.20.
Triadic colors.

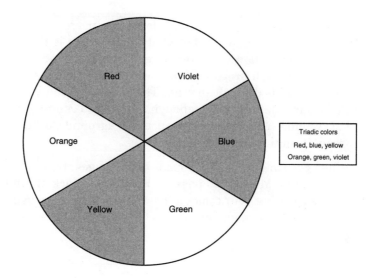

Understand that a color wheel can (and does) actually contain more colors than
I've shown here. You could show multiple iterations of intermediate colors, as
shown in Figure 2.21. When you break the color wheel up into more iterations, you
have more color choices for your graphics and pages.

Figure 2.21.
*A more accurate color
wheel.*

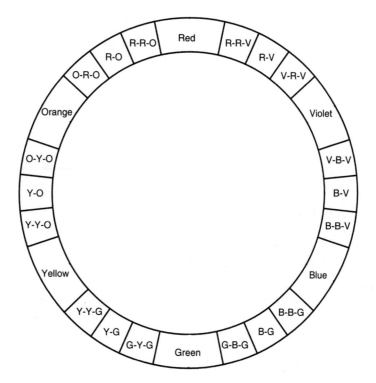

When you are choosing colors for your images and pages, one of the most significant determinants for what colors to use is the color of the background. Certain colors show up better on certain backgrounds. If you are using a reddish background, you probably won't want to use text that is red. Red text on a red background is difficult to read. That doesn't mean you can't use red text; just make sure the contrast is enough so that you can read the text that is over the background. You'll read more about backgrounds, particularly using tiled backgrounds, in the next chapter.

When choosing colors for your text or images, take a look at the color of your background. Many Web pages simply use a black or white background, which makes choosing your colors a little easier. If you are using one of these, look at Table 2.3 and consider one of the following combinations of colors.

Table 2.3. Color use on Web pages.

Number of colors	Black background	White background
1	Cyan	Red
	Green	Green
	Yellow	Magenta
	White	Violet
		Black
2	Cyan and white	Red and magenta
	Green and white	Green and magenta
	Yellow and cyan	Violet and black
	Green and black	
3	Cyan, green, and white	Red, violet, and green; yellow, black, and white; green, magenta, and black

The Negative Aspects of Color

Using color can help or hinder the effectiveness of your pages. You've already read about some of the problems caused by using color in your pages. As you are planning your page colors, consider the following:

- The various associations and interpretations that can be drawn from your colors. Because every user's background and experiences are different, there are a myriad of ways that the audience can interpret the colors that you use. The main consideration is that the interpretation of the content is not heavily based upon your colors. If much of your message is dependent upon color, you might want to note it or provide a legend that describes what your colors mean.

- Overuse of color on a page distracts the user and can inhibit the message you are trying to convey. Use color sparingly. Also, using similar colors across multiple items in your page will help reduce distractions.

- Large sections of color can cause eye fatigue. If large sections of your text are in color, it can make it extremely difficult to read. Colorized segments should be short, to the point, and not overused.

- The extent to which color is perceived is relative and based on the individual and his or her environment. Every device that receives color is not the same. Eye problems, surface colors, lighting, and any number of other factors affect how color is perceived both in the natural world and on the computer monitor. As you read in Chapter 1, "Graphic Design," the monitor itself and the platform and browser can affect the way a color is displayed. Subtle differences in color are often difficult to perceive due to the number of extraneous factors involved.

Theoretical Color Spaces

Up to this point, you've looked at the perceptual side of color, those things that our eyes perceive and that we interpret from those colors. You've also seen that the three attributes of color allow us to specify different colors. In the theoretical domain, any set of colors, more accurately called a gamut of colors, can be described by a three-dimensional model composed of coordinate points.

This chapter has defined the three primary attributes of color: hue, value, and saturation. You read that any color can be defined by these three values. Because there are three values, one can plot those values in a three-dimensional coordinate system (which also uses an X,Y,Z coordinate value) to cognitively define and analyze color.

In Figure 2.22, you see a color space defining all colors by hue, value, and saturation. This color model is called the Hue, Lightness, and Saturation model (HLS). Note that the word lightness has been substituted for the word value. In the model, you'll note that values are described around the circumference of the color space. As you move around the circumference, the hue changes. The purest saturation, or 100 percent saturation level, is found in the middle of the cylinder. As you go up in the model, colors desaturate and lighten (tint). As you go down in the model, colors darken and desaturate (shade).

Figure 2.22.
The HLS color model.

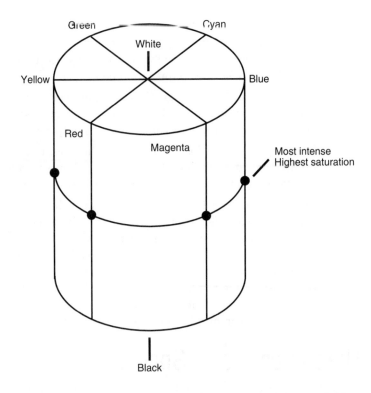

In Figure 2.23, note that a light blue is selected and a portion of the model has been removed. The point shown in the figure lies in the gradated plane. This particular color has a coordinate value of 240,67,13. This means it has a hue of 240 (blue), a lightness of 67 (67 percent white), and a saturation of 13 (13 percent, pure blue hue). If we moved the point, which represents the color, toward the white pole, its lightness would increase; toward the black pole, the color's lightness would decrease. If we moved the color closer to the center of the cylinder, its saturation would decrease; if the color were moved toward the outside of the cylinder, its saturation would increase. And lastly, if we moved the color around the circumference of the cylinder, its hue would change from blue to the next color.

Color models were designed to accurately describe the gamut of colors for any particular device. With each device, whether a computer monitor, a printing press, or your eyes, all of the colors that exist in nature can be described using three-dimensional models. This allows us to completely define all of the colors that a particular device can create or receive.

Figure 2.23.
A color in the HLS model.

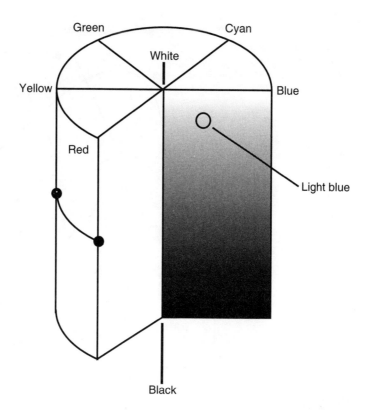

All of the color models that you will deal with work similarly to the HLS model. Some look different because they describe a different gamut of colors. Each and every device has a number of colors it can discern or produce, but not all devices can display the same number of colors. If we laid out all of the colors for various devices, the differences would become apparent, as shown in Figure 2.24. For example, some colors can be displayed but cannot be reproduced in a print. Some colors can be printed but cannot be displayed on a computer monitor. This is because of the differences between additive and subtractive colors; not all colors in one type of color reproduction can be reproduced in another. In addition, there are many more colors that occur in nature than what our eyes can perceive. In nature, there are an infinite number of colors. Our eyes can only perceive a small portion of the ones that exist. Even a trained eye can only discern between 50,000 colors. So, as you continue, keep in mind that the various color models are a theoretical device to help us analyze color and that they each contain their own gamut, or set of colors.

Figure 2.24.
Various device gamuts
overlapped upon one
another.

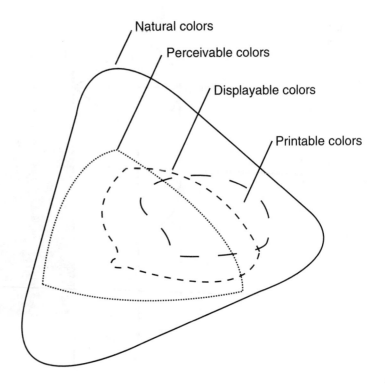

Natural colors

Perceivable colors

Displayable colors

Printable colors

Munsell

The Munsell color model, created by Alfred Munsell in 1905, was the first color model designed to systematically define colors. This particular model was designed to represent the colors in nature; however it was soon found to be inadequate for describing the millions of colors found in nature. Although frequently mentioned in the U.S., the Munsell color model is not used in modern computer applications or devices.

As shown in Figure 2.25, the Munsell color model is an onion-shaped model that describes pure saturation on the outer boundaries of the three-dimensional space. Value changes as the black and white poles are approached, and saturation changes as you move deeper into the color space.

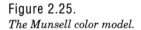
Figure 2.25.
The Munsell color model.

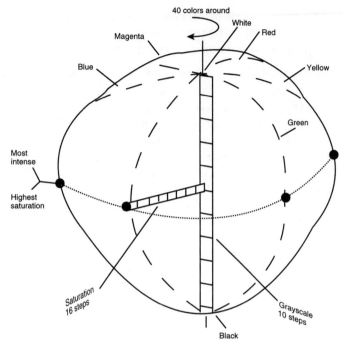

Device-Dependent Color Models

Most of the color models used today are an effort to describe the actual devices that are used to replicate color. As you have already seen, the HLS model is one of the easiest to understand and is commonly used in computer applications. The Macintosh system color picker closely resembles the HLS model.

In addition to the HLS model, two other color models are probably the most frequently used ones in the computer graphic and Web development arenas. These include the CYMK color model, which describes the color space for four-color process printing and the RGB model, which describes the color space for displaying graphic images and Web pages on a computer monitor.

The CYM and RGB Color Models

As previously discussed, CYMK (Cyan, Yellow, Magenta, and Black) comprises the four colors used in process printing. The model used to describe these devices excludes the K in its name. Because the printer color model uses only cyan, yellow, and magenta for its primary colors, it is titled the CYM color model. Alternatively, the RGB model is the model used to describe the colors that are replicated on a computer screen using red, green, and blue phosphor guns.

Because each printing device is different (due to manufacturing variability), each printer has a particular gamut of colors that it can effectively print. In general, however, the CYMK color model satisfies the use of any four-color printer. Notice in Figure 2.26 that the model is shaped quite differently than the previous models you've seen. In this model, the three primary colors are cyan, yellow, and magenta. To change the values of these colors, you approach the poles labeled black and white. Any other movement changes the saturation of the particular color.

Figure 2.26.
The CYM color model.

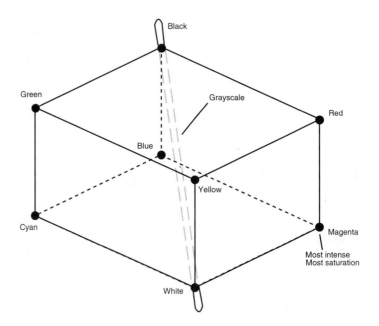

Similar to the CYM model, the RGB model is the exact opposite, having red, green, and blue as primary colors and cyan, yellow, and magenta as secondary colors. (See Figure 2.27.) You'll note also that the model works the same as the CYM model. Approaching either the black or white pole changes the value of a color, whereas any other movement changes the saturation of the color.

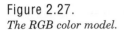

Figure 2.27.
The RGB color model.

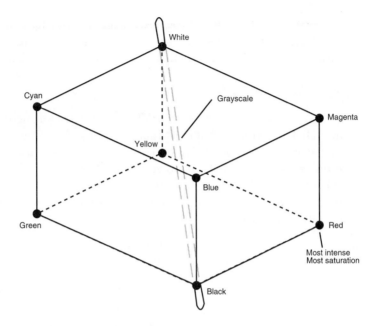

Browser Color

In Web graphics, the definition of colors in the image are a function of the raster editor that you use. Some allow you to use the RGB model and specify your colors by red, green, and blue values. Others use the HLS or CYM models for color specification. However, with bitmap graphics included on Web pages, there is no direct color definition in the HTML file. The colors are defined in the image editor when you create the bitmap. Therefore, all colors are inherent to the bitmap itself as you will see in Chapter 5, "Raster-Based Graphics." However, with text elements, backgrounds, and horizontal rules defined by the HTML coding, you must work with something called hexadecimal color. Hexadecimal color is a base-16 mathematical numbering system used to define and describe HTML colors for the browser. Unless you have worked in some area of computer programming in the past, it is likely that this will be your first acquaintance with hexadecimal color.

As you will find, it is much easier to work with colors in a bitmap editor than it is to work with colors in HTML coding. In a raster editor, colors get defined when you select them with the mouse, as described. In HTML, however, you must mathematically define colors using abstract letters and numbers such as FFFFFF for white or 000000 for black. We'll take a closer look at defining hexadecimal color a little later. Just realize that it is easier to use a paint editor to create bitmaps than it is to define hexadecimal colors in HTML code.

Hexadecimal Color

As discussed, creating colors in HTML code is more difficult than the visual point-and-click environment of most image editors. To define colors in a Web page, use hexadecimal code (base 16) to define the colors—something that you probably didn't even know existed until you started designing Web pages. Probably one of the least favorite tasks of any Web developer is dealing with hexadecimal color, because in the age of graphical user interfaces, it is not a natural way to work graphically based ends.

All browser colors are defined using hex. Colored text, colored links, colored outlines, and anything that is not a graphic and that you want to be a color on the Web page, must be defined using hexadecimal code. In reality, hexadecimal code is nothing more than three two-number sequences that represent our normal decimal numbering system. It sounds simple, but to many it is a point of confusion. Really, the only thing you have to do is convert your normal method of representing graphic color (RGB) to a hexadecimal representation.

If you have used an image editor at all, you've probably seen how the raster environment defines colors. Using RGB or CYMK sliders, as shown in Figure 2.28, you combine additive or subtractive primaries to create a single color. In hexadecimal, however, each color requires a unique hexadecimal code to define it. To do the conversion, you will need to start with an RGB-based color definition.

Figure 2.28.
Sliders used to define colors in a bitmap editor.

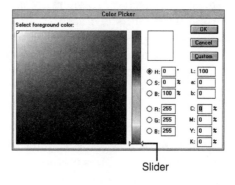

Slider

For example, in RGB, white is defined as R:255, B:255, G:255. The hexadecimal representation is FFFFFF. For black, the RGB definition is R:0, B:0, G:0. The hexadecimal representation is 000000. You'll find that hex is an abstract way to represent color and is one that many of us despise. Probably the only ones that you will remember from memory are black, white, and Netscape Gray (CCCCCC). As a definite hex-hater myself, there is a quick method that you can do with a calculator that will give you accurate results every time. Note, however, it won't make it any more fun!

Calculating Hex

To calculate hexadecimal values, you'll need to know two specific things. The first thing you'll need to know is the RGB specification of the color you want to convert to hex. For this, you can use a bitmap editor. Choose a color visually and then write down the RGB color values shown in the editor. The second thing you'll need is a scientific calculator. If you've got a machine running Windows, you have it already (in the Accessories group). Unfortunately, for Macintosh users, there isn't a system calculator that can work in scientific mode. There are, however, several shareware and freeware calculators that have this capability.

To convert an RGB color to a hexadecimal color, do the following:

1. Find the red, green, and blue values for the color in your image editor, as shown in Figure 2.29. I chose an RGB color defined by R:222, G:39, and B:151 for this example, but any color will do.

Figure 2.29.
Finding the red, green, and blue values for the color conversion.

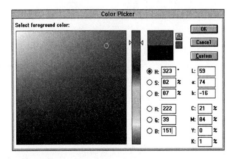

2. Next, open the calculator from the Windows Accessories group.

3. Select Scientific from the View menu.

4. Make sure you are in DEC mode and enter the red value into the calculator. From the color in Figure 2.29, you would use the red value of 222.

5. Next, click HEX, which will show you the hex value of the red decimal value. A red value of 222 gives you a hex value of DE. Jot down this hex value.

6. Repeat steps 4 and 5 with the green and blue values. The green value of 39 gives you a hex value of 27. The blue value of 151 gives you a hex value of 97.

7. After you have converted the red, green, and blue values to hex, write your results as a single string. This is the hex value of the color. In the example, an RGB color of R:222, G:39, and B:151 is represented with hexadecimal code as DE3997.

8. You would then use this value in your HTML code. If you wanted the background color of the browser to be this color, you would enter

```
<BODY BGCOLOR="#DE3997">
```

This makes the background of the browser the specified hex color.

Web Resources

In addition to the calculator method, there are several sites on the Web that have online RGB-to-hex converters that you can use to calculate hex values from RGB values. Check out these sites to help you calculate hex values:

- http://www.bga.com/~rlp/dwp/palette/palette.html
- http://www.echonyc.com/~xixax/Mediarama/hex.html

Summary

In this chapter you have taken a brief look at color usage. Aside from the major attributes of color, including hue, value, and saturation, you have also seen many of the ways that we define color in our daily workings. Whenever you choose a particular color, you must consider its visual, psychological, and physiological implications prior to integrating it into your design. By carefully choosing colors, you can make your Web designs effective and appealing.

3

Typography

As discussed in Chapter 1, "Graphic Design," typefonts
and typefont styles (such as bold and italics) play a key
role in the look of a Web page. Imagine designing a
Web page that used no fonts to communicate. If
everything was delivered using graphics, you would
have to base much of your communication on assumptions,relationships, and past experiences, making interpretation very difficult. Communicating entirely with graphics, although very primitive, was one
of the first methods of communication, as shown in
Figure 3.1. From cave drawings to ancient Egyptian
hieroglyphics, communication occurred through
picture-type drawings.

Figure 3.1.
Early communication
through pictures.

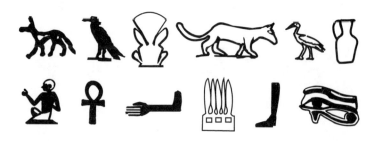

Because of the difficulty of interpreting graphics-only communication, however, graphics alone often do not communicate as efficiently as a combination of text and graphics. The text, style of text, and amount of text that you use on your Web pages are very important.

It seems that on the Web, there are really two camps of individuals. The first camp is those who design almost everything on the Web page with text. Big text, little text, decorative text, and standard text comprise much of what is on the page. If you've seen a page with all text, you know how blasé it is. No doubt, pages are more visually appealing with some graphics.

The other camp of developers inserts very little text and many, many graphics. Everything on the page is an icon, picture, symbol, or other graphic. Aside from downloading very slowly, pages made entirely of graphics are also often difficult to interpret and navigate. Designing pages this way makes it very difficult to determine what, if anything, is being communicated.

Web page design and communication requires a balanced combination of text and graphics. This is no surprise because much of the communication in the 20th century has been based upon the printed page, combining both static text and graphics. However, during the past 20 years, we have also seen the emergence of a new media element that can be used to help us communicate—multimedia. Today, we can not only use static graphics and text but also sound, animation, and video. Because this book is about multimedia, in addition to graphics (and text), pages should also include multimedia elements that enhance, complete, or complement the content being presented.

As you surf the Web, be conscious of the pages that communicate effectively. What would you say about a page that contains only text? Or only graphics? What if the page contained only dancing bullets and animated items? Notice that a page that contains too much of any one of these three items (text, graphics, or multimedia elements) will likely communicate poorly. You must balance your use of each of these elements to effectively and efficiently communicate to your audience.

When moveable type was first invented, it was revolutionary. Prior to its invention, the look of a font was based upon the skill of the scribe who was hand-writing the particular string of text. When moveable type was introduced, there was a single style of text. Yet, as moveable type became more widely used, people started creating text that was taller, wider, more ornate, or less ornate to help communicate and draw attention.

As the number of different styles of text increased, a method for identifying different types of text was established by naming these different text styles to distinguish between them. Each set of characters that have a particular look, or set of defining characteristics, is called a *font,* or *typefont.* Each typefont is named, such as Helvetica, Times, or Courier. Figure 3.2 shows examples of these three types of fonts. Notice the overall difference in the way these fonts look. Most often, the type is named after the individual or company that created it.

Figure 3.2.
Different types of fonts.

Helvetica
Times
Courier

As you surf the Web, you'll find pages that use any number of fonts on a particular page. Have you ever noticed how much a design is based on the fonts used? Much of the tone of the page or site depends upon the use of fonts. Fonts often convey a particular look and feel based on their aesthetic qualities. Although it is often the minute features of the font that contribute to this look, take a look at the overall effect of these features. Then you'll take a look at all the various characteristics of a font that contribute to this look.

As you look at the various typefonts in Figure 3.3, you can see how the way the font actually looks can determine the look and feel of the page. The thickness, style, weight, and height all contribute to presenting a feel of the font. For example, the Technopunk font suggests the meaning of the word. If you were creating a site that had New Age content, you might want to use a font like this. The connotation in the words "Old West" is aided by the look of the font. As you are choosing fonts to use in your pages, use the fonts that you have to your advantage. However, using special fonts requires more work on your part, as you will see in the section titled "Computer Fonts," later in this chapter.

One thing you must note is that the determination of how the font implies something, such as a feeling or other meaning, is somewhat subjective. In Figure 3.3, note the font chosen for Old West. To me, this font, infers the old West simply because it reminds me of the letter type used on many of the Wanted: Dead or Alive posters. However, if you've not seen one of these posters, the look of the font won't have much meaning to you.

Figure 3.3.
Various fonts can be
used to connote tone.

Bold & Beefy

TECHNOPUNK

Technical Graphics

LEGAL BEAGLE

ELEGANT NIGHTS

Old West

Because the Web is a worldwide medium, you must be cautious about the connotations you make. With fonts, most decisions made concerning fonts won't offend or exclude your audience. However, some decisions about colors or the icons used to represent buttons are due to cultural differences. With fonts, the style will have less meaning when viewed outside your intended audience. When you begin reading about graphics in Chapters 4, "Vector-Based Graphics," and 5, "Raster-Based Graphics," and interface design in Chapter 12, "Interface Design and Metaphors," this issue will become more important.

Aside from the type of font you choose, the styles (bold, italics, and so on), colors, and sizes you choose also affect the way your Web page is interpreted. Two of the biggest things that draw attention to a font are color and size. In the previous chapter, you saw how color affects perception and interpretation—but what about the size of a piece of text? For example, what would happen if the size of the word Why were changed in Figure 3.4? The overall presentational image would be lessened, right? Of the things on the page in the figure, the word "Why" instantly grabs your attention. If you access this page on the Web, you'll see that the color of the word also contributes to attracting your attention.

Figure 3.4.
Various styles, colors, and sizes also affect the presentation of the site.

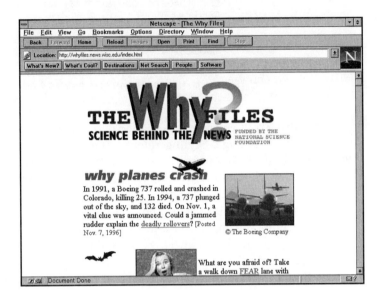

There are two other things that you should note about the fonts used in Figure 3.4. In addition to color and size, you can affect the visual appeal of a page by changing the case of a letter. Case refers to upper- and lowercase letters. In the figure, notice in the title that the words are all uppercase and the byline, "why planes crash," is all lowercase. How does this affect the look of the page? The uppercase letters in the title help contribute to drawing your attention, whereas the lowercase byline, although still attractive, is somewhat subdued.

Generally, type treatments such as upper- and lowercase effects are reserved for titles, headings, and subtitles. They must, however, be used in moderation. Have you ever tried to read an entire page of body text that is all capital letters? Or tried to read a Web page where every other word was all capitalized? It makes my eyes sore just thinking about it. Figure 3.5 shows an example of what I mean. Compare the uppercase version of the text to the lowercase version. Which is easier to read? In general, use oddly placed uppercase letters sparingly. An entire page of capital text becomes very difficult to read after a few paragraphs. Generally, retention is best when there is a combination of upper- and lowercase letters.

Figure 3.5.
Reading large segments of uppercase letters is more difficult than reading lowercase letters.

GENERALLY, TYPE TREATMENTS SUCH AS UPPERCASE AND LOWERCASE EFFECTS ARE RESERVED FOR TITLES, HEADINGS, AND SUBTITLES. THEY MUST, HOWEVER, BE USED IN MODERATION. WHAT DO YOU MEAN, YOU ASK. HAVE YOU EVER TRIED TO READ AN ENTIRE PAGE OF BODY TEXT THAT IS ALL CAPITAL LETTERS?

Generally, type treatments such as uppercase and lowercase effects are reserved for titles, headings, and subtitles. They must, however, be used in moderation. What do you mean, you ask. Have you ever tried to read an entire page of body text that is all capital letters?

The last thing that you can note about Figure 3.4 is the styling of the various text elements on this page. Styling refers to boldfacing, italicizing, and underling. Note that underlining usually denotes a hotlink on almost all Web pages. The same problem that occurs with uppercase letters also occurs with type styling. If you bold or italicize a large body of text, it becomes very difficult to read. Also, developers will sometimes insert hotlinks within body text, which is effective, but only when done sparingly. In Figure 3.4, note there is only one hotlink embedded within the paragraph of text. This is acceptable. However, if the developer of the page had inserted four or five hotlinks, trying to read the paragraph would be more difficult, as shown in Figure 3.6.

Figure 3.6.
Too much text styling can also be distracting to the reader.

In 1991, a Boeing 737 rolled and crashed in Colorado, killing 25. In 1994, a 737 plunged out of the sky, and 132 died. On Nov. 1, a vital clue was announced. Could a jammed rudder explain the deadly rollovers?

In 1991, a Boeing 737 rolled and crashed in Colorado, killing 25. In 1994, a 737 plunged out of the sky, and 132 died. On Nov. 1, a vital clue was announced. Could a jammed rudder explain the deadly rollovers?

When you have a significant amount of hotlinks related to a paragraph or want to stylize many items to draw attention to them, consider using lists rather than embedding them in body text. Understand that moderation is a key to good text design. Ultimately, anything that disrupts the user's focus on your content is not good. Remember, it is your content that the audience wants. Your design and your media elements are simply tools to help the audience comprehend, interpret, and digest your content.

When you began reading this chapter, you read that you can create or support a page's tone with fonts that you choose to use as well as draw attention by varying the size, case, style, and color of the font—but using these effects requires discretion. The way you present titles, subtitles, and other text elements can change the effectiveness and communicability of your Web page.

Typefaces

All of the attributes discussed thus far are really external characteristics that can be changed relative to a single font. But what makes each font different from another? And how do you know when a particular font is better (for a specific task) than another? To help you determine what types of fonts to use in your pages, look at the font itself and understand the characteristics of it so that you can effectively choose fonts for your Web page designs. As you will find, there are many fonts available. With some, the differences are very minute.

In general, there are two types of fonts, as shown in Figure 3.7. The biggest distinguishing characteristic is the presence or absence of serifs. *Serifs* are the small feet and tails that appear on the characters of a font; serifs increase readability. Fonts with serifs are called serif fonts. Fonts without serifs are called sans serif fonts. Let's take a look at a couple of pages to exemplify the differences between them and how they are used.

Figure 3.7.
Serif versus sans serif typefonts.

Serif Fonts
Sans Serif Fonts

As shown in Figure 3.7, the difference between serif fonts and sans serif fonts is the presence or absence of feet and tails on the fonts. So when should you use these fonts? Figure 3.8 shows a page that predominantly uses sans serif fonts, fonts without feet and tails. Notice that the larger the sans serif font is, the easier it is to read. Notice the small list towards the lower left of the screen that begins with the "United States." This size of text is more difficult to read than larger appearances of the sans serif font. Note the list that begins "Worldwide Express." It is also difficult to read. Sans serif fonts become more difficult to read as they get smaller. Therefore, sans serif fonts are most often used for titles, headlines, and subtitles or text strings that are displayed larger than body text.

Figure 3.8.
*Using predominantly
sans serif fonts on Web
pages.*

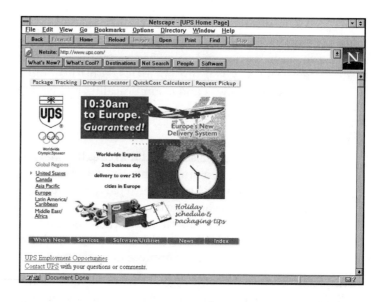

Figure 3.9 shows the opposite of what Figure 3.8 does. Figure 3.9 predominantly uses serif fonts throughout the page. Notice that the body text (in the middle of the page), although quite small, is easier to read than the sans serif fonts shown in Figure 3.8. This is what the feet and tails are for on serif fonts. The serifs on serif fonts make the font easier to distinguish and read at small sizes. However, notice the serif fonts used for "Today's Lead Story." Does this text look busy or crowded to you? Notice that the serifs on the text almost get in the way of the text. This figure shows you that serif fonts are best for small text or for text bodies, but if the text is displayed very large, serif fonts can become very busy and distracting.

The previous two figures showed pages that predominantly use either sans serif fonts or serif fonts. Most pages, however, combine the fonts, using sans serif for titles and headlines and serif fonts for body text and text that is displayed at a small size. Keep in mind this is a general rule and not an absolute. Many designs, like the ones shown in Figure 3.4 and in Figure 3.10, break the rules by using large serif fonts to attract attention. Don't be afraid to bend the rules to create a design; however, be discretionary about whether you are using a serif or sans serif font.

One final thing to consider is that you really only want to use a couple of different fonts on a single page. If you get too many different fonts on a page, it will often be distracting and difficult for the audience to read. It might also present a contradictory tone to your audience. Try to use fewer than three fonts on your page unless you have a valid reason for doing otherwise.

Figure 3.9.
*Using predominantly
serif fonts on Web pages.*

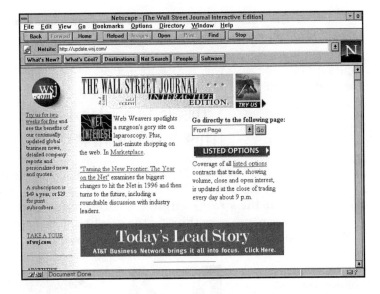

Figure 3.10.
*A combination of fonts is
most effective.*

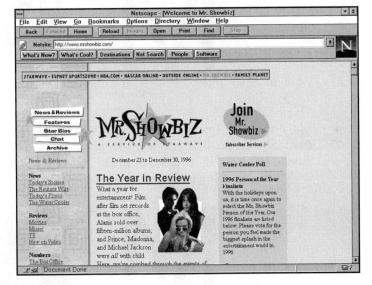

Characteristics

Aside from the global distinction between serif and sans serif, there are also several other font characteristics that I should define. I have looked at at least one of these (point size). These characteristics include the following:

- The overall size of the font is called the point size, measured in points. (See Figure 3.11.) Note that 72 points equal one inch. The first section of this chapter, "Typography," discussed size. Changing the size of a font is also called changing its point size.

Figure 3.11.
The point size of a font.

This is 8 point text.

This is 12 point text.

This is 14 point text.

This is 16 point text.

- The weight of a font is the width of the strokes composing the lines and curves of the letters. (See Figure 3.12.) Each particular font has certain widths to the strokes within the letters. Some fonts have wide strokes, and others are very thin. As the point size increases or decreases, this thickness can become more or less apparent.

Figure 3.12.
The weight of a font.

- The horizontal space of a font is the relative width of the letter M in the font. (See Figure 3.13.) In any given font, all the characters in the font have a relationship to the size of the letter M in the font. The letter M is used because it is the widest character in any font.

Figure 3.13.
The horizontal space of a font.

- Letter spacing is the defined spacing between letters. (See Figure 3.14.) Each font has a defined amount of space that occurs between its letters. Notice in the top row, some characters are closer together than others.

For example *in* has less spacing than does the *ng* combination. Adjustments in letter spacing help users read words easier. Letter spacing can be adjusted, as shown in the other lines shown in Figure 3.14. Some fonts use the same amount of spacing between every letter. These are called monospaced fonts and can be more difficult to read at small sizes. An example of a monospaced font is Courier, which resembles type from a typewriter.

Figure 3.14.
The letter spacing of a font.

Letter spacing
Letter spacing
Letter spacing
Letter spacing
Letter spacing

- Leading is the spacing between multiple lines of text. (See Figure 3.15.) Leading is also one of the font characteristics that can make text either easier or more difficult to read. There is an optimum amount of space that is required to read any paragraph of text. Leading is measured in points. Usually, the default leading is one to two point sizes greater than the point size of the text. For example, a Times font with a point size of 12 is optimally read at a leading of 13 or 14 points. When the point size is equal to the leading, the text overlaps or *crashes* with the lines above and below it.

Figure 3.15.
The leading of a font.

Leading is spacing between lines.

Leading is spacing between lines.

Leading is spacing between lines.

Leading is spacing between lines.

Leading is spacing between lines.

Leading is spacing between lines.

- Alignment is the physical arrangement of a body of text. (See Figure 3.16.) Although alignment is not considered to be a true font characteristic, it is a characteristic than can affect the readability of a body of text. We are familiar with left-justified text, but there might be times you will want to use center- or right-justified text.

Figure 3.16.
The alignment a body of text.

This is left-justified text.
This is left-justified text.
This is left-justified text.
This is left-justified text.

This is right-justified text.
This is right-justified text.
This is right-justified text.
This is right-justified text.

This is center-justified text.
This is center-justified text.
This is center-justified text.
This is center-justified text.

As you are creating Web pages, many of these characteristics are the very things that cause problems on Web pages across browsers and platforms. As you saw in Chapter 1, HTML text that is laid out on a Web page can shift significantly from browser to browser, as well as across platforms. This is something you cannot control because it is dependent upon the user's machine and not the way you code or lay out your HTML code. There will always be some variability from browser to browser and from platform to platform. If you need precise placement of text elements, particularly for composed graphics and text elements, I suggest using a bitmap of the font, discussed in the next section.

Computer Fonts

Now that I have described the various elements that affect the tone, readability, and effectiveness of text, take a look at some more technical concepts concerning computer fonts. This chapter briefly showed how fonts affect the tone of a page and how the various characteristics of the font create its unique look.

Fonts that you use on your pages can be incorporated into the page in two ways. HTML pages can actually present fonts as either vector or bitmap representations. *Vector* fonts describe every character in the font via line descriptions, whereas *bitmap* fonts describe the font with pixels, as shown in Figure 3.17. In the figure, notice the visual differences between the text that says The Weather Channel and the underlined text that says The Weather Channel City of the Day. The jaggy edges on the latter of these strings tells you that it is a vector, whereas the prior is a bitmap. Note that whenever text is inserted as a bitmap it is just like any other inline image. It is a graphic image rather than a result of code.

Figure 3.18 shows another example of bitmap versus vector fonts. Notice the top word, "bitmap." See that the edges are smooth? This indicates that it is a bitmap; it was created in a paint program and inserted as an inline image. Notice the second word, "Vector." It is pretty easy to see the jagged edges on the font. This clues you in to the fact that it is a vector font. To create this word, HTML code was used to create the word rather than creating it in a paint program.

Figure 3.17.
*Bitmap versus vector
fonts in Web pages.*

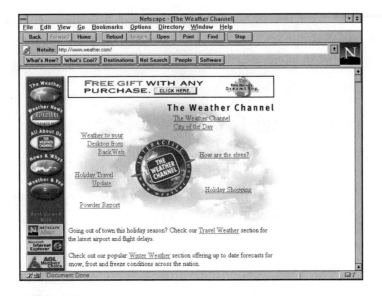

Figure 3.18.
*Bitmap versus vector
fonts.*

Bitmap
Vector

Vector Fonts

The fonts that are used as part of the HTML code are created and laid out per the user's machine. Once the HTML file is accessed, the browser begins by laying out the Web page. Within the HTML code file, HTML tags describe text that is to be fluidly laid out on the Web page for the user to view. The browser calls for the font, and it is created in the browser per the definition of the font on the client machine. These fonts are called vector or PostScript fonts.

The PostScript description of the vector font itself is resident on the user's machine. It is part of the operating system, and is a small file that describes each and every character in the font. This description tells how the font looks, how tall it is, how wide it is, and so on, by defining the outline of every character in the font.

It is a vector description of every character. Because the font description is a vector description, it can be created at any size. This is why you can specify various font sizes in the HTML code. However, with vector fonts, you are also limited to the fonts on the user's machine. In addition, as the font gets larger, the jagged edges become more apparent.

Types of Vector Fonts

As you work on the PC and Macintosh, you will find that there are several different types of vector fonts available. Note that browsers do not specifically know what types of fonts are on the user's machine. In reality, the browser only knows the names that define the different types of fonts.

As you are working in the design field, you'll probably hear about three types of vector fonts: PostScript, TrueType, and Multiple Master fonts. These are all different types of vector fonts, but each has its own special characteristics.

PostScript fonts were originally created by Adobe and were the first type of vector fonts available. Prior to PostScript fonts, all fonts were defined with bitmaps. For those who might remember, for each size and style of a font you wanted to create, you had to have a bitmap representation to be able to use it. In addition, because most personal printers were 300 dpi, each bitmap font representation had to be 300 dpi. This meant that if you had very many fonts at all, a significant amount of your hard drive was eaten up by these font bitmaps.

Seeing a need to save resources, Adobe created the first vector font system that allowed various styles and sizes of a font to be generated from a single vector description of the characters in a font. This made computer desktop publishing much easier in that a single vector definition file replaced numerous bitmap files that defined all instances of a particular font.

Following Adobe's introduction of the PostScript font, Apple decided to enter the font market by creating a new type of font that was faster and more efficient than Adobe's PostScript technology. In the late 1980s, Apple introduced TrueType technology, which boasted all of the features of PostScript, except that it was faster and the files were smaller. These two technologies are the most widely used fonts in the computing industry. In reality, PostScript fonts are beginning to die out because of the exclusive use of TrueType fonts on both the Macintosh and Windows operating systems.

The last font type, Multiple Masters, is a technology that seemed to never really blossom. Introduced as a technology that would allow designers to adjust all of the various font characteristics, such as width, height, and horizontal space, Multiple Master fonts are not very widespread in use.

Creating Fonts as Bitmaps

As you read, with vector fonts, you are limited to those fonts that are on the machine. So what happens if you want to use a font that the user's machine doesn't have? In that case, you create a graphic of the font. Using an image editor, create a graphic of the font and insert the image as an inline image using the <IMG> tag.

There are advantages and disadvantages to using each type of font. Font bitmaps allow you to incorporate any type of font into a Web page, but bitmaps take longer to download because they are graphics rather than code. You'll also notice that bitmap fonts appear much smoother than vector fonts, as shown in Figure 3.19.

Figure 3.19.
Bitmap fonts appear much smoother than vector fonts.

Styles

I am amazed at the number of Web pages that make reading the content very difficult. On of the most common problems on Web pages is the use of tiling backgrounds that make it impossible to read the information on the page. If you decide to use tiling backgrounds in your Web pages, keep in mind that this feature was designed to improve the look of your Web pages, but it can easily distract your audience if it is too busy. Tiled background images must be very subdued to work well. Figure 3.20 shows an example of a Web page that uses background tiles effectively. Notice in the figure that the image is noticeable but that it does not detract from the information being presented. Again, it's your content they want!

Figure 3.20.
A example of a Web page that uses background tiles effectively.

One of the things that you can do in your Web pages, and I highly suggest it if you are using tiled backgrounds, is the use of shadows behind your text. This effect only works if you make bitmap images of your text, but it creates a way to separate your foreground items from your tiled image without having to change the styling of text (such as boldfacing or changing the color). In Figure 3.21, notice that the developer has added some drop shadows behind many of the items to help draw attention to them as well as separate them from the background.

Figure 3.21.
Drop shadows can help draw the user's attention.

Finally, the HTML language allows you to perform various effects on text such as color changes and blinking text. As with many of the other type treatments, use these effects sparingly. An entire page of red text or several blinking text strings can significantly annoy your audience.

Choosing Fonts for Communication

Be aware that effective typographic treatments simply require being aware of some general rules of thumb. As you are designing, keep in mind the following:

- You should use sans serif fonts for items that are usually large in point size such as titles, headlines, and subtitles.

- You should use serif fonts for items that are usually small, such as captions or references, and for large bodies of text.

- You should choose typefonts that contribute to the message you are trying to convey. The fonts and font treatments should not distract the audience or make the information difficult to obtain.

- You should refrain from using large amounts of bold, italic, or underlining on your page. Use a list instead.

- You should not use many different fonts on one page. It will distract the reader.

- You should vary the size of the font in proportion to the importance of the message you are trying to convey.

- For large text use bitmaps or inline images of your text so that it appears smooth.

- Use drop shadows instead of text treatments to draw attention.

Summary

In this chapter you have taken a look at the various aspects of typographic design. Many of the type treatments apply to specific instances. In this chapter I have given you some of the rules of thumb concerning typography. Again, keep in mind that these are not absolutes. As you find yourself creating a page, don't be afraid to try various effects, even if they break the rules. Design is a fluid process. Seldom does a designer create a single layout or type treatment and quit. Often there are several iterations of a particular design and text treatment. I am surprised by the number of individuals who give up when they are on the verge of creating a masterpiece.

The most frequently used typographic treatments will require you to use bitmaps of fonts because you cannot depend on a particular font being on the audience's machine. If you use bitmaps, keep in mind that the more of them you use, the longer your page will take to download.

4

Vector-Based Graphics

For the traditional artist new to the computer world, it often takes time to get used to the digital illustration tools and techniques available for the computer. Indeed, there is much that can be done on the personal computer that makes the creation of graphics easier.

When graphics are created on the computer, the developer has many more options than that of the traditional graphic artist. As with traditional tools, computers give many options for how a graphic is created. However, one other distinct advantage emerges—that of editability. After a digital graphic has been created, the range of changes that can be made to it is quite diverse. From changing small portions of an image, such as adjusting a color or moving an element, to revising the entire work, the computer gives the developer the ability to change any number of aspects concerning the digital graphic.

This chapter covers vector-based graphics, one of the first methods that was available for creating graphics and illustrations. The predominance of illustrating, for many years, required defining specific elements, such as lines, arcs, and circles, using coordinate descriptions. Each individual element required the user to enter code descriptions for an element such as a line. Thankfully, computer illustration has evolved into a visual rather than a code-based process. Today we can draw and paint using any number of input devices such as the mouse, trackball, or pressure-sensitive tablet.

This chapter begins by introducing the two major types of computer illustrations—vector- and raster-based—and proceeds to discuss the former of these two. Chapter 5, "Raster-Based Graphics," continues the discussion by introducing raster-based graphics and the issues associated with them.

The Nature of PostScript

Being a multimedia specialist, I love working with graphics. Hopefully, you do, too. As you begin creating graphics, you will find that there are basically two ways to create them, each with its own advantages and disadvantages.

Concerning graphics, the two main types of graphic images are raster, or bitmap, graphics and vector (also called PostScript) graphics. Bitmap graphics are graphics in which the smallest drawing element is the pixel or picture element, as shown in Figure 4.1. Notice in Figure 4.1 that the entire image is composed of small picture elements or pixels. The enlarged area of 16 pixels shows an individual pixel. The whole example shows an image that is 241 pixels wide by 424 pixels high. Most bitmap images are specified in pixels. The image in Figure 4.1 is a 241-by-424 bitmap.

Figure 4.1.
The smallest element of a raster graphic is the pixel (picture element).

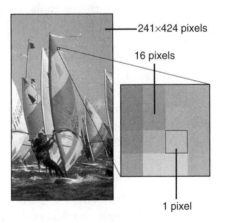

241×424 pixels

16 pixels

1 pixel

The creation of raster graphics is much like traditional painting. The artist working with a raster-based application has a wide range of tools that have many commonalties with traditional painting and drawing tools. In Chapter 5, you'll read more about the various aspects of bitmap graphics.

Vector graphics, on the other hand, are graphics in which the smallest drawing elements are points and when connected create lines, arcs, circles, rectangles, and polygons, as shown in Figure 4.2.

Figure 4.2.
The smallest elements of vector graphics are objects such as points, lines, and circles.

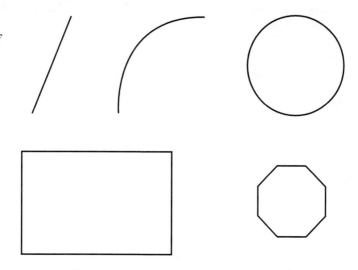

In a vector-based environment, all the elements used to create drawings are defined as elements or objects in the drawing. Each element, such as a line or an arc, is defined by points and other properties such as line thickness, line style, and color. Figure 4.3 shows the points, often called handles, used to define the lines. In the drawing file, the line is specified by a beginning point, an ending point, and a thickness or other property (such as linetype).

Figure 4.3.
Points, denoted by handles, define the elements in a vector drawing.

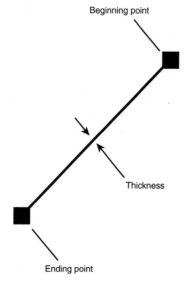

Beginning point

Thickness

Ending point

In a vector drawing, there are two basic types of points. The points that you saw in Figure 4.3 are normal, or straight, points. To create curves in a vector drawing, special points, called Bézier points, are used to create arcs and circles. The Bézier points define Bézier curves that can be adjusted by moving the control handles for the curves, as shown in Figure 4.4.

Figure 4.4.
Arcs and circles are
composed of Bézier
curves.

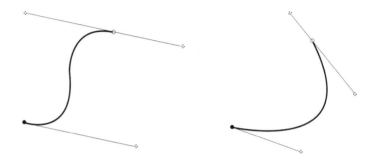

Vector and Raster Images on the Web

The predominance of graphics found on the Web are raster-based, although new technologies exist and are being developed that allow the developer to distribute vector-based illustrations as well. However, often a vector-based drawing will be created and then converted to a raster graphic for use on the Web. The last section of this chapter, "Rasterizing Vector Images," covers how it is done, but before it is discussed, you must understand the differences between these technologies and how you create vector images.

The comparison of these two illustration technologies shows some significant differences between the results generated by each. By definition, you can see that raster and vector drawings are different because of elements that define the image, but it is the visual differences and the way that they are created that are the predominant contrarieties.

The first major difference between these types of graphics is the way that they are displayed on-screen. Raster images are characterized by a more photo-realistic representation of the image, as shown in Figure 4.5. Because raster images use anti-aliasing (blurring of edges), elements within them appear much smoother. Alternatively, vector images are characterized by jaggy or stair-stepped edges on the elements in the image.

In Figure 4.5, on the left you see a raster representation of a raccoon. This portion of the figure is a photograph of a live animal. Because raster graphics define each and every pixel in the image, complex colors and blends can be defined, creating a very photo-realistic graphic. The right portion of Figure 4.5 is a vector drawing of a raccoon. Notice that this portion of the image is not as realistic as the portion on the right. This is one of the biggest differences between bitmap and vector drawing.

Figure 4.5.
*Raster versus vector
graphics.*

Most vector-based drawings do not give a photo-realistic representation, but it
can be obtained and requires painstaking work and very close attention to detail,
as shown in Figure 4.6.

Figure 4.6.
*Achieving photo-realism
with vector drawings is
much more difficult than
with raster-based
drawings.*

Because vector drawings are defined as discrete elements, the amount of realism
that can be portrayed is limited. Because each element is discrete (see Figure 4.7),
color blends between the elements are quite difficult. In the vector environment,
each element has a depth position. In other words, each element is placed on top
of another to create the final image. In Figure 4.7, some of the elements are
exploded so that you can perceive the depth that occurs between various
elements. Notice the elements that are in front of and behind other elements.

Figure 4.7.
Figure 4.7.
*Vector drawings are
composed of discrete,
separate elements.*

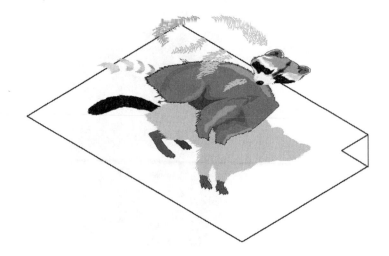

In Figure 4.8, notice that the flat environment is what you perceive. In Figure 4.7, only some of the elements are exploded. Actually, each colored portion is a separate element. But in the drawing environment, you perceive the drawing, as shown in Figure 4.8. In vector drawings, elements can easily be arranged by moving them forward and backward in the environment. Again, keep in mind that you don't actually see this arrangement in a 3D view, even though it occurs this way.

Figure 4.8.
*What you perceive is a
flat environment, even
though it is not.*

To better understand the natural depth that occurs in a vector environment, an example is fitting. In this example, a gray square is created. Then a black circle is created overlapping the square, as shown in Figure 4.9. The circle appears in front of the square because it was created after the square.

Figure 4.9.
Some simple objects to reveal the natural layering that occurs within a vector environment.

To move the square in front of the circle is a simple task. When you select the square and tell the software to move it to the front of the drawing, it appears in front of the circle as shown in Figure 4.10. All vector programs work this way. Illustrations are created by layering elements that are most often varying colors or shades. The compilation of the layers is what creates the final image. Keep in mind, however, that although a vector image looks a certain way (due to layering), any object can be moved to the front or back at any time. All of the objects remain discrete and moveable.

Although raster images present images in a more photo-realistic way, there is a price to pay for this characteristic. Because the smallest element in a raster image is the pixel, each pixel must be defined. A single raster image can contain thousands of pixels, and each pixel has data associated with it. This makes the raster image's file size quite large as compared to a vector drawing. A single 640×480, or full-screen raster image can require up to 40KB of hard disk space. This file would then require approximately 7 seconds to download over a 28.8K modem, which doesn't seem too bad, until you compare it to a vector version of the same file, which is less than 10KB.

Figure 4.10.
*Moving the square in
front of the circle is an
easy task.*

Resolution

The biggest advantage to vector graphics is their flexibility. Vector graphics are designed to output to many types of devices with quality representative of the output device. To understand this statement, you need to understand what *resolution* is.

Probably one of the most misunderstood graphic terms is resolution, because it can mean many things. In general, the term *resolution* describes the quality of replication for any particular device. It also describes the quality of multimedia elements such as graphics, sound, and video. Printers, monitors, images, sounds, and even video have a resolution. Resolution simply describes the clarity or quality of any of these devices or objects. By the time you are finished with this book, you will have read how resolution relates to all of these items.

Concerning graphic images, resolution describes the number of dots per inch (dpi) in the image. This is image resolution. The number of dots that are replicated on a monitor or on a printed page determines the quality of the replication of the image on the particular device. This is device resolution. The quality of image output is dependent upon both the image and device resolution.

Most common desktop laser printers have a device resolution of 300 to 600 dots per inch. Most computer monitors display a device resolution of 72 or 75 dots per inch. The more dots a device can print or display, the higher the quality of the reproduction.

To see how image resolution affects quality, take a look at Figure 4.11. The left image has an image resolution of 300 dpi, and the right image has an image resolution of 72 dpi. Notice the significant degradation in the lower resolution image. You can see that the quality of the image is affected by its resolution. The lower the resolution, the less data that is maintained about the image.

Figure 4.11.
Seeing the effects of image resolution by comparing a 300 dpi image and a 72 dpi image printed on a 300 dpi laser printer.

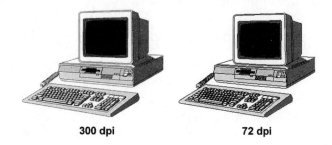

300 dpi   **72 dpi**

The quality of an image is dependent upon its resolution. However, you must also understand that the perceived quality is dependent upon the device on which you are outputting it. In Figure 4.11, you could see a noticeable difference between the two figures due to a difference in the dpi of the image. Do you know why? Notice that the image was being *printed* on a device equivalent to the higher resolution image. This example works if you are comparing two images with varying resolutions from a device equal to the higher of the two resolutions. What happens if you display both images on a 72 dpi monitor, where the device is equivalent to the lower of the two resolutions? As Figure 4.12 shows, you will be unable to perceive any difference between the two files, even though you know that one is 300 dpi and the other is 72 dpi.

Figure 4.12.
Comparing a 300 dpi image and a 72 dpi image displayed on a 72 dpi monitor.

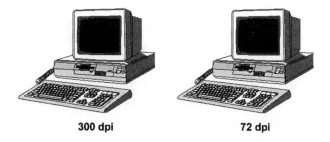

300 dpi   **72 dpi**

Whenever you are dealing with computer graphics, the perceived quality of a graphic is dependent upon two things: the resolution of the image and the resolution of the device. These two are completely independent, but they can greatly affect the results you get from either vector or bitmap graphics. For optimum quality in your graphic images, you really want the resolution of your graphics to match the resolution of the device you are outputting it to. This will give you the optimum quality in your images.

Knowing this, Web distribution of all of your graphic images (those displayed in your pages) only needs to be 72 dpi. As you saw in Figure 4.12, anything more than 72 dpi will not be displayed and is just a waste of bandwidth. The more data you push over the Net, the longer your audience will be waiting for your pages to download. And with unused data, your audience will likely be disgusted by having to wait for large images to download.

Device Independence

As you have seen, resolution plays an important part in the quality of graphic images. As you will see in the next chapter, resolution is one of the most important attributes of concern with bitmap graphics. In bitmap graphics, the resolution is defined when the image is created and can only be changed by adjusting the size of the image. Bitmap graphics are dependent on resolution (device). However, with vector illustrations, resolution is fluid, meaning that the dpi can be increased or decreased on-the-fly. It also means that vector images can be scaled without any concerns about affecting the resolution of the image.

When vector graphics are created, they are displayed on a 72 dpi monitor. The designer might then choose to proof the drawing on a 300 dpi laser printer. Finally, the finished product for which the image was created is produced on a 1200 dpi printer. For vector graphics, this does not create a problem. In most vector packages, resolution can be changed by either changing the target printer, in which case the application automatically senses what dpi is needed, or the desired dpi for the image can be set somewhere in the software. The main concern when dealing with vector graphics is that the dpi of the vector image match the dpi of the output device for maximum image quality.

Advantages and Disadvantages of Vector Illustration

As you have seen, vector graphics present many advantages over bitmap images due to the way that they are defined. Vector graphics are advantageous because of the following:

- They are device-independent, meaning that their dpi and size can be changed without affecting the quality of the image or the size of the file.
- They generally have a smaller file size than bitmap graphics, meaning that they can be downloaded much more quickly when incorporated into Web pages.

- A single vector graphic can be used for many different purposes, and its quality can be manipulated to match the varying qualities of a wide range of devices. Keep in mind that optimum quality is obtained when the resolution of the vector graphic is equal to the resolution of the output device.
- A vector graphic is often easier to create and manipulate given a situation where a photo-realistic image is not needed.

As with anything, there are also disadvantages to using vector graphics. As you have seen, one of the disadvantages of vector graphics is that photo-realism requires painstaking work. Because each object in a vector graphic is self-contained and discrete with its own properties and defined characteristics, it is very difficult to create blends and other graphic effects between objects. For example, in Figure 4.9, it would require a lot of work to create a blend between the circle and the square—however, it could be done. This is one reason that vector graphics are generally less than photo quality. It requires much more work to create smooth, photo-realistic blends in a vector environment. Yet, the biggest disadvantage to vector illustrations is the aliased edges that appear stair-stepped within the graphic, which also contributes to its less than photo-realistic nature.

To understand aliasing, take a look at Figure 4.13. Notice in the graphic the comparison of the aliased and anti-aliased lines. Aliased lines are characteristic of vector drawings while anti-aliased lines are characteristic of bitmap graphics. This is one of the most significant details that clues you into whether a graphic is a vector or bitmap image. Notice that the aliased line looks stair-stepped or jaggy, whereas the anti-aliased line looks smoother. Let's take a closer look at the lines in the illustration to understand why one appears smoother than the other.

Figure 4.13.
The comparison of an aliased line to an anti-aliased line.

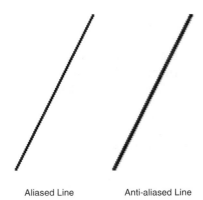

Aliased Line   Anti-aliased Line

As shown in Figure 4.14, you see a closer look at the two lines. Notice that the anti-aliased line has pixels added that are a blend between the black color of the line and the white background. This makes the line appear smooth. Anti-aliasing occurs in raster environments to make objects look smoother and more photo-realistic. Because the raster environment is based on pixels, anti-aliasing is possible. However, in the vector environment, where the drawing is defined by objects rather than pixels, there is no anti-aliasing that occurs. All objects appear with typical jaggies.

Figure 4.14.
A closer look at the two lines reveals what is happening to the anti-aliased line.

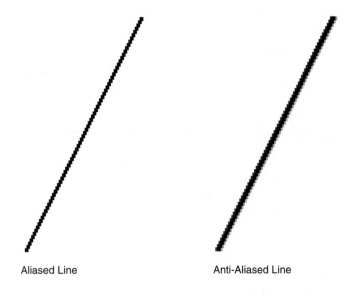

Aliased Line   Anti-Aliased Line

Because this is a negative aspect of working with vector drawings for use on raster devices (such as a monitor), many PostScript drawing packages include anti-aliasing effects within the vector environment. As I am writing this, I am aware of at least one vector drawing program (Macromedia FreeHand 7.0) that allows the developer to specify that anti-aliasing occur. It must be noted, however, that vector programs that perform anti-aliasing are slower than programs that don't, due to the amount of information that must be generated with the PostScript drawing.

The Nature of Vector Objects

In the aliased vector environment, you will notice that only certain elements display the stair-stepped nature of aliased edges. In the vector environment, angled lines, arcs, and circles have the characteristic jagged edges, as shown in Figure 4.15. Note that straight lines, both horizontal and vertical, do not show jagged edges.

Figure 4.15.
Elements that reveal
aliased edges.

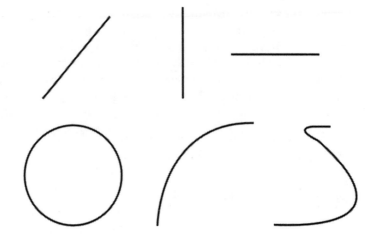

Closed Areas and Fills

As you have seen, in the vector environment, everything is based upon points and paths. Every line, arc, circle, and square, as well as any other element that can be created, is the result of points with interconnecting lines (or Bézier curves), as shown in Figure 4.16. All objects are points that are connected using either normal lines or Bézier lines that have control handles.

Figure 4.16.
All objects are composed
of points.

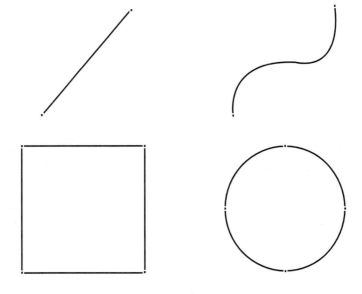

Whenever you are drawing in a vector environment, all the things that you do, both in creation and in editing, are based upon either specifying point elements, such as defining points for a line, arc, or circle, or defining the characteristics of a particular element, such as specifying the linetype or thickness of an element. In general, the creation of a vector drawing requires that you define points that make up the element you are creating and specify the characteristics of that entity.

One of the things you have not read about so far is how colors, blends, and other drawing characteristics are created in the vector environment. How do you create an area of color in the vector environment?

All areas of color within a vector environment are based upon closed areas. A closed area can include a circle, rectangle, polygon, or another path that is closed, as shown in Figure 4.17. Once a path is closed, it becomes an object that can have more than just a simple line thickness or linetype. Closed areas are specified so that they contain fills, patterns, and other special effects aside from line attributes.

Figure 4.17.
Closed areas in the vector drawing can contain fills, blends, and other effects.

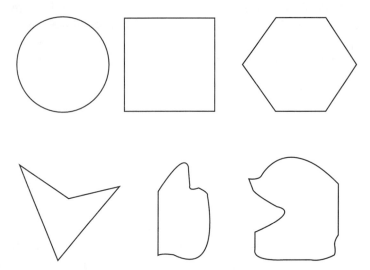

Note that once a path becomes a closed entity it can have two types of attributes: line and fill attributes. The line is the characteristic or way that a line looks. Most often, the line attributes include thickness, style (such as dashed or continuous), and color. The fill characteristics can include simple fills of flat color or gradient color, as well as patterned fills and PostScript effects. Figure 4.18 shows several circles with varying line and fill characteristics. By varying the colors and styles in both line and fill, complex vector drawings can be created, such as the one shown in Figure 4.19.

Figure 4.18.
*Line and fill attributes
are the two main
characteristics of closed
vector elements.*

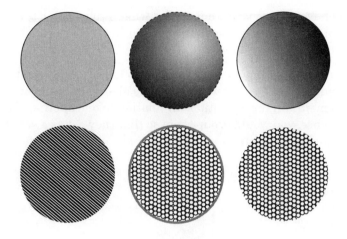

Figure 4.19.
*Varying line and fill
attributes yields complex
vector drawings.*

Grouping, Joining, and Boolean Operations

One of the fundamental capabilities within a vector environment is the capability
to join or merge basic elements such as lines and arcs, or even entire objects, to
create other objects. Most vector programs allow three basic types of operations:
grouping, joining, and Boolean operations. Each of these creates a specific type
of entity, and each behaves a little differently.

The first of the fundamental operation is grouping. As you saw earlier in this
chapter, the entire vector environment is a layered environment wherein objects
have depth position. The objects' depth position determines the look of the
illustration. In addition, you have seen that each discrete object in the database

behaves as a separate entity. But what if you wanted to change a set of objects and not just one, such as scaling or moving a set of objects? This is where the grouping function becomes important.

In Figure 4.20, you see several objects that are discrete and function independently. Let's say you want to reduce all of the objects by 50 percent but you want to maintain their positions in relation to one another. To scale all of the objects at once, you would group them so that they act as a set of objects rather than as individual objects.

Figure 4.20.
Discrete objects can be grouped to perform an operation such as scaling.

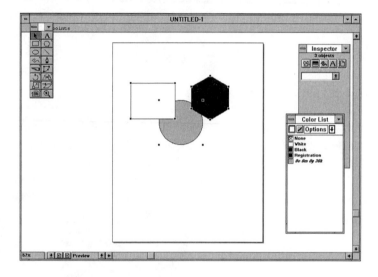

In Figure 4.21, the objects have been grouped. Notice that the objects now behave as a single entity rather than as multiple objects. The nice thing about grouping is that objects can be grouped, manipulated, and then ungrouped. Grouping objects does not get rid of the discreteness of the objects in the group. It creates a set of objects that are affected together but maintain their discreteness, as shown in Figure 4.22. Notice that ungrouping the scaled objects separates them so that they become independent objects again.

The second major capability of vector programs is that they can join objects together. Unlike grouping, joining objects destroys the discrete nature of the objects. In essence, a new object is created from the old objects.

Figure 4.23 shows several independent lines that are discrete, even though they look like a closed polygon. Let's say you wanted to create a fill within the object. Fills can occur within closed areas only. In this case, you must join the elements to make a closed area. Then a fill can be assigned to the newly created object. Joining elements destroys their independence. The characteristics such as thickness and colors that were associated with the individual elements are gone. The new element has characteristics of its own.

Figure 4.21.
Once objects have been grouped, they behave as a single entity.

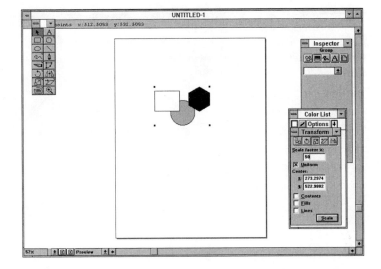

Figure 4.22.
Ungrouping previously grouped objects restores their discrete natures.

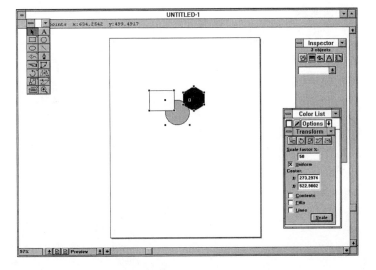

Then, there are vector operations that are performed on closed objects. The operations, called Boolean operations, allow the developer to create unique objects from a set of lower objects. Figure 4.24 shows the three basic operations that can be performed on vector objects: union, subtraction, and intersection. Notice that uniting two objects merges the objects. The common area of the two objects is called the *welding point.* In the subtraction, notice that one object is physically subtracted from the other, while the intersection causes only the overlapping area to remain.

Figure 4.23.
Joining elements creates a new unique object from a set of lower objects. All characteristics associated with the lower objects are destroyed to create a new discrete object.

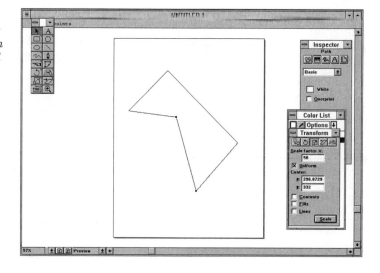

Figure 4.24.
Utilizing Boolean operations on closed vector objects.

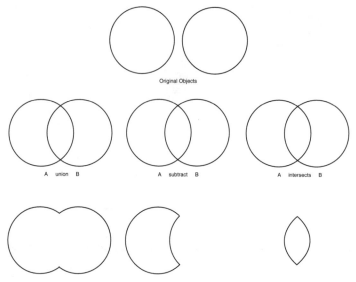

Almost every vector program allows these three vector editing capabilities. The ease with which they can be performed varies. If you are planning to purchase or use a vector program, you will definitely want to examine the package for these types of capability as well as how easily they can be performed.

As you surf the Web over the next couple of years, you will probably begin seeing more and more vector elements used on the Web, as plug-ins are developed and as browsers begin to support their use. However, there are some vector elements that are already being directly used in Web pages. Do you know what they are?

Vector Elements and the Web

One of the reasons vector images have not been used exclusively on the Web is because of their poor quality at 72 dpi (monitor resolution). However, vector elements are the basis for much of the text that is used in Web pages because of the speed at which vector information can be delivered on the Web. In fact, the text specifications that are used in the HTML coding, with tags such as <H1>, <P>, and so on, are actually specifications for the browser to create vector text on the Web page.

Figure 4.25 shows a Web page that displays vector fonts. Can you spot the vector items? Remember, look for the characteristic jaggies. Notice that the text in this Web page is composed of vector text. So, you can see that although vector graphics are not yet exclusively used on the Web, much of the text is vector-based. All of the HTML tags that allow you to insert text are vector-based. Knowing this, you can see that the larger the text is in the Web page, the more it will display the characteristic vector jaggies, as shown in Figure 4.26.

Figure 4.25.
Can you spot the vector elements in this Web page?

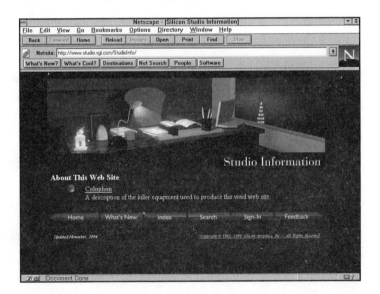

In addition to the vector fonts that are used in Web pages, new technologies, such as Macromedia's Shockwave for FreeHand, can enable you to include vector images on the Web. Once an illustration has been created, to include it on a Web page requires the use of a filter called Afterburner, which prepares the file for Web distribution. The filter gets rid of some information that is not relative to Web delivery and compresses the file. The effects achieved by the use of plug-ins are quite nice, such as zooming capability and higher-resolution printouts; however, plug-ins do not get rid of the characteristic jaggies of vector illustrations.

In Figure 4.27, you see a page that has a Shockwave for FreeHand file in its upper portion. Notice that the illustration exhibits the characteristics of a vector file.

Figure 4.26.
The larger the HTML text is, the more it looks like vector text.

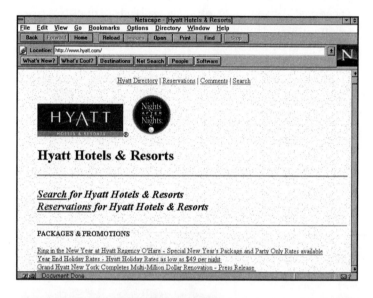

Figure 4.27.
A vector image embedded within a Web page using Macromedia's Shockwave for FreeHand plug-in.

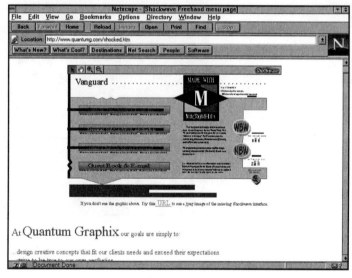

Rasterizing Vector Images

The biggest problem with the conversion of vector graphics to raster is that you end up with jaggies—edges that are often severely pixelated. However, you can get rid of the jaggies if you convert them correctly. Most vector graphics can be imported or opened into Macromedia FreeHand and Adobe Illustrator. These two tools are the predominant illustration packages used for vector illustration. The first step in using vector graphics is the conversion process from vector to raster. I am going to show you how to do it in Macromedia FreeHand because it has a very good filter. You can also import certain vector files into Adobe Photoshop, which also rasterizes vector illustrations quite nicely.

Begin the conversion process by opening the image into the vector program. One of the advantages of Macromedia FreeHand on the PC is that it allows you to export a vector drawing as a TIFF file. The program automatically converts the image to a pixel-based raster drawing. You also have control over resolution and bit depth, which are discussed in the next chapter. However, to make this whole thing work correctly, scale the image up to a larger size than you need, as shown in Figure 4.28.

Figure 4.28.
Scaling the image up in the vector program.

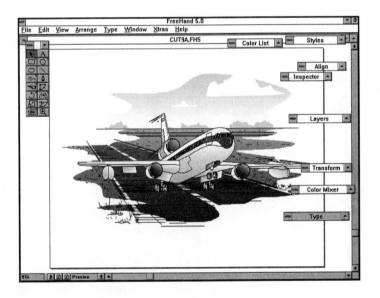

After scaling it up, use the File | Export option and export it as a TIFF image. Now you have a raster image of a drawing; open it into Adobe Photoshop. (Figure 4.29 shows an example.)

Flyure 4.29.
Opening the rasterized TIFF image.

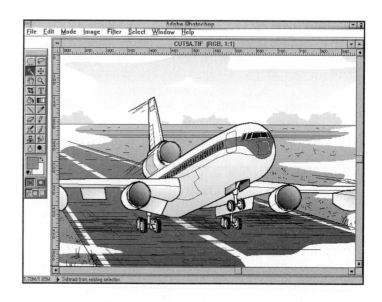

After opening the image in Photoshop, you can see that the jaggies are quite evident. Notice that the edges of the illustration display the characteristic stair-step edges.

To solve this problem, create a new layer. Then, select the images and move them to a new layer by copying and pasting. After the elements are on the new layer, scale them. The purpose for scaling the image up in the vector program is so it can be scaled back down in the raster package. What happens when you scale the image down in the raster package? The raster editor automatically blurs the edges of the image and, voila! No more jaggies. (See Figure 4.30.)

Figure 4.30.
The finished, scaled, and rasterized vector file.

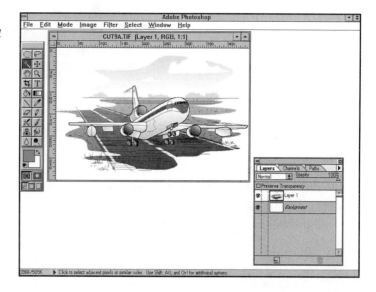

If you do not have access to Macromedia FreeHand, here are a couple of other ways to do this conversion:

- Convert your raster image to an Adobe Illustrator file and open it directly into Adobe Photoshop.
- Do a screen capture of the vector file as it is open in the vector editor.

Summary

In this chapter you read about the positive and negative aspects of vector drawing. Vector drawings are advantageous because of their small size, device independence, and the relative ease with which they can be created, assuming photo-realism is not an issue. However, vector drawings are often characterized by jagged edges and less than photo-realistic quality. Achieving photo-realism in a vector drawing often requires more time and resources than a comparative bitmap drawing of the same image. Keep in mind that although vector drawing is not widely used for illustrations on the Web, many times vector drawings can be successfully used either through the use of plug-ins, such as Macromedia's Shockwave for FreeHand, or by conversion to a bitmap, as described in the end of this chapter.

5

Raster-Based Graphics

In the previous chapter, you were introduced to vector and bitmap graphics and the many ways in which vector graphics are unique. Although vector graphics are important, most of the graphics found on the Web are raster graphics. Figure 5.1 shows an example of a Web page where all the graphic elements are composed of bitmaps. For every vector graphic found on the Web, there are probably ten times as many raster graphics. This is no surprise.

The main reason that raster graphics are used on the Web is because of the output device. The HTML language only includes recognition for bitmap graphics because the devices intended to display Web pages are themselves based on bitmaps. All the computer monitors that you use on a daily basis, whether they are PC, Macintosh, or UNIX-based, utilize raster graphics displays. It is then no wonder that a communication medium whose primary means of output is display-based chooses to directly support only raster-based graphics. Figure 5.2 shows an example of a Web page that is impossible to display as clearly and impressively with vector graphics.

Figure 5.1.
*Bitmap graphics are
the most widely used
graphics type on
the Web.*

Figure 5.2.
*Photo-realistic graphics
look less impressive if
vector graphics are used.*

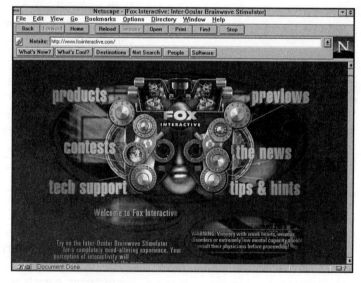

In this chapter, you will read about the various aspects of bitmap graphics. Probably one of the most misunderstood elements in Web design is raster-based graphics. With hundreds of different raster editing applications, each program works a little bit differently. However, the way a bitmap image is defined and manipulated is constant.

While reading this chapter, you are presented with the three common attributes of the raster graphic: image resolution, image size, and image bit depth. You read a little bit about image resolution in the previous chapter. Here, you'll delve a little deeper into its implications and how it relates to bitmap graphics.

You'll also find that bitmap graphics differ from vector graphics in that there is a fixed relationship between the image's resolution and its size. The final attribute of raster graphics you'll examine is bit depth, something that was irrelevant to the vector environment. Bit depth is one of the hardest things to understand when working with bitmap graphics as well as audio and video. Here, you begin looking at how it affects the bitmap graphic. In Chapter 13, "Sound," and Chapter 14, "Video," you'll see how bit depth relates to these two media elements.

In addition to the attributes of the bitmap graphic, you'll also take a look at some of the common characteristics of sizing images as well as features you should be looking for in a prospect raster application. Toward the end of this chapter, you'll also take a look at a myriad of file formats that can be used to house your raster data as well as ways to reduce the sizes of these files using compression.

Prior to moving into some of the advanced topics concerning bitmap graphics, you need to begin by looking at the pixel itself and how it is defined in the raster environment. Then, you'll look at image resolution, image size, and image bit depth.

The Nature of the Pixel

As was highlighted in the previous chapter, "Vector-Based Graphics," bitmap graphics are graphics in which the smallest elements in the drawing are pixels. No matter the size of the bitmap image, it is composed of many pixels, as shown in Figure 5.3.

Some of the standard sizes of bitmaps include 320 pixels by 240 pixels, 640 pixels by 480 pixels, and 800 pixels by 600 pixels. However, the graphics you include on your pages will often be nonstandard sizes.

Understand that when images are specified this way, these numbers represent exact image sizes, such as an image that is 640 pixels in width by 480 pixels in height. Computer monitors are also specified in a similar manner. However, the second number is interpreted as number of lines, or scan lines in the monitor's screen area. For example, a monitor screen area that is specified as 640 by 480 means 640 pixels by 480 scan lines. Each vertical pixel represents one scan line of horizontal pixels.

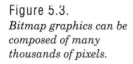
Figure 5.3.
Bitmap graphics can be composed of many thousands of pixels.

Pixels themselves are akin to dots that are used to create a printed picture. To be completely accurate, when you are talking about images that are displayed on a computer monitor, you are talking about pixels per inch (ppi). As you saw in the last chapter, when you are talking about output from a printer, you are talking about dots per inch, or dpi. In reality, dpi equals ppi. If someone says that an image is 600 dpi, it is the same as saying the image is 600 ppi. Dpi equals ppi.

Device Dependency

In the last chapter, you saw that vector images are device-independent. This means that the dpi can change and the image can be sized without greatly affecting either the quality of the image or the graphic's file size. In addition, the vector file doesn't have a relationship between the dpi and the size. They are independent, yet bitmap images work exactly the opposite of vector files.

Bitmap graphics are device-dependent. This means that when the raster graphic file is created, a fixed relationship between the image's size and its dpi is established. The image is created for a specific output size and device dpi. In addition, the quality of the image is also affected by the bit depth at which it is created. These very important details are set when you create the bitmap image.

Once bitmap attributes are set, the range of usefulness for the graphic becomes limited. With bitmap graphics, the issue of dpi and size can be a complex issue. Improperly sized images are the most common problem found on the Web, and this is exhibited in graphics that display with much lower quality than was intended or those that require a significant amount of time to download. In the following sections, you'll take a look at the three vital attributes of all bitmap images. Note that these attributes not only affect the quality of the displayed image, but they also affect the size of the graphic file itself. Therefore, these attributes can either increase or decrease both the quality of the graphic and the efficiency at which it downloads.

Imaging Terms

Undoubtedly, the biggest hurdle you'll encounter is designing your bitmap graphics so they download quickly and display qualitatively for your audience. As you read in the previous chapter, bitmap graphics are much larger than vector graphics because of the way they are defined—pixel by pixel. Many of the following attributes directly affect file size, so they also affect download speed. These attributes also affect image quality. Optimally, you want to design your graphics so that your audience can view them without waiting for long periods of time for your pages to download. However, if the file is too small, too little data is contained in the graphic file and the aesthetic results of the image can be self-defeating.

Image Resolution

The first term that you must understand is dots per inch (dpi). To be technically accurate, it is generally called pixels per inch (ppi). However, in this section, I call it dpi for continuity between chapters. Keep in mind that dpi equals ppi.

As you saw in the previous chapter, dpi is commonly associated with graphics and desktop publishing output. Dots per inch, or dpi, is a measurement used to describe the number of physical, printable dots per square inch of the image.

The image resolution that you need for a graphic image, whether vector or bitmap, is basically dependent upon your output device. Understand that for most Web development tasks, all you need is 72 dpi because that is the maximum resolution of almost all computer monitors. Anything more, and you're just wasting bandwidth on the Net.

Alternatively, if you want a graphic to print very cleanly from the Web, the dpi must be higher. Figure 5.4 shows a 72-dpi graphic image printed at 300 dpi and a 300 dpi graphic image printed at 300 dpi. Notice the significant difference between the clarity of the two images. The image to the left is a 72-dpi image and the pixels that make up the image are easily seen. The image to the right is much sharper and photo-realistic. It has more dots (or pixels) to represent the image at the given size.

Figure 5.4.
*A 72-dpi image versus a
300-dpi image.*

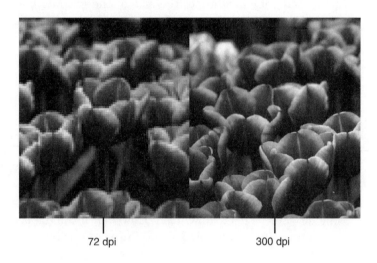

72 dpi   300 dpi

Another difference between the 72-and 300-dpi images, one you can't see in the displayed image, is the file size. Creating raster images at a high resolution exponentially increases the file size. In the previous chapter, you saw that adjusting the dpi of vector images does not affect the file size. With bitmaps, this is not the case. In the previous figure, the file size of the high resolution image is about four times the size of the low resolution file! When you're designing bitmap graphics, design for the lowest common denominator. Only include high-resolution files if you intend for the audience to download them and view them separate from the Web browser. Do not include high-resolution images, ones with a dpi greater than 72 dpi, as inline images in your pages.

As you're creating graphics for the Web, sometimes you might choose to use bitmaps that were created for another purpose. This is perfectly fine if the image is large enough or has sufficient resolution to support the size at which you want to display it. If you want to display it at a certain size, the dpi must be 72 at that size. Most often, you use images that have more than an adequate resolution, so in most cases, you simply need to reduce the dpi and scale the image for use on the Web. What happens if you want to display an image in your Web pages larger than it currently exists?

To solve this problem, often an enterprising person might say, "Just increase the dpi on the low resolution image so it'll display correctly." Unfortunately, that won't work. Bitmap graphics are device-dependent graphic files, meaning that once the graphic is created (or exists) at a certain resolution per image size, you cannot increase the dpi without reducing its size. The image is dependent upon the size at which it was originally created. Figure 5.5 shows what I mean. Notice that the smaller version of the image looks fine when displayed at its original size. When you increase the size of the image, notice that the image becomes fuzzy and unclear.

Figure 5.5.
Increasing the dpi on a low resolution file doesn't increase the output clarity.

Take another look at scaling an existing bitmap by using an example inserted into a Web page. In Figure 5.6, you see a graphic created and inserted into a page at multiple sizes using the HEIGHT and WIDTH attributes of the <IMG> tag. First notice that the center graphic was inserted at its true size. The graphic to the left has its HEIGHT and WIDTH attributes (of the <IMG> tag) set at half the value, so the image appears 50 percent smaller than the true size. The graphic to the right is set at 150 percent larger.

In the case of the small image in Figure 5.6, specifying a reduced size displays okay, although the image is a little ratty and rough. Think about this for a minute. Using what you know about scaling an image up and down, is bandwidth being wasted here? For the image to be displayed this way, all the image data must be downloaded. The data being downloaded has enough dots to display the middle image. However, the browser is shrinking it so that it can display it at 72 dpi at the specified size. You could save downloading time, as well as display a nicer graphic, if the image were sized before you bring it into the page.

Figure 5.6.
*Scaling a bitmap up
causes image
degradation.*

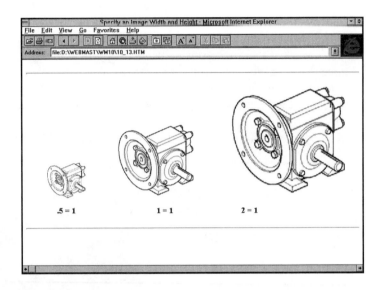

Now look at the other image. The image that is displayed at 150 percent larger
has visible problems. This is the one that has the least visual appeal. Specifying
that the browser scale the graphic up as it is displayed causes the dots to separate
in the image. There is not enough data (dots) to fill the specified size with pixels.
Therefore, the browser must display the existing data with larger pixels. This
makes the image appear grainy and quite frankly, pretty poor. Again, it should
be sized in a raster program and displayed at the true size in the browser. Code
your HTML so that graphics on pages use the exact, or true, size of the image.

It seems appropriate to mention here that the device dependency of bitmap
graphics is the biggest single problem with using them. This is why vector images
are appealing to a point. Vector graphics are device-independent, meaning that
the dpi can be increased or decreased based upon the output device. This makes
sense because vector files are based upon objects rather than absolute pixel
definitions.

Because most Web developers design for screen use only, dpi might not be a great
concern. It usually becomes a problem when you use source images created for
another purpose. However, I am sure that some of you want to design for multiple
purposes.

In any case, develop any and all bitmap graphics at 300 dpi. This gives you
flexibility—in case you want printable versions in the future. Again, you will
notice an increase in file storage requirements as well as decreased processing
speed, but you give yourself more options of reusing the graphics later by
designing at a higher dpi. Prior to inserting the images into your Web pages,

decrease the dpi or image size to an appropriate amount for Web distribution. A good file management technique is to maintain both high and low resolution versions of your graphics.

Image Size

Something directly related to dpi is the image size. There is a fixed relationship between the image size and the image dpi once the image is created. The device dependency of raster images forces you to plan your raster image sizes prior to creating any bitmap graphic.

Image size is the physical height and width dimensions for the raster image. Figure 5.7 shows a graphic image whose image resolution is 72 dpi and whose image size is 2 inches by 2 inches. The first image you see is printed at true size and looks pretty clear. Suppose you decided to print or display the image at that scale. Everything would be okay. Suppose that someone wants to print or display it at larger than 2 inches by 2 inches, maybe at 4 inches by 4 inches. Could you simply scale the image up?

Figure 5.7.
A 72 dpi, 2"×2" image printed at true size and scaled size.

Unfortunately, scaling a bitmap image up will almost always cause the image to break up, as shown in the right portion of Figure 5.7. Any time you scale an image up, you can only scale it up until the dpi equals the resolution of the output device. In the example, the image could be scaled up until its dpi equaled 72. As soon as the dpi begins to drop lower than 72 (or the resolution of the target output device), as a result of scaling, the image begins to break apart and the pixels in the image become noticeable.

Why does it do this? It is device-dependent, or in other words, there is a fixed relationship between the dpi and image size. Remember that dpi is related to the physical size of the image. As the physical size of the image changes, so does its area. As the area changes, the dpi must also change. As the area becomes wider or taller, the dots spread out and more data is needed. As the image becomes thinner and shorter, the area is lessened, so fewer dots are needed.

Figure 5.8 shows how scaling the image or changing its area affects its dots. At the 2 inch by 2 inch layout, the dots are just like they are supposed to be. The original fixed relationship is 1:1. In the second image, scaling or stretching the image causes the dots to separate and the resulting image becomes blurry. The reason it becomes blurry is that the image editor must add dots to the image to maintain the dpi/size relationship. It adds dots by interpolating a dot (or more than one if necessary) between two existing dots. Interpolation is the process of creating data based upon the surrounding data. This is why edges and other features become blurry. Stretching or scaling a bitmap image to a larger size causes the fixed dots to separate, requiring interpolation, and the image becomes blurry. Alternatively, shrinking or scaling the image down causes the dots to become more condensed, requiring some dots to be deleted or merged into surrounding dots. Often the image becomes more sharp and clear as a result. However, when this happens, data is being deleted from the image. Concerning scaling, bitmaps always work this way.

Figure 5.8.

Scaling a bitmap up spreads out the dots; scaling a bitmap down compresses the dots.

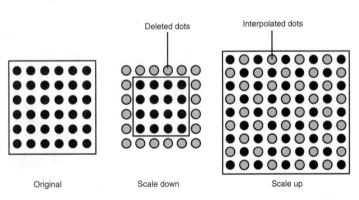

Deleted dots

Interpolated dots

Original   Scale down   Scale up

A final comment related to bitmap image size is just a statement of the obvious. As either dpi or image size increase, so does the size of the file due to an increase in the amount of data, or dots. As size or dpi decreases, so does the file size. Most of the time, you want to create your bitmap images at true size—the size that they will appear in your Web pages. You might also want to create them larger than needed (for those just-in-case print purposes) and create reduced versions for inclusion on your Web pages.

Image Bit Depth

The final concern with bitmap images is an issue totally unrelated in vector graphics. This is the issue of bit depth. For most people, bit depth is a confusing topic, akin to the dpi and image size relationship. I hope I can clear up any misconceptions through a somewhat lengthy explanation.

First, understand that bit depth concerns much more than just graphics, although that's what you are reading about right now. Bit depth is an issue in digital video and digital audio as well as you will see in Chapters 13 and 14. Bit depth defines the physical number of bits that can be used to describe a sample, regardless of whether it is a graphic, sound clip, or video clip.

Before you see bit depth and its relevance to raster graphics, look at the underlying reason that bit depth is an issue at all when you deal with digital data.

Everything the computer deals with must be digital data. The only thing that the computer can understand is binary data, composed of 0s and 1s. However, everything that our natural senses can interpret (such as sound, video, and graphics) must be presented to us as analog data composed of waves. (See Figure 5.9.) What is the difference between these types of data?

Figure 5.9.
Digital data is composed of a series of 0s and 1s, whereas analog data is composed of frequency variations (waves).

01010110
01000010
00101001

Digital data   Analog data

Digital data is data that is represented mathematically as a series of 0s and 1s, or off and on states. Analog data is data that is defined by a series of variations of frequencies (refer to Figure 5.9). For example, the colors you see in graphics are perceived by the rods in our eyes. The colors actually emit waves which are specific frequencies that you can perceive, as shown in Figure 5.10. This is one example of a frequency variation, or analog data. Our senses interpret analog data such as sound or visual imagery.

Binary data, on the other hand, doesn't mean much to us because our physical senses can't interpret it as it really is. A long string of 0s and 1s makes little sense to us, but to the computer, it means something. For example, a single alphanumeric character is represented with a series of 8 bits called a byte. The series of eight 0s and 1s means little to us, but to the computer, it represents the letter A, as shown in Figure 5.11.

Figure 5.10.
*Colors you see and
sounds you hear are
composed of waves
(analog data).*

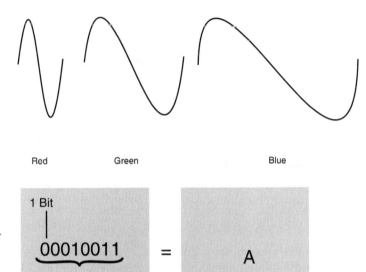

Red   Green   Blue

Figure 5.11.
*Binary data, such as an
alphanumeric character,
is composed of a series of
0s and 1s.*

1 Bit

00010011   =   A

1 Byte

Digital data   Analog data

For you to be able to work with computers at all, one of the two parties, either computer or human, must be able to speak the other's language. All the various input and output devices you use on a daily basis are designed for this purpose—to allow communication between the computer and the operator.

Much of what the computer does revolves around the conversion between analog data—that we can interpret—and digital data—that the computer can interpret. Computing is not just processing data. It is also managing the digital-to-analog and analog-to-digital conversion process. Special chips within the computer, called ADCs (analog-to-digital converters) and DACs (digital-to-analog convert-ers), handle the process of converting data between analog and digital and vice versa. The ADC is used in input devices, whereas the DAC is used in output devices as shown in Figure 5.12. ADCs and DACs are not always actual chips, but sometimes, they are a result of software. In any case, this conversion is what makes computer use possible.

What does this have to do with bit depth, you might ask. Knowing the conversion process is really a prelude to understanding bit depth and its relationship to imaging. Any time you want to represent analog data digitally, you must sample the analog data into the computer. Sampling is the process of converting between the two data types. Most often, sampling means converting from analog data to digital data.

Figure 5.12.
*Analog-to-digital
converters and digital-
to-analog converters are
necessary for computer
use.*

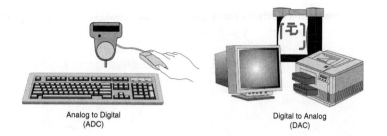

Analog to Digital
(ADC)

Digital to Analog
(DAC)

For example, digitizing audio into the computer requires sampling the audio
(converting it from an analog source, such as a tape recorder, to a digital file on
the computer). The sampling process requires taking small chunks of that data,
at specific intervals, and converting it to digitally represent the analog data. (See
Figure 5.13.) The more frequent the chunks or samples, the more the digital audio
is like its analog counterpart. The frequency, or how often we take those samples,
is called the *sampling rate*. The higher the sampling rate, the more accurate the
finished audio clip, because you take more frequent samples of the analog source.

Figure 5.13.
*The sampling process
requires converting
chunks or samples of
data at specific intervals.*

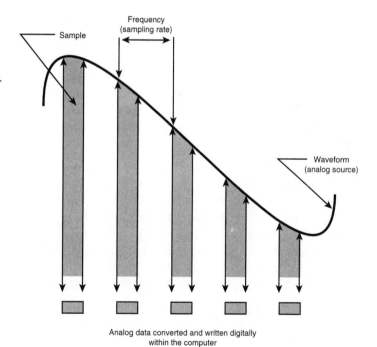

Sample

Frequency
(sampling rate)

Waveform
(analog source)

Analog data converted and written digitally
within the computer

Once you have a sample, you must digitally describe the sample. It doesn't matter
whether it is a graphic, audio, or video clip. Describing the sample is how bit depth
relates to graphics, audio, and video.

Bit depth defines the number of physical computer bits you can use to describe the sample that you have. The more bits you can use to describe the sample, the more representative that sample is. Figure 5.14 shows an audio sample from an analog source. Below it are three representations using various bit depths. In the figure, which wave is more like the analog source? The answer is the one with the highest bit depth.

Figure 5.14.

The wave form that is most like the original analog source is the one with the highest bit depth (and sampling rate).

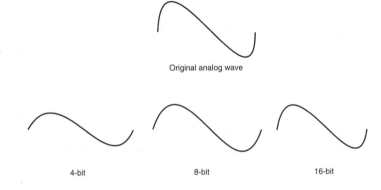

Original analog wave

4-bit   8-bit   16-bit

For any ADC sampling process, the higher the bit depth, the better the digital representation of it because you have more digital bits to describe the sample. This is true with audio and video as well as graphics. The overall conversion of analog to digital data is dependent upon the sampling rate—how often you take a sample—and the bit depth—how many bits you have to describe that sample. Sampling rate describes frequency of samples; bit depth describes descriptiveness of the samples.

Now that you understand what bit depth is, look at it in relationship to imaging. Most images that you work with are either 24- or 8-bit images. These measurements describe the number of bits that you can use to represent the image. In a 24-bit (true color) image, each pixel in the image can be any one of 16.7 million colors; there are 16.7 million color possibilities for any pixel. In an 8-bit (indexed) image, each color can be any one of 256 colors. Notice that a 24-bit image allows for a better representation of an image because it has more bits with which to describe the samples in the image. (See Figure 5.15.)

Because bit depth is a common area of confusion, I want to interject one more example to help explain. This is a simple example, but I believe it'll get the point across.

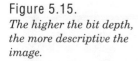
Figure 5.15.
The higher the bit depth, the more descriptive the image.

Imagine that I give you a set of 16 crayons (yes, I said crayons), to create an image. I also give a set of 72 crayons to someone else to draw the same image. Assume that your sketching ability matches that of the other person. Whose image will be more representative, the one with 16 different colors or the one with 72 different colors? In theory, the one with 72. This is also how bit depth works.

The more bits you can use to describe the image, the more colors with which your image can be described. The more colors that can be in your image, the more representative, or photo-realistic, the image. Fewer bits are less descriptive; more bits are more descriptive.

Throughout the previous section, you saw that bitmap images are device-dependent; their resolution (dpi) and image size are fixed. Changing one changes the other. Bit depth is also a one-way street. If you reduce the bit depth of an image, you decrease the amount of data that can be described, which in turn reduces the amount of data in the file. For example, if you have a 24-bit image and you convert it to 8-bits, you decrease the quality of the image. If you try to convert it back to a 24-bit image, in effect, you will have 8-bit data in a 24-bit file. (See Figure 5.16.)

As you work with bitmap graphics, you must be aware of the number of colors supported by various bit depths. Table 5.1 shows the various bit depths used in raster editing and the number of colors supported.

Figure 5.16.
*Reducing the bit depth
decreases descriptiveness
of the image.*

24-bit   8-bit

Table 5.1. Scaling an image in 256-color mode (8-bit).

Image Bit Depth	Name	Number of Colors
1-bit	Bitmap Mapped	1 (black and white)
2-bit		4 (shades)
4-bit		16 (shades)
8-bit	Grayscale	256 grays
8-bit	Indexed color Palletized color	256 colors
16-bit		64,256
24-bit	True-color RGB color	16.7 million

True-Color Images

As you browse the Web, the two predominant image files that you find in use are the GIF and the JPEG graphics formats. The use of these files will probably decrease over the next couple of years due to the new Portable Network Graphics (PNG) format (see "The Portable Network Graphics (PNG) Format" later in this chapter), but GIF and JPEG are the most prominent today.

These two formats, GIF and JPEG, will clue you into what bit depth the graphics are in any particular Web page. Each of these formats supports a different amount of descriptiveness for the pixel data (different possible bit depths) and therefore can display different qualities of images due to the number of colors that are supported.

Without a doubt, the most widely used raster graphics file format on the Web is the Graphics Interchange Format, or GIF, for short (pronounced "jif"). It's no wonder that this format has become a Web standard because it was developed by CompuServe to deliver graphics over its online service. The GIF file format is a computer graphic file format that allows up to 8-bit image data to be delivered. This means that it can only support up to 256 colors. However, it can also support something called transparency, as you will see later in this chapter. All browsers directly support the GIF format, meaning that the browser can display them directly as inline images.

The second most widely used format on the Web is the Joint Picture Experts Group, or JPEG format (pronounced "j-peg"). This format is much more robust than the GIF format, allowing 24-bit quality by using compression. (See the section "Compression," later in this chapter.) The JPEG format alone allows you to create true color images that can be integrated as inline images in your pages.

One of the things you need to note is that depending upon which format you choose, your graphics can appear differently when viewed from the audience because of the number of colors supported.

Remember earlier you read that to achieve the highest quality display of the graphics you create, the image's dpi must match the dpi of the output device. Because most monitors are 72 dpi, matching the dpi is not a problem. However, there is something more you must consider when dealing with raster graphics.

With computer monitors, you must also deal with bit depth. When you print a page, bit depth is irrelevant, but with computer monitors, it is very important. To achieve the highest quality output of your graphics on a computer monitor, the dpi must match that of the monitor, which is not a big deal because all monitors are 72 dpi. The bit depth must also match that of the computer monitor to achieve the highest quality output. If the bit depth of the image is greater than the bit depth of the monitor, the image will look poor, as shown in Figure 5.17. Notice the 24-bit image displayed in the browser set at 24-bit versus the 24-bit image displayed in the 8-bit monitor. In the second case, the computer must interpolate for color information because the monitor cannot display all the colors in the image. Therefore, the browser must replicate the 24-bit nature of the image with only 256 colors.

Figure 5.17.
The bit depth of your images, akin to the dpi of your images, must match the bit depth of the intended output device.

24-bit at 24-bit   24-bit at 8-bit

The color depth of all computer monitors is controlled using operating system settings, and they are usually either 8-bit or 24-bit. Probably 35 to 50 percent of the Web surfers use 8-bit monitor settings. For example, on Windows 95, the display's color depth is controlled through the Control Panels | Monitors | Settings tab. On the Macintosh, the display's color depth is controlled through the Monitor's Control Panel. Figure 5.18 shows both the control panel for Windows 95 and the Macintosh OS.

Figure 5.18.
Monitor settings in Windows 95 (a) and the Macintosh (b).

(a) ———

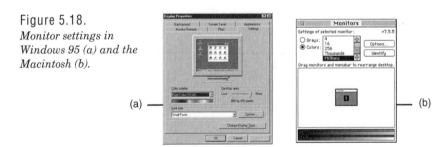

——— (b)

When you display true-color images on devices of lower bit depth, you often get one of two results: banding or color shifting. Sometimes you'll get both! Banding is the result of too few colors for interpolation and shows up as noticeable bands or stripes that appear in the image, as shown in Figure 5.19. Often, they occur in large gradations of color, such as an area that is blended from white to black or light blue to dark blue.

Figure 5.19.
Banding is a result of too few colors to represent high color images.

Original 24-bit   Banded 8-bit

The second of these problems due to bit depth differences, color shifting, is when the interpolated colors look nothing like the original colors. Note that when interpolation occurs, the browser does its best to fake the colors of the image using the colors it has at its disposal. In the next section, you'll see where it gets these colors. However, when the colors in a 24-bit are so unique and so different from the colors available to the browser, discoloration often occurs in the image. The image often has severely discolored pixels, as shown in Figure 5.20. Hey, the browser is doing the best it can.

Figure 5.20.
Color shifting also results from too few colors in the display bit depth.

Original 24-bit   Color-shifted 8-bit

Now you might be asking, "How do I avoid this little problem?" I'll first define the circumstances under which it occurs.

The only time that bit depth problems occur is when the audience's machine is browsing the Web at a lower bit depth than what you designed the pages for. For example, if you design your pages assuming the audience is browsing at 24-bit, you won't notice any problems. In fact, if you browse the Web with your computer set at a bit depth of 24-bit color, or even 64,000 colors, you will probably never run into this problem. However, many people don't have a video card that supports more than 256 colors. If these individuals browse your pages designed at 24-bit, they will probably have a low opinion of the graphics on your pages due to interpolation problems.

Alternatively, if you design your pages focused at the 256-color audience, individuals browsing your pages will perceive no ill effects. Why? When a 256-color image is displayed on a 24-bit monitor, there are more than enough colors to represent the image. You might notice some graininess because there are only 256 colors representing the image, but the images do not have any significant problems. Figure 5.21 shows an example of a 256-color image displayed at 24-bit. Notice the slight graininess of the image. Even though it is grainy, it is still a presentable image. It has no significant degradation even though it is 256 colors.

Figure 5.21.
A 256-color image displayed at 24-bit looks a little grainy, but it is still presentable.

When you develop raster graphics for the Web, your biggest concern is the lowest common denominator. You must design around the lowest link in the chain that can be found among the majority of your audience. Chapter 10, "Interactive

Multimedia Design Process," discusses more about analyzing your target audience. However, before you leave the subject of bit depth, take a look at why 256-color (8-bit) images and devices cause problems.

Palettized Color

As you saw in the previous section, the most troublesome part of designing effective pages is making sure you don't exclude the target audience by designing graphics that display poorly for them. In this section, you read more about palettized images, or 256-color images.

Every 8-bit image is limited to 256 colors simply because the allotted bits to describe the image is only enough to allow each pixel one of 256 possibilities. Therefore, every 8-bit image has a range, or palette, of 256 colors that every pixel in the image draws from. This is also called the Color Lookup Table, or CLUT. Figure 5.22 shows an image and its palette. Note that each pixel in the image is assigned to one of the 256 colors in the palette.

Figure 5.22.
An 8-bit image and its palette or Color Lookup Table (CLUT).

The problem with palettized images as well as palettized operating systems is that not every image uses the same palette. The particular palette used for one image may not be used for another image because the colors in each image vary. For example, an image with many blue hues has a palette with many blue hues. Yet, an image with many red hues has a palette with many red hues. Figure 5.23 shows an image with predominantly blue hues, an image with predominantly red hues, and their respective palettes. Note how the palettes differ in the colors they contain. Also note that some colors are the same.

Figure 5.23.
*The palettes of two
images of varying colors.*

The colors that are the same in the two palettes are special colors that are used for the operating system. In fact, an operating system that is set to 8-bit has a palette called the system palette, as shown in Figure 5.24. The system palette is where all the various applications get their colors when the machine is running in 8-bit mode. In most operating environments, 40 colors remain stable from palette to palette. However, the remaining 216 colors can be anything. It depends upon the palette. You must also be aware that these palette colors vary from machine to machine.

Figure 5.24.
*The system palette is
specific to the operating
system.*

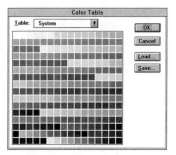

If all this weren't enough, you must realize one other important thing about palettized color. First, the palettes used for a particular image can be changed or remapped. For example, I can specify that a particular image stop using its own palette and start using the operating system's palette (or any other palette). Figure 5.25 contains an image where the palette was remapped. Notice in the image with the new palette, some color shifting or discoloration occurs. Also note, as with dpi, once you change palettes, you cannot go back to the image's original palette. Remapping colors destroys the image's original palette.

Figure 5.25.
Remapping palettes might cause discoloration due to a lack of similar colors.

When you remap palettes, the colors in the image must conform to the new palette, and sometimes they look extremely discolored, particularly if you change an image from one 8-bit palette to another. This happens because the new palette doesn't have the colors that the old palette did. The imaging application must do its best to match colors from the old palette to the new palette and often it doesn't work well.

Seldom do you need to change an indexed color image from one palette to another, but this example shows how palettes affect the image. In application, you most often reduce the bit depth from 24-bit to 8-bit for distribution. Note that when you do this, you often have the option to specify what kind of palette to create for the image.

Adobe Photoshop offers several options. Figure 5.26 shows the palettes that were specified for each of the images and how they affect the resulting image. The first image shows the original 24-bit image. In the 24-bit image, there are so many colors that no palette is needed, so no palette is shown. The second image was assigned to an adaptive palette. In this case, during the reduction in bit depth, the software created a custom palette for the image. The custom palette contains only colors in the image. In the next instance, the image was mapped to the system palette, which is defined in the operating system. The image changed according to the palette instead of the palette changing according to the image (as in adaptive). The last image uses an arbitrary palette for the image using the

Custom option. Notice in the later two images that the palette does not have enough colors to represent the image descriptively. The later images look less appealing.

Figure 5.26.
Using various color palettes during bit depth reduction.

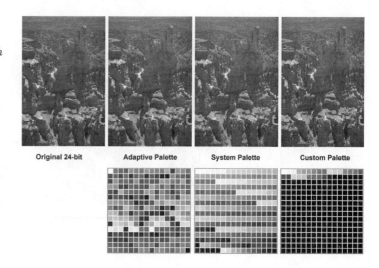

Original 24-bit   Adaptive Palette   System Palette   Custom Palette

One final note about bit depth reduction is that any time you reduce the bit depth, you must choose a palette of colors for the image. One of the things you can do to make your images look sharper during reduction is to use something called dithering. You can use many types of dithering, but your choice mostly depends upon the imaging application you use. Some give you a choice, whereas others do not. Figure 5.27 shows the dithering options in Photoshop. Notice the results in the image due to the dithering option selected, as shown in Figure 5.28.

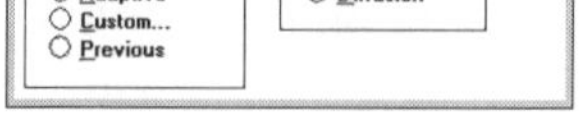

Figure 5.27.
The dithering options available in Photoshop.

Figure 5.28.
The results of the various dithering options.

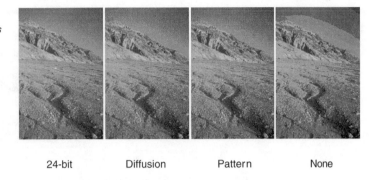

      24-bit   Diffusion   Pattern   None

Browsers, Palettes, and Displays

As if there aren't enough issues to handle already—you must be aware that in the 8-bit environment, whenever a PC displays an image, it attempts to use its own system palette to do so. The Macintosh also tries to display the image with its own palette. What about the browser? It also tries to utilize its own palette when displaying images in the 8-bit environment.

You may say, "Several different browsers might try to access my pages. How do I create a palette that works nicely for all of them?" Although it is not officially documented anywhere, several books contain browser-safe palettes that you can use to define your colors. Using browser-safe color palettes, you can keep the browser from picking awkward colors with which to render your graphics. By specifically selecting colors from these types of palettes, you can ensure a more successful inline graphic.

What graphic does this browser-safe palette improve? Well, in reality, photo-realistic graphics are not helped much by browser-safe palettes. Due to the complex blends and other features of photo-realistic raster graphics, there is always some graininess that appears within them. Browser-safe palettes are most helpful for graphics that have smooth blends or fills. Most often, they help bitmap graphics that were generated from vector graphics.

Figure 5.29 shows an example of a bitmap image that uses an adaptive palette, a system palette, and a browser safe palette. Because there are large areas of flat color, the graininess can be easily seen when viewed on a display screen. This graininess could be eliminated with a browser-safe palette. Using pure colors from the browser-safe palette, the browser does not attempt to dither the colors because they exist in the browser's color palette.

Figure 5.29.
*A browser-safe palette
and the results of
using it.*

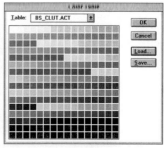

If one of your design constraints is designing around an 8-bit environment, you definitely want to be aware of the browser-safe color palette and how it can help make the graphics on your pages look better. If you are looking for a browser-safe color palette for a particular application or imaging program, try performing a Web search for color palettes or related information. More than likely, you'll run across a site that contains information about your particular application. They might even have hotlinks that allow you to download palette files or other utilities.

File Size

The three primary attributes of raster images that you examined all contribute to how big your graphic files are, not just how they look. On the Web, size and appearance are your two biggest concerns. The smaller the graphic file size, the quicker it downloads to your audience. As image resolution, size, or bit-depth increase, so does the file size. Shrink any one of these image variables, and the file size also shrinks. When you design graphics, the two most important issues are the speed at which the graphics download and how visually appealing the graphics are. One of goals is to find the medium in which your graphics look good but also download with relative speed.

When you create graphics for Web pages, you must be aware of how your audience will connect to the Web. If most visitors connect via modems, be careful how many graphics you use. A good rule of thumb is that it takes approximately 10 seconds to download 50KB of data via a 28.8Kbps modem. Double that figure for a 14.4Kbps modem. If users have to wait too long, odds are that they will dodge your site. Be careful using large bitmap graphics, which require large amounts of time for modem users to download.

Conclusions Concerning Raster Image Use

Before you learn about layering and image sizing, I'll summarize the important items concerning bitmaps that you have learned so far.

- There is a fixed relationship between the image resolution and the image size of a bitmap. Increasing the size decreases the dpi, causes interpolation, and results in a blurry image. Reducing the size of an image increases the image's dots per square inch, causes data to be deleted, and sharpens the overall image.

- Akin to dpi, bit depth also affects the quality of the image. The higher the bit depth, the more colors the image can have and the higher the quality of the image. The lower the bit depth, the fewer colors you can use and the lower the image quality.

- Image resolution, image size, and image bit depth all affect the size of the digital file. Increasing one attribute increases the size of the file. Decreasing one of these attributes decreases the size of the file.

- Always maintain a high quality version of your graphics for future editing, even if you distribute the images on the Web as lower resolutions. You may decide in the future that you want to reuse a graphic. Decreasing size, dpi, or bit depth reduces the data in the file and it cannot be regained without resampling the analog source or recreating it.

- Each 8-bit image has a Color Lookup Table (CLUT), also called a palette. All the pixels in the 256-color image are assigned a color from the palette.

- The palette for any given image may be changed by mapping the image to a new color palette. The software does its best to match the existing colors to the ones in the palette through various types of dithering. If the palette contains too few relative colors, some banding or color shifting may occur.

- Be aware of browser-safe color palettes and how they can aid you in designing around the 8-bit display environment. Keep in mind that most often, 8-bit display problems occur with graphics with large, flat color areas.

Layering and Sizing Images

As mentioned earlier in this chapter, it is important that you size your images to the size they need to be in your Web pages before you actually try to use them. This helps alleviate graphics that waste bandwidth and display poorly in your pages.

Calculating image sizes is relatively easy if you plan your pages. The first step is to know what size images you need in your page. The second step is to scale the images to get them to the right size.

There are two basic ways to determine the size that your images should be, the first step to scaling images. The first way is to actually lay out all your graphical elements right in your image editor. This is the method I prefer. The second is to use grid paper to sketch out your elements on the page. I'll explain why I prefer to lay out my pages in an image editor by first explaining one of the most important features of a raster editor—the capability to layer raster drawings.

The Flatland Raster Environment

In some raster-editing packages, you can create the various elements of your page using a special capability called layers. Layers give you the ability to draw your various bitmap elements, such as a series of inline images, a banner, or even each individual element, on different layers. Layers are like acetate sheets. Each sheet is transparent until you start drawing on it. Drawing on layers in a raster editor overcomes a lot of the negative aspects of working with bitmap images.

To understand the importance of layers, look at one of the biggest raster editing problems via an example. Figure 5.30 shows a raster image that is a banner for a Web page. Suppose you want to move some of the things around a little. You want to move the text "Joe's Vacation Hideaway." To begin, you select it using the wand tool.

Figure 5.30.
Selecting elements to
move in a raster image.

Now you drag it to where you want it to be, as shown in Figure 5.31. What happened to the area that was behind the text? In a flatland raster editor, anything that is drawn automatically deletes the pixels behind it. In essence, that which is placed in front deletes that which is behind.

You'll also notice in Figure 5.32 that the shadow for the text didn't move either because it wasn't selected. Notice how the shadow is a blend between the shadow color and the colors around it. In other words, it is anti-aliased. Anti-aliasing creates small blends between foreground and background elements to make them appear more photo-realistic. You could select the shadow with the text so that it moves with the background. As shown in Figure 5.32, the image still has problems when you use this technique. What is known as an anti-aliasing halo is one of the biggest problems with raster editing. Anti-aliasing is the slight blurring of edges to create smooth edges between raster items. This can work against you when you work in a flatland environment.

Figure 5.31.
Dragging the text reveals that the background elements are deleted.

Figure 5.32.
Selecting the shadow with the text and moving it causes problems.

In Figure 5.33, I placed a gray circle on a white background. Notice the blow-up of the edges of the circle. A blend is created between the circle and the background. This is the anti-alias.

In the second image in Figure 5.33, the gray circle was copied and placed on a black background. Notice the discolored pixels floating around the edges of the circle. This is an anti-alias halo. Because I created the circle on the white background, a fixed anti-alias was created between the gray circle and the white background. When I copied and placed the image on the black background, the fixed anti-alias was copied with it. I need a way to "un-fix" the anti-alias so that when I paste the circle on the black background, the anti-alias is a blend between black and gray instead of white and gray.

The Layered Environment

To solve the anti-aliasing problem, as well as resolve the issue of foreground objects deleting background objects, you need to use layers. Creating your graphics using layers makes your graphic design tasks much easier, as well as much more fun. The layered environment is why I choose to lay out my Web pages in an image editor. Layers make working with raster graphics more fluid, helping to support the design process.

Figure 5.33.
A circle created on white and copied and pasted onto black creates the same problem.

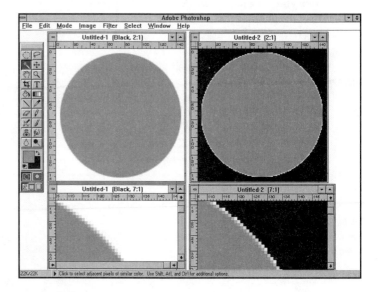

Recreate the illustration task of moving the circle from one background to another using layers. I begin by opening a new image with a white background in a layered image editor such as Photoshop. Here, I add a new layer that contains my circle, as shown in Figure 5.34.

Figure 5.34.
Opening the Layers palette and creating a new layer.

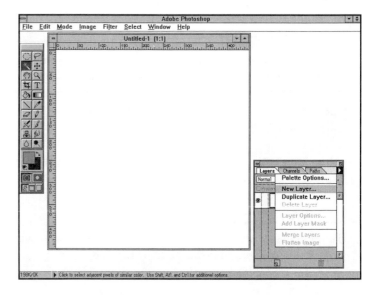

Once I add a layer, it is added to the Layers palette, as shown in Figure 5.35. First, you see a small icon representation of the contents of the layer in the palette. Because both layers are blank, all you see is white. Second, notice the layer that is highlighted or white. It is the current drawing layer. If I start drawing right now, whatever I draw is placed on this layer. You can change the current drawing layer by clicking it. In the Layers palette, you can also turn each individual layer on or off by clicking the small eyeball to the left of the layer's image. This is how layers work in Photoshop, but they function similarly in other editing packages.

Figure 5.35.
A new layer in the Layers palette.

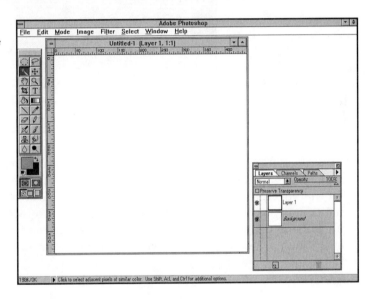

Some of the other controls are showing in the Layers palette. Notice the small drop-down menu and the slider control at the top of the palette. The drop-down menu allows you to create compositing effects between layers. The slider allows you to control the opaqueness of a particular layer. Often layers-capable editing environments add special features that you can use between the layers, and Photoshop has quite a few.

One final note before I continue: The other layer that is showing in the Layers palette, the background, is somewhat special. This layer cannot be deleted or moved. If you begin creating drawings with several layers, you can change their order by simply click-dragging them up or down the layer list. However, the background layer cannot be moved or deleted.

I am in the process of creating the gray circle on a white background and then transferring it to a canvas with a black background. I begin by checking to make sure the new layer I created is the current layer. Next, I create a circular mask and fill it with gray using the paint bucket, as shown in Figure 5.36.

Figure 5.36.
Creating the circle on Layer 1.

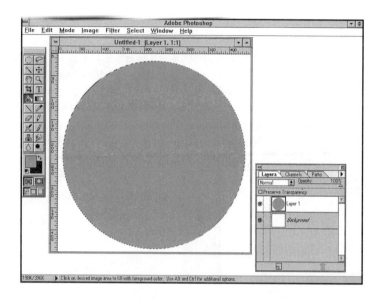

As in the flatland example, the circle's edges were automatically anti-aliased to make it look smooth. Now, turn off the background layer by clicking the eyeball for that layer. Figure 5.37 shows that the anti-alias created around the circle is not actually a blend between gray and white as it appeared, but rather, it is a blend between gray and transparency. The gray and white boxes mean that everything surrounding the circle is transparent or no color.

Figure 5.37.
The anti-alias is a blend between the gray circle and transparency or no color.

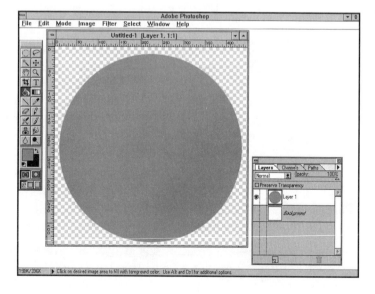

Analyze what happened with this transparent blend. Because the anti-alias is between the gray circle and transparency, I can copy the circle from the layer in this drawing to a new layer in another drawing without an anti-alias halo causing problems. (See Figure 5.38.) In effect, the anti-alias becomes fluid, helping to support a fluid design tool and process.

Figure 5.38.
*Copying the circle. Hey,
no anti-alias halo!*

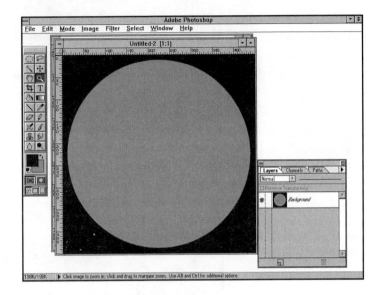

What does this mean to the Joe's Vacation Hideaway example from Figure 5.30? Take the image from Figure 5.30 and design it on layers. Figure 5.39 shows the way it was actually designed. Look at the layers in this particular image.

Now try to move some of the elements that were moved earlier. Move the text again, but notice that the background items don't get deleted and the shadow and highlight for the text also move without deleting the background. (See Figure 5.40.) I'll explain how and why this works. As you saw with the circle example, using layers doesn't create a fixed anti-alias. It also doesn't delete the items behind the objects. Because portions of the graphic are on separate layers, all the parts are kept intact no matter where you move them. They are treated as objects rather than definitive pixels. Layers give the bitmap environment the editing ease of a vector environment.

Figure 5.39.
The layers used with Joe's Vacation Hideaway.

Figure 5.40.
Moving items on layers doesn't delete the background or create an anti-alias halo.

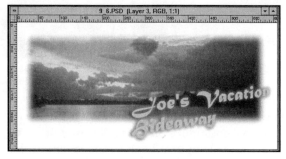

As you can see, an imaging application's layering capability creates a fluid way to design raster images. I use a raster environment to lay out entire pages because of its fluidity. Once I lay out the pages, I can simply crop and save the images for use in my Web pages.

How do you size your images if you don't have a layers-capable image editor? One of the best ways to plan your pages is to use grid sketching paper. Using grid paper, you can draw your screen resolution, setting 1 grid box equal to 10 pixels or something similar. Lay out your screen elements by hand and then just count the boxes to calculate the sizes that the images need to be.

Once you determine the size for your images, use your image editor to size them. In Photoshop, you use the Image | Image Size option, which opens a dialog box, as shown in Figure 5.41. Adjust the width and height of your image. Make sure the Constrain File Size option is unchecked. If it is not, scaling an image down increases the dpi. When you scale an image, you should notice a decrease in file size.

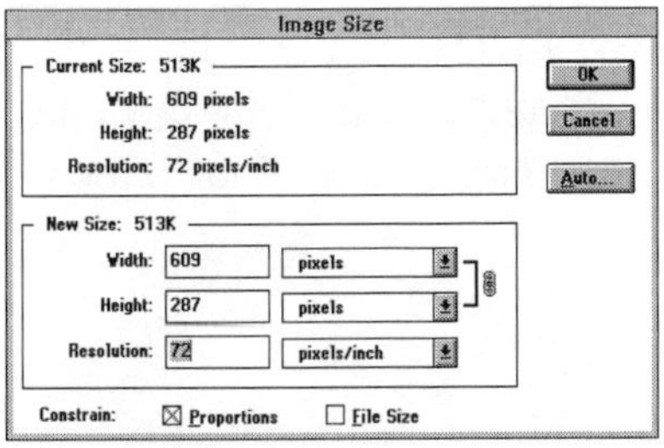

Figure 5.41.
Sizing images using Photoshop.

One of the nice things about Photoshop is the way it blurs images as they are reduced. As in any image editor, reducing the image size too far results in a blurry blob. For Photoshop (or any image editor) to resize properly, you must make sure you are in a 24-bit mode prior to scaling. Prior to resizing any image, go to the Mode menu and select RGB Color (24-bit) if you're in Photoshop. This gives the editor more colors to choose from during the blurring process. Blurring a 256-color image looks pretty bad, as shown in Figure 5.42. Again, prior to changing the size of any image, change the image to high-color, 24-bit, or RGB mode (which are all the same thing) to get the best graphic images.

Figure 5.42.
Scaling an image in 256-color mode (8-bit).

Formats

No discussion of graphics is complete without a discussion of the various file formats you'll run across on the Web. Undoubtedly, you can use a myriad of file formats to distribute your files, but it's not guaranteed that your audience can view those files unless you stick with one of the more standard graphics file formats. Take a look at some of the various computer graphic file formats and their positive and negative aspects.

Graphics Interchange Format (GIF)

As you have seen, the most widely used raster graphics file format on the Web is the GIF format. Keep in mind that the GIF format supports 8-bit image data as well as transparency.

GIF Transparency

The GIF file format can actually come in a couple of different variations. The most widely used version is the GIF 87a, which is just standard raster image data. A later version of the format, called GIF 89a, supports a special function called transparency, or transparent GIFs.

The special GIF 89a format was developed to allow users to create bitmap images in which certain elements can be transparent, as shown in Figure 5.43. Using a special filter, the user can assign a particular color in the bitmap to be transparent, allowing the background color or tiled image in the browser to show through the inline graphic. It's really a pretty inventive feature for this little format. Even with transparency data, GIF files generally remain small due to the low bit depth data that they contain.

Figure 5.43.
Using the GIF 89a format to deliver transparent bitmaps.

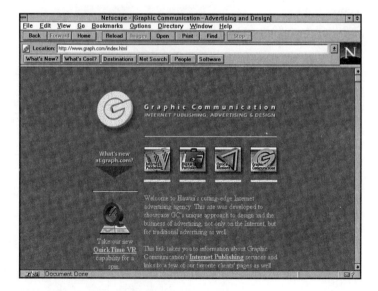

Joint Picture Experts Group (JPEG)

In addition to the normal JPEG format discussed earlier, a relatively new type of JPEG image called a progressive JPEG is appearing on the Web.

Interlaced GIF and Progressive JPEGs

The new JPEG files, called progressive JPEGs, allow the browser to create low resolution representations of the graphics, which become clearer and higher quality as the browser downloads more of the file. Much like focusing the lens on a camera, the image begins blurry and then becomes clear when the image is completely downloaded, as shown in Figure 5.44. JPEG files themselves can contain both 8-bit and 24-bit information, which makes them a good candidate for delivering graphics at more than 256 colors.

Figure 5.44.
Interlacing allows progressive downloads.

To enable a progressive download, the image must be digitally recorded or saved in a special way. The interlace option in any graphic file format causes the data to be saved non-sequentially. Rather than store each line of pixels as it appears from top to bottom in the image, interlacing stores every 4th, 8th, or 16th line, in that order. Rather than store line 1, 2, 3, and so on, an interlaced file stores line 1, line 8, line 16, and so on. It then repeats at the top of the image with line 2, line 17, and so on, as shown in Figure 5.45. This way, the image is progressively drawn as the image is downloaded.

Figure 5.45.
Interlacing saves the file a special way.

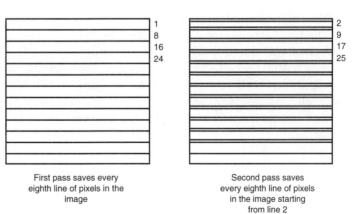

First pass saves every eighth line of pixels in the image

Second pass saves every eighth line of pixels in the image starting from line 2

Many of the latest imaging applications such as Adobe Photoshop 4.0 support this new rendition of the original JPEG format. The progressive JPEG is quite impressive, but data loss can be a negative because it uses lossy compression.

Other File Formats

Although GIF and JPEG images are the most common formats found on the Web, you can run across many other file formats as you surf. You'll find that each format has its own quirks and advantages.

BMP

The BMP, or Windows Bitmap, graphic file format allows you to store up to 24-bit image data. This image format, originally designed for Windows graphic images, is used by a wide range of applications on the PC. This particular image format can also incorporate a special internal compression scheme called Run-Length Encoding, or RLE.

TIFF

Tagged Image File Format, or TIFF (pronounced "tif"), is a special computer graphic file format that was designed to support the output of high-resolution raster images. This particular file format allows up to 32-bit data and is very robust. It is not uncommon for TIFF files to be quite large. Because it is designed to hold image data for printing, the TIFF format uses a special internal compression scheme called Lepel-ZivWelch (LZW) compression.

PICT

Most of the formats mentioned so far are raster formats—holding only pixel data. The PICT format, used predominantly on the Macintosh, is a special type of file format called a metafile format. Metafile formats allow either raster or vector data within them. In fact, they can store both simultaneously. PICT files are very popular in both vector and raster imaging on the Macintosh due to their very small file sizes. However, take PICT to the PC and you'll be lucky to find software that can open it. If you work across platforms, PICT is not a good choice for a file format.

The Portable Network Graphics (PNG) Format

One noteworthy occurrence has developed in the world of Web graphics: a new graphics format. Just what you need, a new format. However, this new graphics format has some very distinct advantages over both the JPEG and GIF formats and seeks to better standardize the graphics on the Web.

The new PNG, or Portable Network Graphics, format is a graphics format that boasts advantages over both the GIF and JPEG formats. The PNG format supports indexed-color up to 256-colors, progressive display, transparency, and lossless compression. The biggest reason for the introduction of the PNG format is to eliminate many of the problems associated with the GIF format. The biggest problem with the GIF format is that the compression it uses is copyrighted. Many of the Web sites and companies that exclusively use the GIF format could be found guilty of copyright infringement if the company holding the GIF copyright (CompuServe) wanted to pursue it. The GIF copyright is the biggest reason for the introduction of the PNG format.

In addition, the PNG format includes several features that also make it a threat to the JPEG format. The PNG format supports RGB color images up to 48-bits, full masking (alpha channels), and image gamma information. It will be interesting to see how quickly this format catches on. The big two browsers (Netscape and Internet Explorer) currently support the new format. In addition, many of the latest image editors allow the developer to generate files in the new format. It appears the GIF and JPEG are on their way out soon. Keep your eyes on the PNG format.

Compression

The previous discussion of file formats mentioned many formats that use internal file compression. Actually, you'll find that Web-based graphics and files use two different types of compression: lossy and lossless. These terms describe how the compression scheme works.

As you have read, one of the biggest problems with raster images is their size. To overcome this hurdle, compression schemes were developed to help reduce the file size of raster images. Almost every raster image has redundant data. For example, an image with a lot of blue hues in it has redundant data in it due to the repeated definition of the blue pixels. Compression schemes take the redundant or repeating data and substitute tokens or representative characters for the repeating data, thus reducing the file size, as shown in Figure 5.46. Each and every compression algorithm works this way.

Figure 5.46.
Compression algorithms substitute tokens for repeating data.

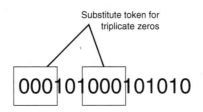

Substitute token for triplicate zeros

0001010001010 10

Compression schemes use an algorithm, or codec, to compress and decompress the image file. A codec stands for compressor/decompressor, which is an algorithm used to expand and compress the file. Most compression schemes, such as the ones used in BMP and TIFF files, are transparent to the user. Many times, you don't even know that the compression is occurring, but the compression can significantly reduce the size of the file.

How does it work? As you've read, compression occurs because of the redundant data in the file. However, the compressibility of a file is dependent upon how much redundant data the file actually has. A file with a lot of similar hues will compress more than an image with a wide variety of colors. Compression is dependent upon the amount of redundant data.

Compression schemes are judged by the amount that they compress the file, or their compression ratio. The compression ratio is the ratio of the uncompressed file's size to the compressed file's size. Many of the compression schemes claim a ratio of 2:1, whereas others can only perform 1.25:1. You must be careful of fantastic claims. Take a look at the difference between lossy and lossless compression and you'll see why.

Lossy Compression

When files are compressed, not all codecs reproduce an exact copy of the original file when they are uncompressed. Some data is lost to attain smaller file sizes. This is the case with lossy compression. Lossy compression is a compression scheme in which certain amounts of data are sacrificed to attain smaller file sizes.

Lossy compression schemes, such as those used with JPEG images and many of the video formats, do not create an exact replica of the original file after decompression. They lose some of the original data. This might alarm you at first, but lossy compression schemes are usually used when the files that are being compressed don't need the extra data. For example, an image that you display on screen requires less data than a file that you're going to print. Therefore, you can sacrifice some of the data for the sake of a smaller file size. This is also true in the digital video realm. Again, a certain amount of data can be sacrificed without significantly hurting the playback performance.

If you decide to use a lossy compression scheme, you do have a choice concerning how much data is lost. Most of these schemes allow you to choose a loss rate or ratio. For example, when you create a JPEG file you can adjust how much data is lost. The same is true if you are creating video clips. Of the file formats I have mentioned, only JPEG uses lossy compression. Figure 5.47 shows three varying qualities of JPEG graphics.

Figure 5.47.
Various qualities of
JPEG images.

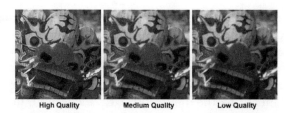

High Quality   Medium Quality   Low Quality

If you decide to use JPEG images, keep two things in mind. First, after compression, if you ever try to print the JPEG file, it will probably look bad. Second, you should keep a backup of your JPEG images in a format that either doesn't use compression or uses lossless compression.

Lossless Compression

As its name implies, lossless compression can be used for image files that you want to print and use in situations where a loss of data is detrimental. Lossless compression is a compression scheme in which a decompressed file creates an extract replica of the original file.

Lossless compression schemes do not sacrifice data. In fact, they create an exact copy of the original file when they are decompressed. Lossless compression schemes are often used with files that need to maintain the highest level of data. Often, they are used in the desktop publishing field for printing purposes, where loss of data is unacceptable. Lossless compression schemes include the TIFF's LZW and the BMP's RLE compression schemes.

Internal File Compression

In addition to looking at compression from a data point of view, you can also examine compression at the file level. All the schemes that I have discussed so far are internal compression schemes. These internal compression schemes generally occur within commercial packages and in effect are part of the file format itself. Internal file compression occurs at the data level. It understands the contents of the file and compresses the data based on redundancy within the data.

External File Compression

External file compression is a second type of compression scheme that you may encounter on the Web. Ever seen a .ZIP file? How about an .HQX, .SIT, or .BIN file? These compression files were created using an external compression program.

External file compression means that the compression algorithm knows nothing about the data itself. It simply looks at the file level to see how the file can be further decreased in size. External file compression is lossless, so you don't worry about data loss.

You can actually take a file that has been internally compressed and compress it even more using an external compression program. However, once externally compressed, the contents cannot be opened by any other program until it is uncompressed. For example, suppose you create an internally compressed JPEG file. Then, you compress it using something like Pkware's PKZIP. Now it is a zip file. You cannot link the file to an HTML file as an inline image because HTML cannot read zip files. You do lose one degree of freedom by externally compressing files. However, you end up with a more highly compressed, smaller file.

If you want to use external compression programs in your file delivery, you have several from which to choose. First and foremost on the PC is Pkware's PKZIP. It's probably the oldest of the bunch. The Macintosh has several that you can choose from, but I suggest Aladdin's Stuffit Expander. For less than a hundred dollars, it beats all the others. Of course, there are others, but these two programs are the most widely used compression and decompression programs on the PC and Macintosh operating systems.

Summary

In this chapter, you examined the various aspects of bitmap graphics used on the Web. The predominance of graphics on the Web are bitmap graphics. As you develop Web pages, you need to be conscientious of the image resolution, image size, and the image bit depth because these attributes affect both the quality and speed of download.

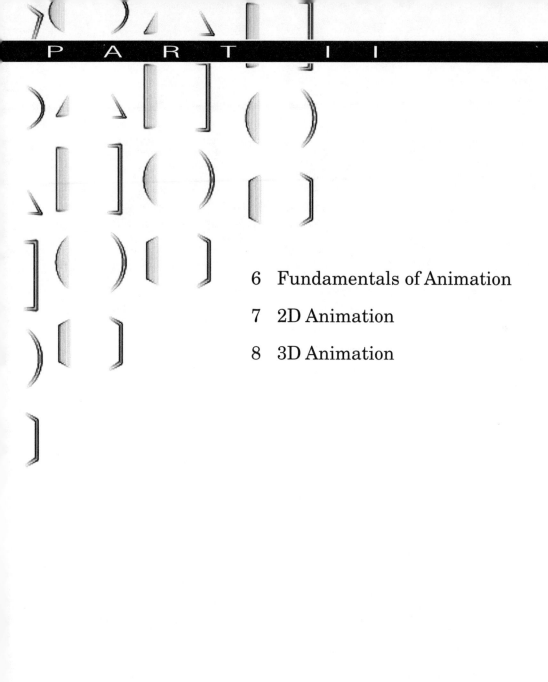

PART II

6   Fundamentals of Animation

7   2D Animation

8   3D Animation

6

Fundamentals of Animation

Animation is one of the most fascinating visual phenomena known. It tricks the human eye and gives the perception of "life" within the single cels that compose an animation. The concept of animation is simple, but the effect that you perceive can be both exhilarating and exciting.

The illusion created by animation is the effect of viewing a series of images quickly so that the eye cannot distinguish between each individual image, called a *cel,* as shown in Figure 6.1. A single cel or frame's contents represents that content's position or condition for a single instance of time in the animation. Making a compilation of many images with changing contents is animation. The images blend together in time to create the perception of movement. This occurs because of a visual phenomenon called *persistence of vision,* in which the eyes and brain continue to perceive an image even after the image has been removed.

Figure 6.1.
*Displaying multiple
images with small
changes across images
creates the perception of
movement.*

To see an example of persistence of vision, look at a static saturated, fluorescent, or bright color for a minute or two and then look at a blank, white page. You'll notice that your eyes will still perceive the color on the blank page even though it is not there. More than likely, the image will appear with less intensity, but it is a noticeable phenomenon for most people. This residual effect is the main reason that animation can be produced at all.

From the mishaps of Wile E. Coyote to the delightful Disney movies, animation has been a source of enjoyment for the young and old alike. Traditional cel animation has been in existence for many years and still thrives today, but animation has been taken one step further with the computer animation on the Web.

Animation on the computer hinges on the same visual principle as traditional animation, but the tools used to create each are a little different. Rather than drawing and painting each animation cel using traditional tools such as pencils and brushes, each frame is drawn on the computer. After each frame is created, the computer can replay them quickly and sequentially, giving the illusion of movement or change over time. Even though you should perceive a gap between the images, persistence of vision causes the rapidly displaying frames to appear as a constant, fluid image rather then a set of individual images playing one after another. Yet, no matter what tools are used to create an animation, the basic concept used to create it is still the same.

Computer animation can include much more than cartoon-type images, although this is where animation started. Many people hear the term "computer animation" and envision cartoon images, but it is much more than traditional cel animation for the computer. Computer animation has been so refined that it can often be difficult to tell if the footage is live or computer-generated. Computer animation allows the developer to create any range of realism in the animation, as shown in Figure 6.2.

Computer animation can include anything the imagination can dream. From entertainment to engineering, computer animation can be incorporated to enhance ideas, concepts, and fantasies. Computer animation has also become a powerful tool in advertising, training, and what were once aesthetically unappealing boardroom presentations. Many people have seen advertisements such as the Lifesavers Minis or movies such as *Toy Story* or *Jurassic Park,* but very few have seen training demonstrations and presentations that were enhanced by the use of computer animation. In addition to its other uses, animation on the Web can be used to help clarify, complement, and complete information distributed on the Web, as shown in Figure 6.3.

Figure 6.2.
Any range of realism can be created in computer animation.

Figure 6.3.
Animations on the Web can be used to help clarify, complement, or complete the content being provided.

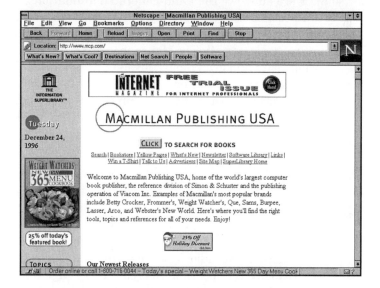

No matter what context, with effective animation, ideas are clarified, perceived, and accentuated because of the power of dynamic graphics. One animation can alleviate thousands of words or add the needed graphic effect to capture your audience's attention.

The Historical Perspective

Many of the principles used in Web animations have existed for a long time and are based upon techniques developed by early cel animation. Most of the terms and techniques are a result of those that were involved with animation long before the intervention of the computer.

In the introduction of this book, you read how various inventions throughout history have had a worldwide impact on many of the things that we take for granted on a day-to-day basis. In this discussion, I mentioned the impact that Thomas Edison's inventions had, particularly the phonograph; however, he was also key in inventing the kinetograph, an early predecessor to today's motion cameras. The *kinetograph* was a device that was capable of recording up to 10 photographs per second, which could then be replayed on a device called a *kinetoscope.* Although at 10 frames per second, the recorded video was somewhat jerky (due to the small number of recorded frames), it was an invention that would lead to the basis of the animations and live footage that is recorded today.

Following Edison's invention, many people began creating hand-generated frames or cels to produce animations. Eventually frame rates, quality, and even sound were added to the hand-generated animations, which culminated to the first full-color animation produced by Disney in the late 1920s. With several hundred artists and painstaking work, the first animation, starring Disney's signature character Mickey Mouse, became a revolutionary success. Over the following years and even today, Disney's techniques and animation style define the standard for animation. In 1995, with the devoted computer graphics specialists at Pixar, Disney once again set a standard in the animation world by producing the first movie-length three-dimensional generated animation, *Toy Story.*

Much of the animation that is generated today is a result of the computer, graphics, and animation capability (as we know it today) that was not available until long after the introduction of Disney's first animation. Only in the early 1980s did it actually become feasible to produce animation and video effects via the computer. This was mainly due to price and availability prior to that time. The technology was not at a price/return level that made it feasible or financially possible for the vast majority to implement these techniques on the computer. However, today it is possible to create any range of animation qualities from computers. Even the most common desktop Pentiums can be used to create animations for broadcast or for the Web, given the appropriate software.

Animation Fundamentals

When you are dealing with animation, remember that it is really nothing more than a series of images in which the contents of the images change. Each frame represents a single instance in the total time of the animation. In the traditional setting, each frame is created first as a drawing, and is then colorized and photographed in its proper position (relative to the other frames). So the traditional animation is a result of multiple, traditionally created images.

Digital animation, akin to traditional animation, is nothing more than a series of digital images that are played in a sequential progression on the computer. For the most part, computer animations contain a series of raster images that have been painted by the animator or generated through the use of a three-dimensional animation. The end result is usually a single digital animation file that is nothing more than many raster images in one file. Sometimes, Web animations can be stored as many individual images files rather than a single large one. In any case, both are based on raster images.

You can also use vector graphics as a basis for Web animations, but they are a little more complex to create. Often, Web animations that are based on vector graphics must utilize external or advanced applications, or languages such as Macromedia Director, Java, JavaScript, or VBScript.

Note that when I am referring to vector- and raster-based animations, I am talking about the end product—the animation file itself. The animation file is what you create and play back on the computer. An animation file might contain information that is based on either vector or raster graphics, as shown in Table 6.1. When I am talking about 2D versus 3D animations, I'm referring to how the animation was created. You'll note that the next two chapters are titled "2D Animation" and "3D Animation." These chapters describe methods of creating the animation, not what's in the produced animation file. The end product of the 2D animation method, or application—the animation file itself—can be vector- or raster-based. The 3D method of creation (3D animation application) always generates a raster animation file.

Table 6.1. Methods of creation and the types of animation files they create.

Animation Method	Animation File
2D Animation	Vector- or raster-based (creating each frame)
3D Animation	Raster-based (based on 3D environments)

Because most Web animations are composed of raster images, most of the discussions in this and the next two chapters deal with them. You'll spend some time reading about vector animations, but they are not as widely used as raster-based illustrations.

As you saw in the last chapter, "Raster-Based Graphics," raster images are painted and defined pixel by pixel. Therefore, when dealing with Web animations that are based on raster graphics, you must understand some of the issues discussed in the chapter, predominantly image resolution, size, and bit depth. Yet, before you see how these relate to Web animation, there are a couple of other animation concepts you'll need to know.

Methods of Integration

When you are utilizing Web animations at your site, there are two predominant ways to include them. You can either include HTML code in your pages that include references to multiple GIF (or other raster format) images or as code that utilizes a single animation file (which houses all the images in a single file).

Normally, when an animation is integrated using multiple GIF images, the browser can directly display the animation, with no help from plug-ins or other browser add-ons. GIF animations are usually quite small and are the preferred method of integrating animations in pages. Most often this scenario will use Java, JavaScript, or even some basic HTML to specify how the images should be played (frame size and rate) in the Web page.

Whenever a single animation file is used, it is a common practice to directly integrate them in an inline fashion within a Web page. Yet, single animation files can become quite large, which can make integrating them directly in a page a detriment for users connected via modems. If you use single animation files, always give the audience the choice to download the file through a hotlink or button. Don't make users automatically have to view the animation when they download your page.

In addition, more often than not, the user will need some type of plug-in or other add-on to view the single file animation. Popular file formats are QuickTime, Video for Windows, and VDOLive. In Chapter 14, "Video," you'll read more about these file formats. Whenever you integrate these types of files, make sure that you specify any plug-ins or other items they'll need to view the animation in the page that the animation link occurs. You might also want to add a hotlink to a site from which users can download the needed plug-in, as well as specify how big the animation file is so they can decide whether or not to download the animation.

Most animation packages give the option of saving the animation you've created as either a set of appropriately named raster images or as a single image file. When you begin looking at Chapter 7, "2D Animation," and Chapter 8, "3D Animation," you'll take a closer look at how to save animations both as single files and as singular files. For now, just realize that you can integrate animations as either multiple GIF images or as a single animation file.

Key Frames and In-Betweens

To understand the concept of keyframe animation, you must understand the sequence involved in creating a traditional animation. Traditional animation usually began with an idea that was birthed by a writer or animator. Then, a storyboard was created showing the storyline and the actions of the characters or objects in the animation. Even today it is common to create storyboards of an animation prior to production.

The animation storyboard is a sketch that shows what the individual frames in the animation will contain, as shown in Figure 6.4. Now, considering that most animations are composed of several hundred frames, it would be impractical to draw every frame from the animation in the storyboard. Therefore, the storyboard usually contains only the main actions of the animation, which are the primary or key actions, called the *keys*, or *keyframes*.

Figure 6.4.
The animation storyboard shows the key actions (key frames) in the animation.

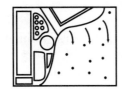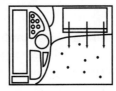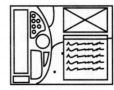

In the traditional process, when the storyboard was created, the master artist would draw up the master or main frames, called keys, that are found in the storyboard. The remaining intermediate frames, called *in-betweens,* or *tweens,* were created by many, many apprentice, or blue-collar, artists. The laborious part of creating the animation was creating the tweens, not to mention that at this point in the process the frames had been drawn but not painted or photographed.

After the frames were drawn, they were then painted and still photographed to create a film animation. To create the movements in the animation, each frame was drawn on a separate piece of acetate. In addition, a single frame could be composed of several sheets of acetate. Usually each moving item in the animation, sometimes called a *sprite,* required a separate piece of acetate to create a layered composite. Much like the layered environment discussed in vector and raster drawings (Chapters 4 and 5), the traditional photographic process used to create animations was layered as well. By varying the combinations of acetate sheets, each frame could be photographed. The combination of frame photographs creates a final animation that when played back, gives the perception of movement because of changes in the elements in the frame.

In Chapters 4 and 5, you were presented with the concept of illustration layering. In reality, it is from the traditional cel animation process that these digital illustration tools draw their layering constructs. As a result of the knowledge gained from the traditional animation process, as well as the logical efficiency resulting from the use of layers, today's digital tools integrate many other traditional constructs, such as rotoscoping, onion-skinning, and chroma-keying, as you will see in the next chapter.

Due to the large amount of drawing, painting, and cel arrangement for photography, the traditional cel animation process requires hundreds of hours, with many people working with painstaking accuracy. This is where the computer

becomes very advantageous. The digital animator can create cel-by-cel animations using 2D tools with more efficiency because the computer most often
reduces the monotony of generating tweens, coloring each frame, as well as
creating the drawing for each frame. With 3D tools, the digital animator can
create photo-realistic animations that are often difficult to distinguish from live
footage.

Frame Rate

As you read earlier in this chapter, the first animations where created by
generating frames at 10 images per second. Every animation has a certain
number of frames that play per element of time. The more frames that play per
element of time, the more smoothly the actions occur within the displayed
animation.

In the animation field, the smoothness of the displayed animation is a function
of the number of frames that play per second (fps), called the *frame rate*. When
you are dealing with cel animation, generally 24 frames are played per second.
The frame rate of video is generally 30 frames per second. On the standard
computer, however, you cannot generally display this type of frame rate. On the
computer, frame rates of video and animations that are independent of the Web
are generally 15 frames per second. On the Web, most animations play at a frame
rate of 8 to 10 frames per second.

The speed at which animations play on the Web are dependent upon two
variables: frame size (image size) and frame bit depth (image bit depth). If you've
read Chapter 5, this should make sense because each frame in the animation is
a single raster image. Note, however, that with animations, you do not need to be
concerned with dpi (dots per inch). Almost all animations are 72 dpi because they
are intended for output on display devices.

Frame Size (Image Size)

In the previous chapter, you read how the image size of a raster image affects both
the file size and quality of the image. Since most Web animations are composed
of raster images, image size also affects the quality and size of an animation.
When you are working with animations, however, image size is referred to as
frame size and affects all the images in the animation rather than an individual
frame.

When you are working with digital video and animations apart from the Web,
frame sizes are specified using standard frame sizes. Frame sizes are generally
specified using standard frame sizes so they can be used for various purposes.
Standard sizes include 160×120, 240×180, 320×240, and 640×480, as shown in

Figure 6.5. Other sizes may be used depending on the intended output (such as broadcast digital video).

Figure 6.5.
Standard digital video sizes.

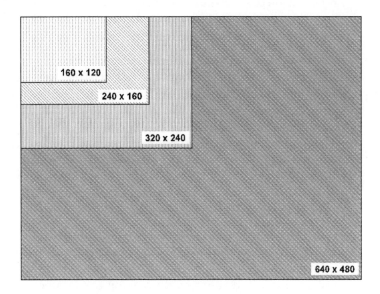

When you utilize animations on your Web pages, you'll more than likely be using sizes that don't conform to the standard sizes for animation and video. In fact, they will probably be quite smaller than 160×120 to get optimum playback over the Web. Figure 6.6 shows an animated banner, which is an example of a typical Web animation.

Figure 6.6.
Web animations must be small enough to download quickly over the audience's connection to the Net.

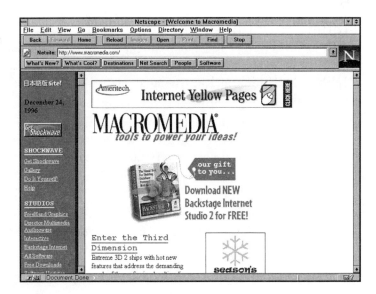

Small sizes for Web animations are predominantly due to the file sizes that occur when you use the standard animation and video sizes. Keep in mind that an animation on the Web must be small for it to download to the audience's machine in a reasonable amount of time. An animation that is the smallest size, 160×120, will probably be too large to integrate directly into the page.

When you are working with animations for Web delivery, you must design around the severe bandwidth limitations that exist for the client, so the files must be small. Most users connect to the Internet via modems that are 28.8 bps (bits per second) or less. With a 28.8 bps modem, it takes about 1 second to download 2KB (kilobytes) of data. So, a 50KB file (one raster image at 160×120 pixels) will take 25 seconds. An animation file will generally have many frames, which can exponentially increase the file size/time to download. This assumes that the server feeding the information is not being accessed by many other users. If a particular Web site is being accessed by many users at a time, it can take longer to download a 50KB file because the server tries to serve everyone equally.

One of the best ways to decrease download times is to reduce the frame size of the animation. Akin to changing the image size of a raster image, changing the frame size of an animation will reduce the size of the digital animation file. You can also decrease download times by decreasing the number of frames (images) in the animation. Number of frames and frame size are the two main factors that affect the size of the animation file size.

Elsewhere in this chapter (see the sections titled "Limitations on the Web" and "Methods of Integration"), you'll take a closer look at how to create efficient animations for the Web and integrate them on your pages.

Frame Bit Depth (Image Bit Depth)

In the previous discussion of reducing file size, you probably wondered where bit depth fits into all of this. Well, with Web-based animation (as well as real-time playback of animations independent of the Web), you are very limited concerning the bit depth of animations.

Almost all animations that efficiently and effectively play on the Web are 8 bits or less. This means that you aren't working with millions, or even thousands, of colors. However, you can get very nice effects creating animations that are 8-bit. A 256-color palette or 8-bit animation has sufficient colors to create effective animations given that the frame size is appropriate for Web use.

Granted, you cannot create smooth-color, full-screen (640×480) or quarter screen (320×240) animation using a 256-color palette. You will note some color shifting and banding using 8 bits for animations of this frame size. But I can guarantee that delivering animations with frame sizes over 160×120 is just wasting bandwidth. If you try to create animations of these sizes and use them in your Web pages, you're asking for trouble. The animation will likely play poorly for your users, if they don't exit your site before the animation plays. The bandwidth of today's Web through a modem connection, and even through most direct network connections, won't be able to deliver the data fast enough to play the animation in real time. The technology is just not there yet.

Plan to deliver any and all animations at a reasonable size, 160×120 (when used in an inline fashion) or less, with a bit depth of 8-bit. This is what the technology can reasonably support and the limitation around which you must design.

Animation Software

Software has been enhanced to enable complex operations and alleviate much of the busy work associated with creating animations. Both two-dimensional and three-dimensional animation packages are available on the market today, but they vary significantly in the way they allow you to create animation files.

2D Animations: Sprite, Vector, and Spline

Two-dimensional animation packages allow the user to mimic traditional cel animation on the computer in that each frame must be created and painted. Some packages allow a limited amount of special effects as well as a wide variety of painting and drawing tools. This type of animation package is by far the most time-consuming method of creating computer animation.

Most nonphoto-realistic computer animations are created through two-dimensional packages. Figure 6.7 shows an example of an image that was generated with a two-dimensional package. It must be noted, however, that although with two-dimensional animation packages it's more difficult to achieve photo-realism, you can add special effects, such as farcles, and intense reflections into photo-realistic animations that were created in a three-dimensional animation package. In Chapter 7, you'll take a closer look at the methods of creating 2D animations such as sprite, vector, and spline paths, as well as techniques that can make 2D animations easier to produce such as onion-skinning, compositing, and other techniques.

3D Animations: Motion Studies and Analysis

Three-dimensional packages, on the other hand, are different because they rely on a three-dimensional surface, solid model, or a three-dimensional scene to create the animation, as shown in Figure 6.8.

Figure 6.7.
Two-dimensional animation packages are generally used to create nonphoto-realistic animations.

Figure 6.8.
Three-dimensional animations are based upon surface or solid models.

Most 3D animation packages released today also incorporate intelligent features that reduce the amount of time the user must physically spend working on the computer. One such feature is keyframe animation.

Keyframe animation in a 3D environment requires that the user first create the objects in the animation and then specify the main movements of those objects in the key frames of the animation. The computer then calculates the intermediate steps of movement automatically, in real time, thus alleviating much of the time-consuming work. The computer also reduces user time by performing the most laborious task, rendering each individual frame. It does this, in most instances, by projecting 3D data onto a 2D plane. It then calculates what the object should look like according to the properties assigned to it. These properties can include the color, texture, lighting, and even atmospheric conditions in some packages.

Figure 6.9 shows an example of an image generated by a 3D animation package. The capability to create photo-realistic images, with every aspect of realism, is readily available for use on most moderate personal computers.

Figure 6.9.
Creating photo-realistic images on the personal computer.

Limitations on the Web

As you have read in this chapter, there are several issues you must be aware of if you want to deliver animations on your Web pages. You must realize that

- The main issue of delivering animations is focused on the size of the file or files that is used to represent the frames of an animation. Remember that it takes approximately 1 second for 2KB of data to download over a 28.8 modem, assuming the server you are accessing is not extremely busy.

- The frame rate of most animations delivered over the Web are significantly less than those associated with broadcast video or animation. If you can attain a frame rate of 8-10 fps, your animations will be effective.

- The frame size of most animations delivered over the Web, integrated in an inline fashion, are generally smaller than 160×120 pixels. Anything larger than this will require large amounts of download time and will play back with unappealing results.

- The file size of an animation delivered over the Web is dependent upon the frame rate and the frame size of the animation.

- Animations in which the file size, frame rate, or frame size make it impractical to deliver in an inline fashion should be linked to the page as independent, compressed files, allowing the user to download and view them independently of the Web browser. These types of animations should never be used in an inline fashion (coded directly into the HTML code of a page).

Choosing Software and Hardware for Animation

After you establish the need for computer animation, consider what kind of computer software and hardware you need to purchase. Many people want to go out and buy all the latest multimedia hardware devices, and then purchase the software to run on them. This can present a significant and costly problem. The type of software is the first choice that needs to be made when planning computer hardware and software purchases. A person can buy all the high-powered hardware devices in the world; but if the software can't run efficiently, the hardware is useless.

The software and hardware dilemma is analogous to buying a new car. When you are deciding what type of car to buy, do you make that decision on the type and size of the engine that drives the car, or the basis of the car's functionality and features? Unless you are a racecar driver, that decision is probably based on the latter of the two.

The software choice is much like the car buyer's choice. Software is what allows you functionality and gives you certain features. Software is what allows you to utilize certain features and functions. Problems can exist when software cannot run on the hardware. If the hardware is chosen before the software, efficiency cannot be guaranteed. This can be a very expensive and trying situation to correct. In most cases, if software is forced to run on lower-level hardware, it will not function properly. The best scenario is to choose software that has all the features that you are looking for and then choose the hardware components to match.

There are many animation packages that are on the market today, and, like any software, they all have features and characteristics that distinguish them from any others. Some features are consistent throughout all the packages, and others have been specially designed by certain companies. But one thing that all of these packages have in common is that they are either 2D- or 3D-based packages. In the following two chapters, you'll continue to learn more about 2D and 3D animation creation and how you can integrate them in your Web pages.

Summary

In this chapter, you took a look at animation and the principles involved with its use on the Web. As with raster graphics, resolution, size, and bit depth are important. The resolution and bit depth are generally 75 dpi and 8-bit for reasons mentioned in this chapter. Therefore, size or frame size is the most important. As you also saw, frame rate is important due to its effect on file size.

CHAPTER

7

2D Animation

As was introduced in the previous chapter, 2D animation describes a method of creating animations that is akin to techniques used in creating the traditional cel animation. In the 2D animation application, the animator must define both the contents of the frames in the animation as well as the changes that occur over time. This means that the animator must design each and every action, element, or change in every frame.

If you are looking at 2D animation as a method of creating lengthy photo-realistic animations, forget it. First, 2D animation packages are generally used to create less than photo-realistic animations as shown in Figure 7.1. Note that creating animations from scratch in 2D programs is somewhat limited because every frame must be defined photo-realistically (if that's what you are trying to achieve). You'll find that it is enough just to create the frame changes in nonphoto-realistic animations using these packages, let alone trying to achieve a high level of realism in them. If you're looking for photo-realism, check out the next chapter, "3D Animation."

Figure 7.1.
A typical frame from an
animation created in a
2D animation package.

Don't be too quick to discard this chapter. Although the animations generated from scratch in a 2D package are not photo-realistic, 2D programs can be very effective in creating special effects over the top of animations generated in a 3D package. In addition, 2D packages are probably the primary generator of animations found on the Web because of the low bandwidth issue. Most Web animations are as a result of 2D animation packages.

In this chapter, you are going to look at three primary things concerning 2D animation packages: cel (frame contents), techniques, and effects. As was mentioned in the previous chapter, 2D animations can include either raster or vector elements. In fact, some packages can utilize both simultaneously. You'll also see how the changes over time are specified in 2D packages to create animations.

Following the discussion of cel contents, you take a look at the techniques used in many of the 2D animation packages. Many of these techniques draw from traditional methods of creating cel animations. Others are as a result of the digital tool itself. You'll find quite a variety of 2D animation packages on the market, and the section on techniques will give you an idea of how the various techniques employed by the software differ.

This chapter concludes with a discussion of the various effects that can be used in 2D animation packages. These effects can be used both on animations generated within the 2D package itself and on animations generated from 3D programs.

Cel Contents

As you look at the tools used to create animations, you'll find that there are three predominant ways in which these applications can create a 2D animation. These include the creation of static raster frames, the use of raster sprites with vector paths, and the use of vector sprites and vector paths. The quality and effects that can be generated using these methods can be quite diverse; but given what you know about vector and raster elements, these descriptions should give you some clue about how the animations are created using them.

Before you look at these three 2D animation methods, note that all 2D animation packages include some sort of drawing and painting tools. Many include a raster editor or paint application in the animation package. This is what allows you to create the contents that appear in the individual frames. The robustness of these editors, however, varies considerably. Some 2D programs include raster editors that are quite complex, whereas others are very crude, only allowing the simplest of selection, painting, and drawing tools. This is definitely something you want to look at in comparisons among animation programs. As you begin to look at the three different 2D animation creation methods, the importance of the drawing tools will become more evident.

Static Frames

The first type of 2D animation package available on the personal computer was the static frame animation package. In this type of 2D animation package, the animator draws each and every element within the animation on a flat canvas, as shown in Figure 7.2. The portions of the animation that change over time must be painstakingly drawn in each frame on the computer. The static frame environment most closely resembles the traditional cel process.

Figure 7.2.
Drawing each and every frame in the static, bitmap frames.

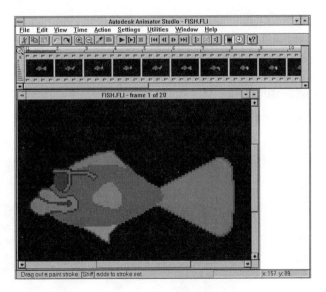

Static frame animation creation also resembles small flip-book animations that we probably all enjoyed as children. In the flip-book animation, every page in the book has a different frame that has been drawn. Thumbing through the book makes the animation appear to move, which is nice. However, someone had to draw every one of those frames. In the static frame environment, as well, someone has to draw each and every frame, which is a time-consuming process.

The static frame environment is the lowest-level and simplest approach to computer animation. It's not much more than cel animation in digital form. Many of the monotonous and repetitive tasks that exist in the traditional process exist in these types of packages. These types of programs integrate very few digital helps when creating the animation. About the only help that the animator has is the ability to copy the contents of one frame to another as well as help such as onion-skinning, as discussed later in this chapter. You will find that this approach to computer animation is pretty time-consuming. For Web animations, most animators want a quick method of creating an animation, especially because Web animations are designed to complement and complete, not to be the sole source of communication.

The static frame environment is normally a flatland environment and exhibits the negative aspects found in flat bitmap editors—those without layering capability. This is the primary reason it takes so long to create animations with them.

For example, an element pasted into the frame removes any pixel information that lies behind it. (See Figure 7.3.) As you saw in Chapter 5, "Raster-Based Graphics," raster editors that work this way do not support the fluidity of graphic design. You cannot easily change, manipulate, or edit graphic elements in this type of environment. Non-layered environments make working with the individual bitmaps harder. Note that any bitmap editor, or application that integrates a flat bitmap editing environment, is more difficult to use than a layered one because of problems with background deletion, anti-aliasing, and other typical raster issues.

Figure 7.3.

*The knock-out attribute
of the flatland raster
editor.*

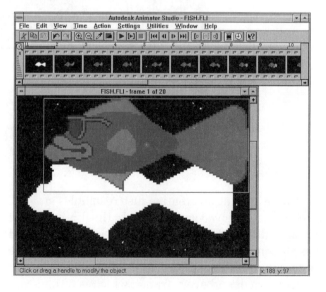

Raster Sprites

The second method of 2D animation creation is the use of raster sprites. A *sprite* is any element in the animation that changes over time. For example, in an animation of a flying bird, the bird is a sprite in the animation.

Using raster sprites in an animation environment provides one unique advantage over the static frame setting: You are working with objects rather than sets (frames) of pixels. Understand that the objects are composed of pixels; however, you can treat sets of pixels individually as discrete objects. Figure 7.4 shows an example of a bird that is a sprite and is composed of a set of pixels. Note that the sprite can be moved over the screen and acts as an independent object.

Figure 7.4.
Raster sprites are groups or sets of pixels that act as independent and discrete objects.

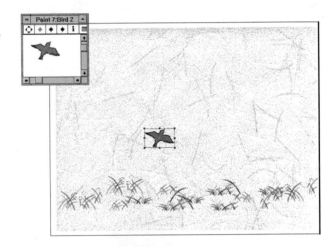

In the raster sprite environment, because there are discrete objects, you are working in a layered environment. Often, multiple raster sprites are composited over a background or other sprites to create a composite frame. There is no deletion of background objects, but anti-aliasing can still be a problem, as shown in Figure 7.5.

Vector Sprites

The last type of 2D animation method is the use of vector sprites. Similar to the use of raster sprites, *vector sprites* are also treated as discrete objects that can be animated over or behind other objects. The vector sprite environment is also a layered environment.

As you saw in Chapter 4, "Vector-Based Graphics," using vector graphics has some significant advantages as well as disadvantages. Remember that vector graphics are defined by objects such as lines, arcs, and circles. They can be easily scaled, but when used as screen output they often appear jaggy and less than desirable, particularly when arcs or circles are involved in the graphic. (See Figure 7.6.) Vector sprites are most effective in situations in which size is the key issue (such as on the Web). Remember that vector graphics are very small because they use vector (PostScript) descriptions.

Figure 7.5.
The layered environment allows sprites to be moved without the deletion of background objects, which enhances animation design.

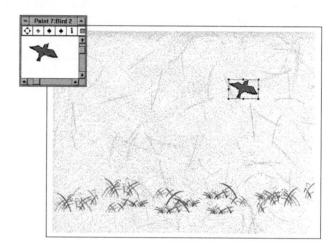

Figure 7.6.
Vector sprites show the characteristic jaggies associated with screen output of vector graphics.

As you are working with animations for the Web, you will most often utilize both raster and vector sprites. You can, in most packages that support sprites, use either one in the creation of your animations. Vector sprites are most useful for rectangular-type objects that are static in your animation, such as a background element. Raster sprites are best for animated items such as characters.

Paths of Motion

Probably the most important part of animation is defining the movements and actions that occur within the animation itself. In raster and vector sprite environments, movements are defined by paths of motion. These paths define the movements of the sprite along a Bézier spline. You can control how tightly or loosely the sprite travels the path as well.

In Figure 7.7, you see an example of a sprite and the path of motion defined for it. Regardless of whether you are using vector or raster sprites, the path of motion is always defined by a Bézier spline, even though it appears to be a linear path. The key positions, or markers, on the spline denote the keyframes of the animations. The number of tween steps that the computer generates between the keys is determined by the number of frames.

Figure 7.7.
The path of motion for both raster and vector sprites is defined by a Bézier spline.

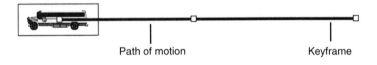

Path of motion   Keyframe

Most computer animation packages do an adequate job of defining the tween steps between the keys that you assign. In addition, many packages allow more than just linear motion, as shown in Figure 7.8.

Figure 7.8.
Most packages allow paths of motion to be more than just linear paths.

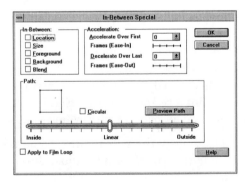

There are two predominant ways of defining the paths of motion within the animation package. The first is to specify the beginning and ending points of the object and let the computer fill in the in-between steps. This will most often cause the computer to create a linear path between the object's beginning and ending points, as shown in Figure 7.9. After the computer has created the in-between steps, you can go back and adjust the in-betweens to your liking.

Figure 7.9.
*Defining a path of
motion through a
beginning and ending
point.*

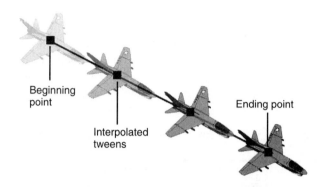

Beginning
point

Interpolated
tweens

Ending point

The second method for establishing paths of motion is through the use of real-time recording. For example, in Macromedia Director, you can place an object in an originating location. Then you simply click and drag the object on the screen to the location at which you want the animated object to end. The computer then creates a path of motion based on your click-and-drag operation, as shown in Figure 7.10.

Figure 7.10.
*Using real-time record-
ing to define a path
of motion.*

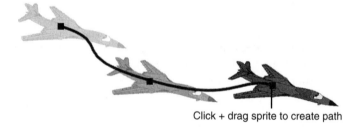

Click + drag sprite to create path

A path of motion is relative to a certain number of frames. Almost all animation packages use some sort of timeline to represent movements that occur within the animation. Most will display a difference in the timeline between frames that are keyframes and ones that are in-betweens. Figure 7.11 shows the animation elements and the timeline associated with what is shown on screen.

Either means of specifying paths will require some adjustment to make the animation look better. Often, you'll want to adjust the path so that it more closely resembles the real world. That requires editing the number of frames per certain segments of the path of motion.

For example, suppose you created an animation of a ball bouncing across the screen. You define the simple movements of the ball using linear paths, as shown in Figure 7.12. However, when you watch the animation, you'll see that it looks unnatural because when a real ball bounces, it does not go on a straight path up and then a straight path down. Some editing needs to be done on the path of motion so that it appears more realistic.

Figure 7.11.
The sprite's relationship to the timeline of the animation.

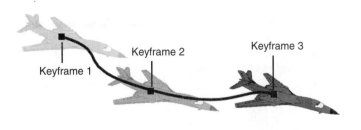

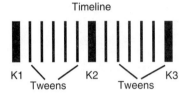

Figure 7.12.
Linear motion paths don't mimic the real world.

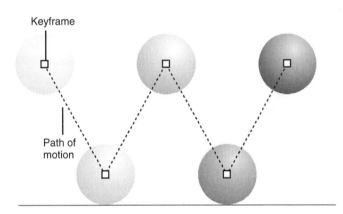

To make the example more like what occurs in the real world, you need to adjust the path of motion so that it is not so linear. Depending on the animation program, you might be able to insert Bézier points on the path of motion to round off the sharp point at which ascent turns to descent. However, you might have to take a more base-level approach and adjust the sprite. In any case, creating a smoother path of motion will make the animation appear more realistic, as shown in Figure 7.13.

Defining Movements over Time

In the example of the bouncing ball, the smoothing of the path of motion made for a better animation—but is there anything else that can be done to make it more realistic? Let's take a look at a couple of things you can do to make an animation even better.

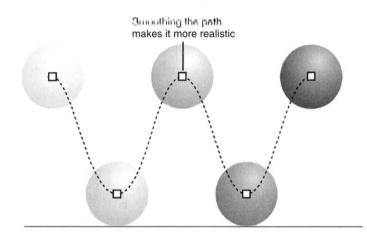

Objects seldom move at a constant rate. Often, there is acceleration and deceleration that occurs on objects that move as a result of friction and other natural phenomena. *Kinematics* is the study of forces on mechanical and other objects that move. If you are looking at the natural movements and ranges of motion as they relate to the human body, you are studying *kinesiology*. In any case, all objects are affected by natural phenomena, which are exhibited as changes in direction and momentum.

To make the ball example more realistic, some of these forces would need to be exhibited in the animation. As the ball ascends, there should be some natural deceleration that occurs as it approaches its apex. As it hits the ground and bounces back up, there should be some acceleration. In addition, on the overall animation, the ball should slow down a little and its bounce height should decrease as it exerts energy in the bounce. Figure 7.14 shows the adjusted path of motion to make the animation appear more natural.

Figure 7.14.

Adding acceleration and deceleration to the path of motion.

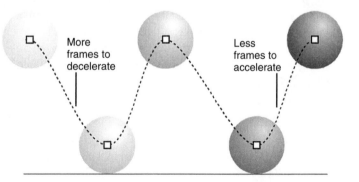

Many of the natural phenomena that occur as a result of forces that act on moving bodies can be simulated within animations. The degree to which you try to replicate them is up to you, but it will affect how realistic your animations appear to be. In the ball example, determining who your audience is will determine to what lengths the bouncing ball should be realistic. Always determine what level of realism your animation should be based upon the audience and the context of the animation.

Along these same lines, many 2D animation packages integrate somewhat sophisticated tools designed to make replication of kinematics easier. Some packages allow you to easily create acceleration and deceleration by affecting a motion path. Creating acceleration and deceleration requires editing the path of motion.

For example, to make the ball accelerate on its incline, fewer frames are needed in the incline sections of the motion path. Moving the key frames makes the ball accelerate. To make the ball decelerate, more frames are needed in the decline portions of the motion path. Moving the keyframes in the path creates more in-between frames making the ball decelerate on its decline, as shown in Figure 7.15.

Figure 7.15.
Changing the path has changed the number of in-between frames causing the ball to speed up and slow down.

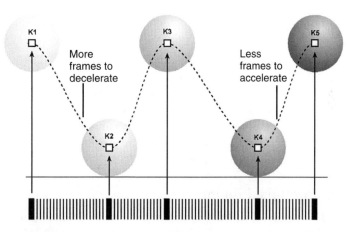

Keep in mind that animations are played back at a constant rate. You cannot increase or decrease the frame rate of the animation; so instead, you must adjust the number of frames per unit of motion. The speed of playback of those frames might also be affected by the bandwith that the end user has. Remember that the motion path defines the movement of an object over a certain amount of time/frames. Decreasing frames is just like decreasing the amount of time, and vice versa.

Translation

Up to this point, you have really read about only one translation method: movement. Although movement in the animation is one of the primary translations in an animation, there are two other translation movements that can be utilized. These are rotation and scaling.

For example, to finish making the ball more realistic, we could make it rotate as it is bouncing. If the ball were truly bouncing in a certain direction, it would be rotating in the direction of the bounce. This could be accomplished by adding a second path of motion defining rotation, as shown in Figure 7.16. With both of these paths defined, the ball would not only follow the bouncing path that you established previously, but it would also rotate along that bouncing path.

Figure 7.16.

Adding a second translation to the ball: rotation.

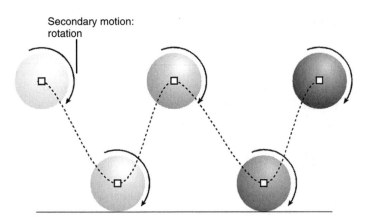

Secondary motion: rotation

Defining multiple paths of motion can be difficult or simple, depending on the animation package. Often, using multiple paths of motion requires the ability to perform hierarchical linking.

Hierarchical Linking

Hierarchical linking is the capability to define relationships between multiple objects and multiple paths of motions. In the ball example, defining multiple paths of motion for the ball would require establishing a relationship between the bounced path and the ball's rotation path. In a package that supports hierarchical linking, you could define the rotation of the ball in relationship to the distance traveled along the bounce path. This would make creating the second path of motion extremely easy. You would simply tell the software that for every X distance traveled on the path, the raster sprite (the ball) will rotate Y degrees. This would automatically create the rotating ball on a bouncing path.

In addition to establishing relationships between paths of motion, you can also use hierarchical linking to create relationships between multiple objects. For example, if you wanted to create an animation of an arm and hand of an animated character moving, you could link the arm and hand so the movement appeared naturally (and more easily). Otherwise, any movement you perform on the arm would also have to be manually created for the hand. In the linked environment, any movements to the arm would automatically affect the linked hand, as shown in Figure 7.17.

Figure 7.17.
Hierarchical linking creates a relationship between two objects or paths.

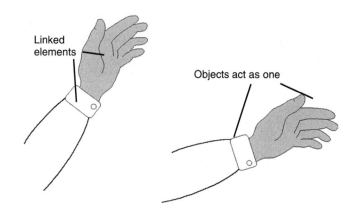

Hierarchically linked objects are always created as a parent and child relationship, as shown in Figure 7.18. A single parent object can have many child objects linked to it, but most packages allow child objects to belong to only one parent. In the hand and arm example, the arm is a parent object and the hand is a child object.

Figure 7.18.
The parent and child relationship of hierarchical linking.

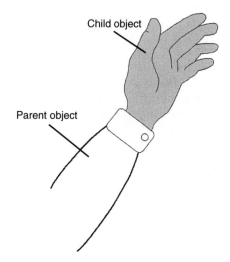

If the hand had fingers, logically they would probably be a child to the hand rather than the arm, as shown in Figure 7.19. Note that any translations made on either parent would also affect the associate child object. In addition, the child itself can be translated, such as wiggling the fingers, without affecting the parent object. As you can see, an animation of the entire human body could have any number of parent/child relationships and would present a significant advantage over having to translate each and every object independently for movement or other translations.

Figure 7.19.
*Establishing more than
a single parent and child
relationship.*

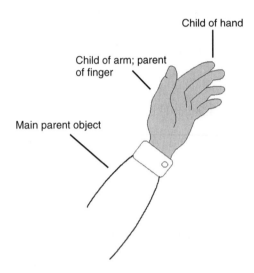

Child of hand

Child of arm; parent
of finger

Main parent object

The relationships that you establish through linked objects can be created in any fashion. Most often, there is a logical method of creating linked objects. The arm moves the hand, so the hand is established as a child of the arm (parent). The hand moves the fingers, so the fingers are a child of the hand. Note that moving the arm would therefore move the hand and the fingers because the fingers are a child of the hand.

Although every package functions a little differently, most hierarchical relationships work this way. Keep in mind, however, that just because a package touts hierarchical linking it still might only support singular parent and child relationships (one parent and one child).

Deformations

The translation of an object can include move, rotate, or scale. The ball example is missing one thing to make it complete. As the ball bounces, more than likely it will deform slightly as it bounces off the table. You could use the scale translation to make it *squish* (for a lack of a better term), but most scaling operations occur with a fixed-aspect ratio. This means that the percentage the X dimension is scaled is also the percentage that the Y dimension is scaled. Both decrease or increase simultaneously. In the animation, the ball would appear to get smaller or larger rather than squish (or *deformate*).

According to Webster's, *deformate,* or *deformation,* means the state of being disfigured—a malformation. This is what you are looking for in the ball. Most often, deformations refer to translations that do not occur symmetrically or across multiple axes at a time. The scaling operation affects two axes; however, to make the ball squish, you need to scale or deform a single axis, as shown in Figure 7.20.

Figure 7.20.
Deformations usually
affect only one axis, such
as the squishing ball.

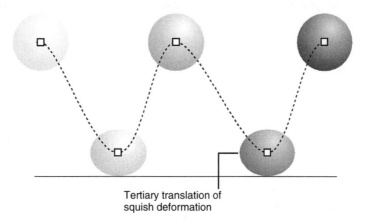

Tertiary translation of
squish deformation

Deformations in animations are usually given technical names like squish, squash, shear, poke, and point. Each one has a specific type of deformation that it will create, and the availability of any given deformation is dependent upon the package.

To finish the ball animation, we need to add a little squish when the ball bounces. Adding a deformation would make the animation complete, as shown in Figure 7.20. Understand that deformations are types of translation and are used for special purposes such as your squishing ball.

2D Animation Techniques

In 2D animation programs, there are several techniques that can be used to transfer the information that appears in one frame to another frame. Much more than simple copying and pasting, these techniques are a means of making 2D animation creation a much easier task. In addition, these techniques enable you to create animations that are more professional.

Most of the techniques described are methods of timing the elements in your animation so they appear to move fluidly. One of the most difficult aspects of animation is creating the appearance of smooth motion. If even one frame is off, the entire animation can look unprofessional. Most timing inaccuracies are a result of moving an element too far too quickly or interjecting an awkward movement in an individual frame. These animation techniques are designed to decrease timing and position problems.

As you take a look at these techniques, keep in mind that more than one might be available to you in a given software package. In addition, one might be more applicable depending on your given circumstances and purposes.

Onion-Skinning

The first 2D animation technique discussed in this chapter is commonly used by static frame animation programs and can also be used in most sprite-based animation programs. *Onion-skinning* is a technique that allows the animator to compare the contents of one frame in relation to other frames.

Onion-skinning is a technique that is a carry-over from traditional cel animation. In the traditional process, prior to creating each frame on acetate, all frames were hand-drawn on special thin paper, sometimes called *trash paper*. Onion-skin paper resembles tracing paper, although it is generally more durable than tracing paper. Because it is a thin paper, it is translucent and somewhat transparent. Laying a piece of onion-skin over another drawing allows the artist to see the drawing underneath it. In this way, the animator can draw the contents of the cel he is working on based upon the contents of the previous cel. Often, a range of cells is laid upon one another to verify the progression of images in the range of drawings.

Because onion-skinning will work with any transparent media, after the drawings of the cels are made, the painters, who paint each cel in the animation, also use the onion-skinning technique to compare and contrast colors for accuracy.

On the computer, onion-skinning allows the digital animator to compare two cels, or a range of cels from the digital animation. Application software that supports this technique will normally contrast the current frame over the top of either the prior frame, next frame, or both, as shown in Figure 7.21. This way, you can check the movements and progressions that occur over a range of frames.

If you are using animation software that does not support onion-skinning, you can perform the same thing in most layered raster-editing environments. For example, you could save several images from the animation as individual bitmaps and bring them into a raster editor to do the onion-skin comparison.

Figure 7.21.
Onion-skinning compos-
ites several frames so a
comparison of actions or
progression can be made.

Blending

Another technique is the ability to perform blending operations between frames of an animation. Using blending, the animator can blend the contents of two frames to create results in a third, as shown in Figure 7.22.

Figure 7.22.
Blending frames creates
a frame based upon
surrounding frames.

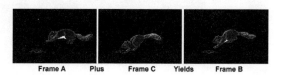

Frame A   Plus   Frame C   Yields   Frame B

The blending technique is generally limited to sprite-based animation programs, but some high-end raster editors in animation programs allow you to create blended frames based on the contents of two surrounding frames. Most often, blending is used to create tween frames, but it can also be used to create keyframes in certain instances.

Transparency

Another type of animation is the use of transparency to create frame contents. Much like the transparency effects created in the GIF 89a format (see Chapter 5), animations that support transparency allow the animator to specify specific colors in a sprite to be transparent. This allows the sprite to pass over other items in the animation, without the rectangular definitions of the sprite bitmap.

Figure 7.23a shows an example of a raster sprite that needs to be animated over a colored background. In Figure 7.23b, placing the sprite on the background reveals the pixels around the sprite. To make the surrounding pixels transparent, the white color is assigned as transparent. This allows the sprite to be animated over the background without the extraneous white pixels appearing. (See Figure 7.23c.)

Most animation packages that support transparency also allow other similar effects. For example, Macromedia Director allows a foreground sprite to take on many different transparency effects, which it terms *ink effects*. A wide variety of effects allows the extraneous pixels, as well as the sprite itself, to create many different combinations when placed on a background, as shown in Figure 7.24.

Figure 7.23.
*Transparency allows
certain colors in the
sprite to appear as
transparent.*

Figure 7.24.
*Some animation
packages, such as
Macromedia Director,
allow more than just
transparency.*

Source Images

When you are working with animations for the Web, you'll probably be creating your own elements from vector and raster elements. Aside from your own custom creations, there are two other main means of generating sprites and other elements for your animations: using cut-outs and clip-art.

Cut-Outs

Cut-outs are a very effective and efficient means for creating animations. Cut-outs can reduce a lot of extraneous work when they are used properly. Cut-outs are another carry-over from traditional cel animation.

When the amount of movement or change from frame to frame is limited, it is often useful to redraw only the portion of the frame that is changing. For example, in an animation of a bird that is flying across the screen, more than likely the only parts of the bird that are changing are the wings of the bird. The remainder of the body stays the same across the screen. Using cut-outs of the wings allows the animator to insert the proper portions of the wings as they are needed within the animation, rather than redrawing the entire bird. Therefore, cut-outs of the various wing positions can be used with the existing body in the animation, reducing the amount of redrawing that occurs from frame to frame.

In character animation, body movements such as a wave of the hand or the legs in various walking positions, provide an opportunity to use cut-outs to reduce the amount of drawing that must occur in the animation.

Clip-Art

In addition to using cut-outs, a frequent practice is to use clip-art as a basis for animation. Although you won't spend a great deal of time reading about them here, copyrights are a major concern when you are dealing with any form of clip-art or other media elements created by individuals other than yourself. You must make certain that you have adequate permission to use graphics and other media elements created by another person, even if you found them on the Internet. Understand that just because something is found on the Internet does not mean that you can re-use it for distribution on the Web. Publishing on the Web is the same as publishing in any other media. Therefore, you must obtain permission to re-use the elements on the Web just like you have to do for re-use in books, CD-ROMs, or other publishing media. For more information on copyrights and other authorship details, see the sections under these headings in Chapter 10, "Interactive Multimedia Design Process."

2D Animation Effects

Aside from the various methods and techniques that can be used to create 2D animation, there are also some other special things you can do concerning your animations on the Web. Most of these effects are somewhat simple to describe but applying them in the various programs can be somewhat difficult.

In the remaining sections, you'll take a cursory look at what each of these items are. They are all common terms you might run across as you are designing Web animations. However, they are implemented a little differently from program to program.

Color Cycling

The first of these animation effects is called *color cycling*. In Chapter 4, "Raster-Based Graphics," you were presented with the concept of 8-bit color. Remember that in a 256-color animation, all the colors are contained within a special matrix called a *palette*. Each color in the palette has a specific number. Each pixel in the image is referenced to one of the colors by the matrix or Color Lookup Table (CLUT) number. This is how the software knows what color each pixel in the image should be.

The color cycling effect causes colors in the animation to be shifted by re-referencing one of the colors in the color palette. For example, you might have a sprite that is assigned a particular green color, which corresponds to a number. In animation programs that support color cycling, you can create an animation that smoothly changes the green sprite to another color in the color palette. You do this by having the software reference a different color in the color palette, using its number, over a specified amount of time. By doing this, you get an animation of the sprite smoothly changing colors over a specified amount of time. In fact, you can have the sprite change colors through the entire color palette.

Rotoscoping and Compositing

Rotoscoping and compositing are closely related and allow you to create various animation effects based upon already existing animation files. The easiest to use is rotoscoping.

Rotoscoping is the ability to draw paint upon already existing animation, video, or film. For example, you might want to go into a view of a city skyline and add a title that remains constant while the background pans the horizon, as shown in Figure 7.25. This effect can be easily created after the video source has been sampled. After you have a digital video clip, animation, or film clip, you can easily paint on the frames of the file because every image is a simple raster image. It's just like painting in any other raster image.

Figure 7.25.
Rotoscoping allows you to draw or paint on top of existing video, animation, or film.

The second of these effects is called compositing. *Compositing* allows you to overlay one animation or video clip over the top of another. Two source frames are combined to create a single frame. There's not much to compositing. It's just superimposing each frame from one source clip over the top of another source clip to create a new animation file.

Chroma-Keying

Compositing alone is not very impressive. Lay image A over image B and get image C. However, chroma-keying adds something special to the compositing capability.

Like compositing, chroma-keying combines two source clips to create a new clip. However, chroma-keying gives you the ability to only replace certain portions of image A with image B as shown in Figure 7.26. Note that only the black pixels in this frame would be replaced by the superimposed frame. This is called the chroma-key, which is the color that will be substituted for in the image.

Figure 7.26.
*Chroma-keying replaces
only a certain color in
the image with the
superimposed image.*

Using a special chroma-key, a special color assigned to be transparent, chroma-keying replaces the chroma-key color in the first clip with the contents of the second clip, as shown in Figure 7.27. This allows you to precisely control what parts of the first animation are replaced with the second animation.

Chroma-keying has been around for many years. It is the basis for the blue screens used in things from the daily weather report to movies such as *Star Wars*. In these settings, the actor stands in front of a large blue screen and is recorded. Then the blue portions of the actor's clip are replaced with contents of some other clip such as a weather map of the United States or the desert sands of Tatooine. In any case, the chroma-keying effect replaces a special color in clip A with the contents of clip B to create superimposed clip C.

Morphing

Morphing is one of the newest effects and is a direct result of the computer in graphics. In morphing, the computer is used to smoothly interpolate between two different images. For example, you can morph a picture of yourself into some animal or other image, as shown in Figure 7.28. The computer can cleanly and precisely create an animation of you morphing into something else in the animation.

Figure 7.27.
*The substituted
chroma-key.*

Figure 7.28.
*Two source images used
to create a morphing
animation.*

To create a morph, you must begin with two source images. Once the source images are loaded into the software, you define a closed vector object defining control points in both of the images, as shown in Figure 7.29. The control points of the polygons of the two images should have the same number of points. The computer uses the pixels around these datapoints to define how the image will be interpolated.

After the control points are defined for the images, you must define the number of steps or frames (which equal the amount of time) it should take to morph from one image to the other. At the 50 percent point, half of the superimposed results are a result of the first image, and the other half are due to the second image, as shown in Figure 7.30. This is how the computer creates a morphing animation.

The effectiveness of most morphs is based upon several attributes such as the position and orientation of the subjects of the base images. For example, morphing your head into the body of some animal will not be very effective. If you morph your head into the head of something else that has similar positioning, size, and orientation, the morph will be effective. Nonetheless, you can basically have the computer interpolate any raster image into any other raster image and save it as an animation.

Figure 7.29.
Defining control points for a morphing animation.

Figure 7.30.
At the middle of the morph, the superimposed image is half image A and half image B.

Filters

The final type of effect that you can use is a filter. A *filter* is a program add-on or feature that creates a specific type of effect. Filters can be used to perform imaging operations on an animation, such as controlling brightness, contrast, and saturation. They can also be used to add special effects such as farcles, highlights, and colorized lights. One of the best filters, and one I use quite frequently, is the lens flare filter in Photoshop, which can be used to create farcles, as shown in Figure 7.31. This is a real cool way of creating timely farcles or that bright and shiny lens flare!

Figure 7.31.
*Photoshop's cool lens
flare filter.*

Summary

In this chapter you took a look at the various aspects of creating 2D animations. Keep in mind that the animations created with 2D animation packages might include either vector- or raster-based animation files. This chapter covered static frames, raster sprites, and vector sprites. You saw how movements are defined using the path of motion. When you are working with 2D animation packages, you can use a variety of techniques and have many options for special effects.

8

3D Animation

As you read in Chapter 6, "Fundamentals of Animation," animations can be created using one of two methods: 2D or 3D software. As you saw in the last chapter, 2D animations are created by utilizing software that requires that the animator define the contents of each animation frame and the changes that occur in all of the frames over time. As you read, animations generated in 2D packages are typically less photo-realistic than animations created in 3D animation packages.

The biggest advantage to the 3D animation environment is the ability to create photo-realistic images and animations without having to painstakingly paint each individual frame or cell of the animation. (See Figure 8.1.) Instead, the animator creates 3D objects, applies textures and other object characteristics, and then lets the computer render the scene based upon the characteristics established for the environment. Although the animator doesn't physically paint each frame of the animation, there are many other things with which the animator must be concerned. In this chapter, you will look at the various aspects of utilizing 3D animation packages.

Figure 8.1.
3D animation packages allow the animator to create photo-realistic images without digitally painting each and every frame.

Every 3D animation package has three basic parts or modes of operation: the modeler, the renderer, and the animator. To create a 3D animation requires creating a 3D model or scene upon which the animation is based. Then you must assign specific rendering properties, such as the texture of those objects, the lights that illuminate the scene, and the view of the scene you want to render. Finally, you establish translations of the objects that define the changes that occur within the environment over time. The changes over time are what you are trying to capture in your three-dimensional generated animation.

Because the process of creating 3D animations includes modeling, rendering, and animating, this chapter is divided into sections discussing each of these. In most packages, modeling, rendering, and animating object occurs within a single 3D environment. However, all the commands within the software are devoted to creating models, setting rendering characteristics, or defining animation attributes.

You'll find that there are various qualities of renderings that can be produced via 3D animation packages. Each animation package contains a rendering engine, which is the code that creates each frame based upon the environment. The rendering engine of each package is a little different and produces varying qualities of images based upon the complexity of the rendering engine. In addition, the capabilities of a 3D package's modeling and animating commands also affects the resulting animation.

Keep in mind that the 3D animation process is a three-fold process. It requires the ability to model, render, and animate the objects within the environment. The process begins with the creation of the models themselves. The resulting animation is based upon the models, their characteristics, and their changes over time.

After models are built, textures and other surface characteristics are assigned to the models to make them look like tangible objects. Finally, the models are given specific translations to enable the software to create a rendered animation. In this chapter, you will look at the ways these three tasks—modeling, rendering, and animating—are performed within 3D animation packages.

The Modeling Environment

The modeling portion of the 3D package allows the animator to create 3D models, as well as import them from other software packages. The modeler is one of the most important parts of the animation software because the whole animation is based on the movements and changes surrounding the model. It doesn't matter how good the software renders or animates; if he can't create a good three-dimensional model, or import one, it is of little use. Because the realism of the model is very important, the modeling capabilities of the software and the ability of the modeler to create a realistic scene is of the utmost importance.

Modeling Environment Variables

In any modeling environment, there are various ways models are created. Most 3D animation packages, as well as 3D CAD packages, contain three main variables that are used to operate within the 3D environment. These include the objects, the coordinate space, and the viewpoint (or display view), as shown in Figure 8.2. The capability of any 3D package is based upon the robustness of these three properties.

Figure 8.2.
The modeling environ-
ment has three main
variables: the objects, the
coordinate space, and the
viewer.

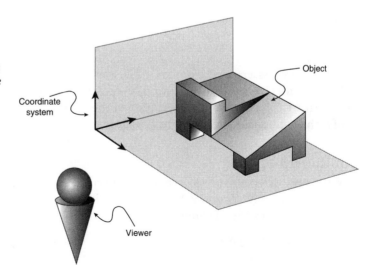

Coordinate
system

Object

Viewer

Objects

As you probably already guessed, one of the 3D environment attributes or variables is the object(s) you create within the environment. This is the focus of all 3D packages—the creation of objects. Although objects in varying packages can be created a little bit differently, objects are one of the primary things that you control within the modeling database.

Within any 3D environment, all objects are unique, discrete, and digitally tangible things that can be manipulated. All the objects created in a 3D database have a location (position in space) and an orientation (a rotation in relation to an axis), as shown in Figure 8.3. This also means that they can be translated by moving, rotating, or scaling them within the database. Working in a three-dimensional environment is akin to manipulating objects in the 3D world in which we live.

Figure 8.3.
All objects have a location and orientation in the coordinate space of the 3D environment.

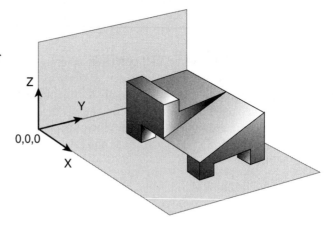

All the objects created exist in a 3D world or conceptual space with no ends. Because all objects have a location or a position, however, there must be a way of tracking the location and orientation of the objects. This is done through the use of a three-dimensional coordinate system.

Coordinate Space

With any 3D package, all space is defined by triplicate coordinates usually denoted by an X, Y, and Z location. This is the second attribute or controllable variable within the 3D environment.

The theoretical space, or coordinate space, extends to infinity in all directions. The coordinate space has an origin (0,0,0), and all object positions are relative to the coordinate origin. In addition, the object's relationship to three-dimensional axes defines its orientation.

In Figure 8.4, you see a simple object created and positioned in 3D coordinate space. Note that the position of the object is relative to the origin and its rotation is relative to the primary axes in the environment. Any corner of the object can be labeled with a coordinate location relative to the origin.

Figure 8.4.
The position and orientation of all objects is specified in relationship to 3D coordinate space.

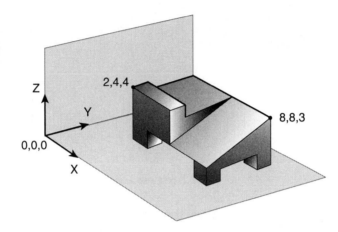

Creating animations in the 3D environment requires translation of objects, such as moving, rotating, or scaling, over a certain period of time. Therefore, understanding 3D coordinate space and how to translate objects within it is very important.

Viewpoint

The final attribute of all modeling environments is the viewpoint. The viewpoint is the variable that controls what is viewed on the computer display screen. Changing the viewpoint within a 3D package changes what is seen on the display screen.

The 3D modeling environment can best be described in the following manner. The 3D environment is a conceptual space without ends. Because your monitor does not have an infinite display area, you can see only a small portion of the conceptual space on your screen. Note that you can build or translate a model anywhere within the conceptual space of the environment. Figure 8.5 shows an object being translated (moved) from one position to another. As objects are translated, what is seen on the screen changes due to the relationship between the objects and the current viewpoint.

Figure 8.5.
*Translating an object in
the 3D environment.*

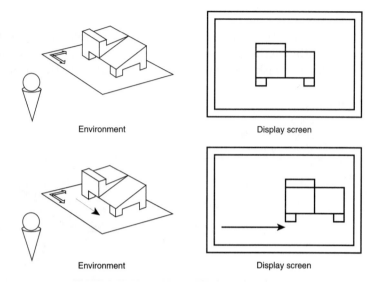

To acquire various views of the environment—to change what you currently see in the window (display)—you must change the viewpoint. The viewpoint is the theoretical viewing position, where you as the viewer are positioned in the 3D environment to look at the model. The viewpoint has both a location and an orientation, meaning that you can change what is currently seen by changing the position or orientation of the viewpoint. Figure 8.6 shows an example of two viewpoints of a model.

Figure 8.6.
*Changing the viewpoint
changes what is seen in
the display.*

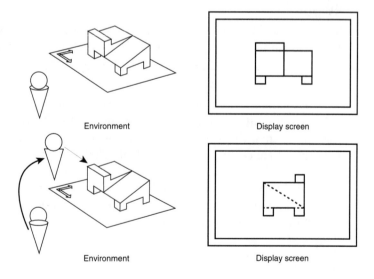

Although this is a cursory explanation, you'll find that all 3D packages have these three variables. The modeling environment includes the objects, the coordinate system, and the viewer (viewpoint). The coordinate space is what is used to define the 3D world. Often, it also affects how objects are created. Both the objects and the viewer have an orientation and location within the 3D world. What is viewed on the screen is a function of the relationship between the position and orientation of the viewpoint and the position and orientation of the objects. Translating either viewer or objects changes what is seen on the display screen.

Types of 3D Models

Most 3D animation software uses surface modeling techniques to create the actual objects or models in the scene. Yet, there are three types of modelers available: wireframe, surface, and solid modelers. Each of these describes a more complex method and type of model.

To better explain the different types of modeling, imagine physically creating a 3D cube out of toothpicks and tape by representing the edges of the cube with toothpicks and taping the vertices to hold them together. The finished product would be similar to building a wireframe model, as shown in Figure 8.7.

Figure 8.7.
A simple wireframe model.

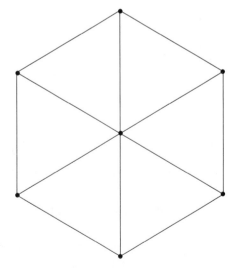

Wireframe Models

Wireframe models are the simplest models to create, but they can also be very confusing in complex situations because the user can see the hidden edges on the back side of the objects, just as with the toothpick model. (Refer to Figure 8.7.) They do not contain surfaces so they cannot be effectively rendered either.

A wireframe model is composed of points and connecting lines that represent the limits or boundaries of the object, as shown in Figure 8.8. So in the toothpick model, the wireframe would be composed of points at the intersection of the toothpicks (where the tape would be), and the toothpicks themselves would represent the connecting lines that are the limits of the form of the cube.

Figure 8.8.
A wireframe model is composed of points and connecting lines representing form boundaries.

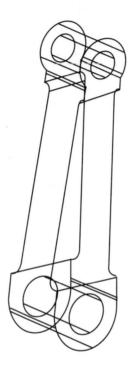

Surface Models

A model can be thought of, in most cases, as a modified wireframe. In most modeling packages, the user can change a wireframe model into a surface model by adding surfaces to it.

For example, imagine taking the wireframe toothpick model and wrapping one layer of paper around it, so that the entire surface area on the outside of the cube is covered by a piece of paper, as shown in Figure 8.9. The toothpick model is now representative of a surface model. The actual surface planes would be represented by the paper, whereas the boundaries or intersections of the planes are represented by the toothpicks. Surface models are therefore composed of points, lines, and surfaces.

Figure 8.9.
Covering the toothpick
model with paper creates
a surface model.

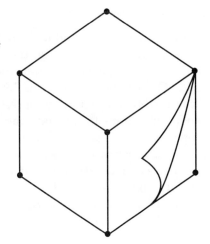

Even though the toothpick model now looks as if it is solid, it is not. If it were cut in two pieces, it would be hollow because it has no true volume or mass on the inside. This is advantageous in 3D animation software because it is the surfaces that software needs to generate the animation.

Most modeling packages, even when building a surface model, display the model as a wireframe—a model that you can see through. This cuts down computation time for regenerating the display screen. The modeler can, in most cases, generate a hidden-line removed display of the model to check its position or orientation, as shown in Figure 8.10. This is very helpful if the user becomes disoriented about where the object is in 3D space.

Figure 8.10.
A normal model view
and a hidden line
removed version of
the same.

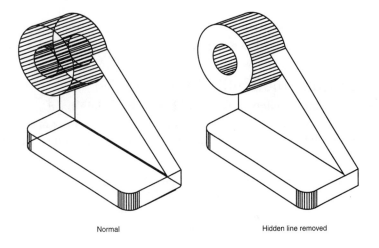

Normal   Hidden line removed

Solid Model

The last modeling type, the solid model, is a computer representation of an object that has a mass and a volume. In most instances, the computer generates a surface model that is assigned a mass and volume and other necessary information to represent the solid. The computer does this by using surface model boundary information, also called B-rep (boundary representation) information, combined with specific, solid algorithms to calculate volume characteristics. It then applies mass properties of the object to the volume data for material-specific information. After these characteristics have been assigned to the model, it becomes a *solid* in the computer's memory. In theory, if a solid model were cut in half on the computer, it would appear solid and its engineering computations would behave like a true solid as well. To make the toothpick model a true, physically solid model, it would have to be filled with some substance.

The user can take a wireframe and place surfaces on it to generate a surface model. It must be noted, however, that most solid modelers cannot take a surface model and simply change it into a solid, even though most (solid modelers) use a B-rep representation to generate solid model information. The computer can, in fact, generate a surface object from the solid model, but not the other way around. This becomes an issue when you import 3D digital files from one package to another.

Most animation packages use surface modeling because of some of the limiting features associated with solid modeling. Solid modeling is the most accurate way to produce 3D models but is limiting because of the number of engineering properties that the computer must calculate and store for each manipulation of the object. To create animations, this amount of data is not needed. What you are really interested in are accurate surfaces on which to base your animation. In most cases, surface models are preferred in 3D animation packages because they are more flexible and less cumbersome than 3D solid models.

Surface Modeling for Animation

Surface modeling is by far the most widely used model type in 3D animation packages. Surface modelers are preferred because of the wide variety of modeling features that can be created within them, as well as the speed at which they can generate a model.

Surface modelers use a pattern of lines, called a *mesh,* to represent the form of the model—and because they are hollow, there are only B-rep calculations to be processed, as shown in Figure 8.11. Boundary calculations are simply calculations required to define the limits of the object. There is no concern about mass or volume. The surface mesh then conforms to the limits of the object and the order of those surfaces.

Figure 8.11.
Surface models use
meshes to represent
surfaces.

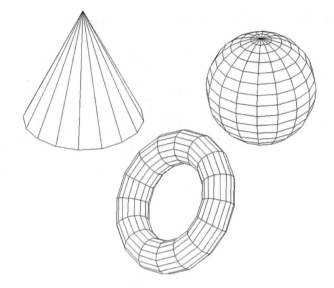

Surface meshes are akin to a pair of panty hose. Whatever the mesh is assigned to is what it will conform to. If it is applied to a bumpy, B-rep form, the mesh will be bumpy. If the mesh is applied to a smooth, curvilinear B-rep form, the mesh will be a smooth curvilinear form.

Surface Meshes

As you read, surface models are composed of surfaces or planes that are covered by a mesh that conforms to the boundary representations of the object. Two types of meshes can be calculated and applied to any surface model. The type of mesh that is used depends on the sophistication of the package and type of model desired.

The first type of surface meshes are polygonal surface meshes. These are the most common meshes and can be created in almost all surface modelers. Polygonal meshes use triangular or quadrilateral polygons to compose the meshes that cover the form, as shown in Figure 8.12. The size of each individual triangle or quadrilateral can be controlled by the user. The tighter the mesh, the smoother the object's surfaces will be, and consequently, the smoother the surfaces will appear in a rendered image.

Figure 8.12.
*Polygonal meshes use
triangular or quadrilat-
eral polygons to compose
the meshes that cover
the form.*

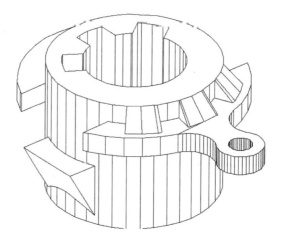

Although the optimum is to have smooth surfaces in your renderings and
animation, the tighter the mesh the more calculations are needed to render the
animation or image. The tightness of the mesh also determines how fast the
software regenerates the display screen while you are working. These polygonal
surface meshes are based on linear functions, which are used to generate the
latitudinal and longitudinal position of the polygons that compose the mesh as
you are working. The more polygons you have, the more computing horsepower
is needed. With some test animations, you can determine the optimum mesh for
your purpose and machine parameters.

The second type of mesh, and by far the most desired, is called a *patch* and is
shown in Figure 8.13. Patches include parametric surfaces such as B-splines as
well as the ever-popular NURBS (Non-Uniform Rational B-Splines), which are
widely used in workstation-based modeling and animation packages.

Figure 8.13.
*Patches create a
smoother and more
representational surface.*

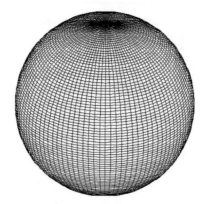

All of these parametric surfaces use high-order, mathematical calculations to generate the geometry patches. By using higher-order functions, the user is allowed to manipulate the shape of any given patch by moving weighted control points at the intersection of the patch's longitudinal and latitudinal lines, as shown in Figure 8.14. In other words, at any intersection on the patch, the user can move a point in any three-dimensional directional, which in turn distorts or changes the patch in real time. These are very effective when the model is organic in nature.

Figure 8.14.
The shape of any given patch can be manipulated by moving weighted control points at the intersection of the patch's longitudinal and latitudinal lines.

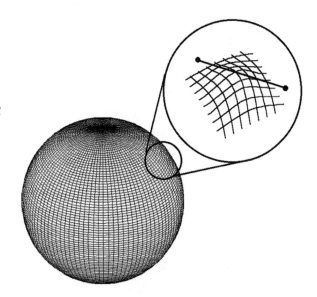

A point can also be inserted into a patch at almost any location as long as the point rests on the patch. Inserted points are also fully moveable, allowing the user to create almost any conceivable 3D model. In fact, this is how most organic shapes are created and manipulated in 3D animation programs. Note that organic shapes can be created using polygonal surface meshes, but they are usually not as realistic and are fairly complex to create. NURBS-based modeling is by far the most desirable type of surface mesh for photo-realistic 3D animations.

Boolean Operations

In the creation of models, Boolean operations are one of the most important modeling features that can be found in 3D animations packages. A Boolean operation allows the user to combine many different models to create composite models. Composite models are simply the combination of one or more models to create another single model.

To understand what a composite model is, take a look at a simple example. To create a drilled hole in a rectangular box, the user would use a Boolean operation and subtract a cylinder from the box. The resulting model would be considered a composite model. Figure 8.15 is an example of a composite Boolean model.

Figure 8.15.
Boolean composites are composed of lower-level elements. Subtracting a cylinder from a box creates a hole in the box.

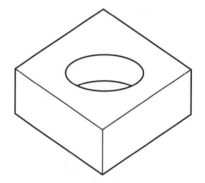

There are three Boolean operations that can be used to model 3D objects. The three Boolean operations are union, subtraction, and intersection. A Boolean union merges two or more existing models to create a composite, and a Boolean subtraction subtracts one object from another to create the composite. An intersection creates the composite by determining the shared or common space of the two entities and deleting or removing the remaining portions of the two models. All of these operations involve the use of multiple models to create a single composite, as shown in Figure 8.16.

Figure 8.16.
Boolean operations include union, subtraction, and intersection.

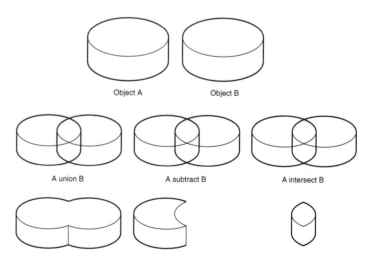

Boolean operations are fundamental modeling techniques. Most animation modeling modules support these basic modeling functions. For the user to be unhindered when creating models for animations, Boolean operations should be available in the modeling portion of the animation package.

Rendering Engines

The second part of the 3D animation package is the rendering portion. The rendering portion of the package includes some unique variables of its own, much like the uniqueness of the objects, coordinate space, and viewer of the modeling portion. Yet, before you can understand the individual elements that the renderer deals with when generating an individual frame from a 3D scene, there must be an understanding of the different types of rendering available. Within each package, the renderer can compose different qualities of raster images such as wireframe rendering, flat shading, gouroud, phong, ray-tracing, and radiosity, as shown in Table 8.1.

Table 8.1. Various types of rendering engines create different qualities of images.

Rendering Quality	Type	Characteristics
Lowest	Wireframe	Based lines rendered
	Flat	Flat shading in over wireframe
	Gouroud	Polygonal faces rendered
	Phong	Shadows and highlights rendered
	Ray-tracing	Realistic reflections, light rays traced, scattered light ignored
Highest	Radiosity	All light rays traced

The type of rendering quality available in each animation package is dependent upon the quality and price of the package. Most animation packages give several of the output qualities. Note, however, that in most cases, the names, when defined by a package, are a generalization. One package might call its rendering technique *phong* but give the quality of ray-tracing, or vice versa. Each type of rendering has specific characteristics that differentiate it from any other, regardless of packaging specifications.

The photo-realism of each type of rendering quality progresses from the simplest, which is wireframe, to radiosity, which is the most photo-realistic and complex. Throughout this progression, each subsequent type of rendering is built upon the lower form, as described in the following sections.

Wireframe Rendering and Flat Shading

Wireframe rendering is the simplest type of rendering to generate. In most cases, the renderer simply removes the hidden lines from the view of the object, as shown in Figure 8.17.

Figure 8.17.
Wireframe rendering simply creates a hidden-line-removed image.

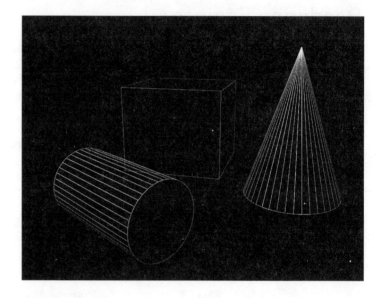

Wireframe rendering can usually be created in all animation packages as well as most CAD packages. This rendering technique is sometimes used as a check to see that all the parts of the 3D scene move correctly and that the objects are in the correct location to one another. As mentioned earlier, most models being built are displayed as if the surfaces of the model are transparent so that there is no lag time when redrawing and regenerating the VGA screen. Wireframe modeling can be a valuable asset when a quick rendering needs to be generated to check location, orientation, and movement of models.

Flat shading is the addition of flat color behind a wireframe rendering of a model by rendering the individual polygons that comprise the objects, as shown in Figure 8.18. This type of rendering is a simple enhancement of the wireframe rendering of an object or scene. By the addition of flat color within the polygons that make up the model, it is somewhat easier to visualize. Yet, this type of rendering is still far from being a photo-realistic image.

Figure 8.18.
Flat shading adds flat color to the polygons used to create a wireframe rendering.

Gouroud

Gouroud shading takes the flat-shaded model one step further. This type of shading takes into consideration the vertices that compose the 3D model in relation to the light sources in the scene. Variation of the individual planes is shown by sharp planar color changes in the rendered image between the vertices of the model. (See Figure 8.19.)

Figure 8.19.
Gouroud shading shows sharp planar color changed between the vertices of the model.

Note that this type of shading does not include shadows or highlights, which is the next step in the progression of rendering capabilities. Gouroud shading can be used to check that all the surfaces of a model are enclosed. This is particularly helpful when the surface model has been imported from another program or generated from a wireframe.

Phong

Phong shading calculates each pixel of the raster image. It is basically a gouroud image with added shadows and highlights. This type of rendering gives smoother face differentiation and calculates shadow characteristics by interpolating surface normals or perpendiculars. It also allows the operator to add, through the use of lights, intense highlights on the object at his or her discretion. This type of rendering is able to utilize light intensities and 3D object orientation as well, which is what allows it to add highlights and shadows in proper locations. (See Figure 8.20.)

Figure 8.20.
Phong shading includes shadows and highlights based upon light sources within the scene.

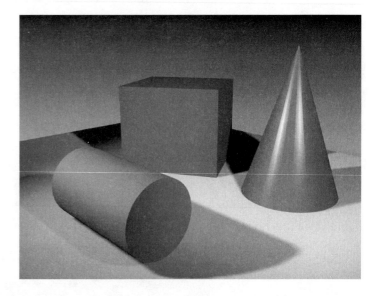

In most packages that are able to produce phong images, shadow and highlight intensities can be adjusted with lighting. You'll take a look at 3D lighting a little later in this chapter. Note that phong shading is the first type of rendering that begins to approach the term photo-realistic.

Radiosity and Ray-Tracing

Ray-tracing is a technique that incorporates the tracking of light rays. In a ray-traced image, the true path of light rays within the image is recorded as the light hits the viewable portions of the objects in the database. This gives an incredible, photo-realistic image, as shown in Figure 8.21.

Figure 8.21.
By tracking light rays, ray-traced images give incredible, photo-realistic results.

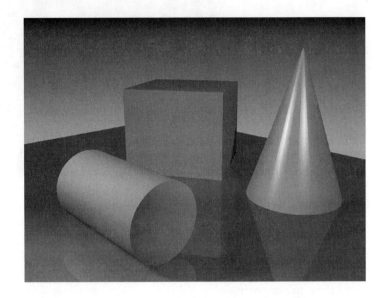

Light rays projected from light sources hit the viewable faces of objects and are scattered. Since this would take a considerable amount of time to render on the computer, most packages trace the rays that hit the viewable surfaces from the light sources and do not deal with the scattered light rays. By tracking only the main light rays, rendering computation time is reduced.

Ray-tracing is important because it allows for more realistic shadows and highlights as well as true mirror-type reflections. This is the most applicable type of rendering quality available for the personal computer because it is feasible in relation to the time it takes to generate.

Radiosity is the highest quality image that can be generated on the computer, but in most cases it takes a tremendous amount of time for each frame of animation to render. A frame that takes 10 minutes to generate using ray-tracing could take 20 minutes to generate using radiosity.

Radiosity differs from ray-tracing in that it traces the light from the light source and also calculates the paths of the scattered light rays as they hit the viewable surfaces. (See Figure 8.22.)

Figure 8.22.
Radiosity tracks all light
rays within the database
to create the rendered
image.

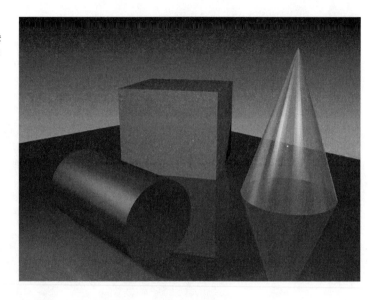

For example, radiosity takes into consideration that the corners of a room are darker than the areas adjacent to light sources. By calculating the scattered rays, radiosity rendering engines are able to determine small light intensity variations as they bounce off of objects within a 3D scene. This type of rendering gives true photo-realistic images, but as mentioned before, it takes a tremendous amount of time to generate.

All these forms of rendering have progressed over time and evolved one from the other. As stated earlier, there is no standardization of the names given previously in animation packages; they are only generalizations in most cases. The best way to determine what type of rendering a package is capable of is by seeing the output generated by it. If the example displays highlights and shadows without reflections, it is safe to say it is capable only of phong-type shading. If the example includes reflections, it is probably capable of ray-tracing or radiosity. Note that it is often difficult to determine whether an example has ray-tracing or radiosity because of the slight differences between the two. In general, if the package can generate a ray-traced image in a feasible amount of time, it is a good package.

The Rendering Environment

The second portion of the 3D animation package is the renderer. The rendering environment is what controls the generation of the raster images from the 3D model. In the discussion of the modeling environment, you saw that the fundamental elements in the modeler were the objects, a coordinate system, and a viewpoint. After the models are built, however, the rendering environment parameters affect how the objects look in the rendered image. Before you look at the attributes of the rendering environment (cameras, lights, and object textures and characteristics), take a look at how the renderer creates a flat image from the 3D environment.

When the rendering of a 3D scene is generated, the renderer is simply projecting the 3D information about the scene onto a 2D plane, making it a flat raster image. This 2D plane is defined by the view that is being rendered and is usually defined by a camera view, as shown in Figure 8.23. Keep in mind that the viewpoint is part of the modeling environment and controls what you see on the screen as you are building models. The cameras are placed within the 3D environment and control what is rendered in the animation file.

Figure 8.23.
The renderer projects the 3D scene onto a 2D plane. The plane is defined by a specified view (such as a camera) within the rendering environment.

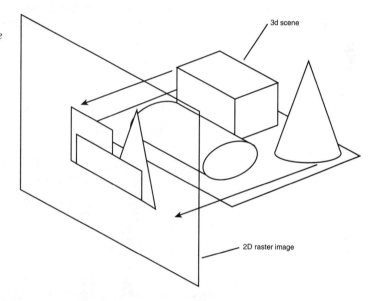

3d scene

2D raster image

In the process of projecting the 3D model onto the 2D plane, the renderer decides what color each pixel of the image is supposed to be, based on the 3D environment. The rendered pixels are affected by the number of lights in the scene, the textures of the models' surfaces, and the location of each object in the environment. Depending on the complexity of the package, it might also take into consideration things such as atmospheric conditions, reflectivity, and other object characteristics.

Each parameter within the rendering environment is defined by algorithms that are used by the program to approximate what color each pixel in the raster image should inevitably be. The true mathematical function for these algorithms and which algorithms apply to each feature will not be discussed in this book, but it should be known that the renderer does use extensive mathematics to determine and calculate the raster image from the 3D model based on the environment characteristics.

Now that you know how the renderer converts the 3D scene to a 2D raster representation, you need to look at the things that affect the rendered image. These attributes include the cameras, which define the view of the scene to be rendered, the lights, which define the amount of light in the scene, and the object textures and characteristics, which define the surface attributes of the objects in the environment.

Cameras

In the discussion of the modeler, you read that what is viewed on the screen is based upon the viewpoint in the environment. As you are building 3D models, most of the time the viewpoint is used to display a view (or multiple views) that is perpendicular to the object. These types of views, called *orthographic views,* are effective for modeling but quite unappealing for rendering animations because they do not reveal depth in the view. Figure 8.24 shows an example of a model being built using multiple orthographic views.

Figure 8.24.
Orthographic views
are commonly used for
building models in a
3D environment.

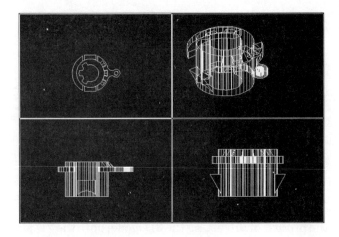

To create animations and rendered views, non-orthographic views are usually used. This creates an image in which three dimensions are perceived. To obtain a non-orthographic rendered image, the renderer uses a special view called a camera view. Much like using a camera in the real world, any portion of the 3D scene may be photographed. The camera can be positioned and oriented anywhere within the 3D environment.

Camera views are special because they display the receding lines of the objects in the scene as converging to common points. Since this is the same concept as a perspective view, they are often called *perspective view renderings*. This type of rendering is more realistic than that of orthogonal view rendering because the human eye perceives the real world from a perspective viewpoint. Figure 8.25 shows an example of a rendered orthogonal view and a rendered camera view (perspective). Note that in the orthographic view, depth cannot be perceived. In the camera view, all three dimensions are perceived. Also note that the image looks more real because the lines that represent the edges of the object converge. Perspective projection is how your eyes perceive the real world, and gives the most effective renderings and animations.

Figure 8.25.
An orthographic view versus a perspective view.

The degree to which the lines converge in a rendered image depends on the types of lenses available for the camera in the renderer. Just as in the real world, you can vary the amount of converge, or the size of the camera shot, by changing the lens of your camera. However, some packages do not allow multiple types of camera lenses. This means that the cameras in these packages are usually limited to 35mm-type camera shots—which can be some what blasé, as shown in Figure 8.26. Note the distortion that also begins to occur at the base of the lantern.

Figure 8.26.
Using a 35mm camera lens doesn't always produce the best image.

Most 3D animation packages allow a wide variety of camera lenses, such as 15mm, 30mm, 35mm, and up to 135mm. This variety of lenses allows both mild and dramatic perspectives or more or less line convergence. Note that the wider or the higher the number of the lens, the more dramatic the perspective. Most camera specifications also allow the user to obtain a dramatic perspective, as shown in Figure 8.27.

Figure 8.27.
An example of a dramatic perspective view generated from a 3D program.

Camera views, as stated before, give the most realistic renderings given the right size lens for the job. They are very advantageous when multiple renderings of an environment are desired without dual modeling databases. They are also helpful when the operator wants to create an animation with a moving camera, such as an architectural walk-through. Keep in mind that camera views are for rendering, whereas the viewpoint is used during model creation.

Lighting

After a camera (or view to be rendered) is defined, you must deal with the various types of lights and their positions. As any professional animator or photographer will tell you, two of the fundamental things that make a good image are the choice of shot (camera position) and the lighting. You'll find that lighting is one of the most difficult things to deal with. Getting the lighting just right in the 3D environment is very difficult. Lighting can be used to set a mood, draw attention, and enhance the overall image.

There are four basic groups or classifications of lights available in animation packages today: ambient, radiant, fluorescent, and spot. Not all packages include all four types, so you should check what you get when buying an animation package. You will find that the realism of most rendered images from 3D packages is based upon realistic lighting. Therefore, the more lighting types supported by a package, the better.

To understand the difference among all the types of lights, one needs to examine the way they are represented in the database. Realize that each light varies in the way light is projected from the source towards the object.

All lights are represented in the database as a point in three-dimensional space, with the exception of ambient light, in which the source is at infinity. Radiant and fluorescent lights are represented as points but usually only radiate light at a limited distance. Spotlights generate a cone from the point of location in the desired direction. The cone is representative of the median of the light that is being emitted from the source. Figure 8.28 shows the way each type of light is represented in the 3D database. Let's take a closer look at the various types of light sources.

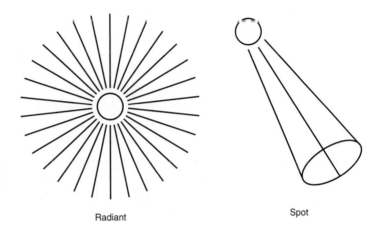

Figure 0.20.
*The two main types
of lights in the 3D
environment.*

Radiant   Spot

Ambient Light

Ambient light is atmospheric light that is radiated within the scene. It provides the minimum amount of illumination within the three-dimensional scene and casts no shadows. It normally has no position in relation to the X, Y, and Z coordinate system. Note that some architectural animation packages allow the user to define a time of day, which results in a specific daytime or nighttime illumination.

In the real world, ambient light would be characteristic of the light that is radiated from the sun or reflected from the moon. Ambient light usually determines the darkness or lightness of the shade areas of a three-dimensional scene. Figure 8.29 shows an object rendered with ambient light only. Remember that the shaded areas of a scene are those areas that are opposite the light areas—areas that are not hit with direct light. (See the section titled "Lighting Effect on Hues" in Chapter 2, "Color Theory and Color Models.")

Ambient light can usually be set from 0 to 255. Note that 0 is black and 255 is white, or total light (using the RGB color model). Because ambient light is based on the RGB (red, green, blue) color model, it can also be tinted or given a specific color, which can be helpful when trying to achieve a sunrise or sunset effect.

Ambient light control is an important factor when creating animations and renderings, and it must be noted that not all packages allow the user to control this portion of the lighting scheme.

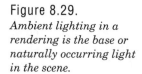

Figure 8.29.
*Ambient lighting in a
rendering is the base or
naturally occurring light
in the scene.*

Radiant Lights

Radiant lights include light sources that simply radiate light, with no specific direction. They project parallel rays of light across the three-dimensional scene. These types of lights mimic simple light bulbs placed within the three-dimensional scene, which means they also have a limited field of projection. They, too, are usually based on the RGB color model, which allows them to be colored light if so desired. These types of lights can be manipulated to give soft or subtle light affects as well as dramatic, intense light configurations.

Fluorescent Lights

Fluorescent lights are a modification of the radiant type light because they exhibit the bluing characteristics of true fluorescent lights. This type of light gives a more realistic effect when using the animation package for interior perspectives and other architectural uses.

Fluorescent light characteristics, such as the *bluing effect,* can be achieved with radiant type lighting although they are sometimes more difficult to set up. In addition, fluorescent lights usually give only the user an on/off choice. Because true fluorescent lighting does not allow color choices (except in neon lights, which are an exception), the fluorescent lighting in animation packages is similar. The lights in some cases can vary in intensity but usually not in color.

Spotlights

Spotlights are lights within the three-dimensional scene that can be directed or pointed at different locations. These lights incorporate the RGB color model, so they can also be colored. These lights attenuate over a specified distance and can cast shadows. Spotlights incorporate two other variables: falloff and highlight characteristics.

A spotlight is usually defined in the 3D package by three cones, as shown in Figure 8.30. The first of these cones, the outermost cone, is the falloff adjustment. The *falloff* adjustment is considered to be the amount of light that is radiated off of main cone of light that the spot is projecting. The falloff adjustment could be thought of as the radiant light that is coming off of the cone, even though the light is a spot. Generally, falloff light creates dull, non-intense light. The second of these two cones is the *hotspot*, or highlight adjustment. This tertiary cone, which is the smallest of the three, determines the amount of intense light that is projected onto the viewable surfaces. The hotspot cone creates intense light in the specified cone. The final cone, the one in the middle, is the median of the falloff and hotspot cones and is generated at a specified intensity.

Figure 8.30.

A spotlight is represented by three cones: the falloff, hotspot, and median.

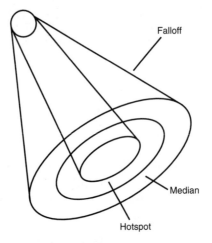

Falloff

Median

Hotspot

In general, the types of lights available in an animation package are limited to the price and sophistication of the package. For the user to be unhindered, it is recommended that any perspective purchase include ambient, radiant, and spotlighting. Fluorescent lighting is very useful if interior designing is the main goal of the animations. Most packages do include the three main types of lighting, but the amount of control varies from package to package.

Object Textures and Characteristics

The final attribute that the renderer must deal with is the characteristics of the objects in the scene. Object characteristics are an important feature of the renderer because this is what makes objects look real in the rendered image or animation.

For example, if the user wanted an object to look like marble, he or she would need to define the marble quality for the rendering engine so that an appropriate marble surface would appear on the object, as shown in Figure 8.31. The two predominant methods of defining surface characteristics in 3D animation programs are through the use of surface mapping and procedural mapping. *Surface mapping* employs the use of external bitmap images that are applied to objects. *Procedural mapping* uses mathematical algorithms to define the textures and characteristics of objects.

Figure 8.31.
Defining qualities of objects makes them look real, such as making an object look like marble.

Surface Mapping

The application of image-based textures to objects is called surface mapping. *Surface mapping* is the process of applying two-dimensional images onto a surface or object so that it looks more realistic. Surface mapping requires the user not only to specify an image to apply to an object but also how the bitmap will be applied to that object.

A surface map is nothing more than a two dimensional bitmap that is wrapped around an object to give it a certain appearance, as shown in Figure 8.32. An image map can be applied in any one of several ways. Note that the way the map is applied can be controlled within the software.

Figure 8.32.

Wrapping an image around an object creates the appearance of a certain texture.

When you are trying to make objects look a certain way, there are actually two techniques that can be used. Up to this point, you've been reading about the most widely used method on PC-based, 3D animation programs: surface mapping. However, surface mapping is more than pasting images onto objects. Surface maps have other characteristics that can affect the way the rendered object looks. These user-defined characteristics include reflectivity, opacity (transparency), bumpiness, and bump mapping.

As an alternative to surface mapping, surface textures can be defined using procedural mapping. *Procedural mapping* uses algorithms to define how an object should be rendered. Procedural mapping is frequently used on workstation-based animation programs and will be explained in a later section in this chapter titled "Procedural Mapping."

Both of these types of surface applications, surface mapping and procedural mapping, allow the renderer of the animation package the capability to generate a completely photo-realistic animation.

Surface Reflectivity

Surface mapping is more than pasting bitmaps on 3D objects. There are other variables that are involved in surface mapping. The first of these variables is reflectivity.

Reflectivity is simply the capability of an object to reflect its surroundings as a true object would in the real world, as shown in Figure 8.33. Some packages allow reflections to be either automatic (calculated from the objects in the scene) or generated from an applied two-dimensional image file (as a result of a surface map).

Figure 8.33.
Reflectivity is an important object characteristic that is involved in surface mapping.

Automatic reflections are by far the most advantageous type of reflection because they are the most photo-realistic. One limiting factor of automatic reflections is the fact that they take a generous amount of time to render, because the renderer has to extensively calculate the reflection object's surface characteristics according to its surroundings.

As an alternative to using automatic reflections, applying two-dimensional image files to the three-dimensional objects is the secondary way to generate reflections and is also the quickest in regards to rendering time. Two-dimensional image files can be used when the quality of the reflection is not important. When you apply the image to the object, it can give the illusion of a reflective surface without extensive computation of the object's surroundings, as shown in Figure 8.34. Note that the image file would have to be somewhat representative of the objects surrounding the reflection object for it to be effective.

Figure 8.34.
*Applying an image map
to create a reflection.*

Applied image reflections are usually used when the environment, such as the sky, would be in the reflection. For clear and precise reflections, the only true way to generate a photo-realistic reflection would be to use an automatic reflection. Note also that not all packages support automatic reflection calculations, which can be an extreme limitation in some instances, because many times surface map reflections produce unappealing results.

Opacity (Transparency)

Opacity, or transparency, is the second variable that defines how a texture is applied using surface mapping. *Opacity* is the amount of light that can be seen through a particular object. Opacity is what allows objects to look transparent, completely solid, or anywhere in between, as shown in Figure 8.35. Opacity is a vital portion of the texture capabilities and should be included in the texture definition variables of any perspective package.

Figure 8.35.
*Opacity controls
the transparency
of an object.*

Bumpiness

Bumpiness is one of the main ingredients in a texture specification that allows a three-dimensional object to look real. This is what makes surface mapping more than pasting an image on a model.

A *bump map* is a bitmap that is either associated with the surface map or applied after a surface map. The bump map's grayscale values are converted to height values, which allow the renderer to give the total surface map a grainy or bumpy look, as shown in Figure 8.36.

Figure 8.36.
*Comparing an object
with and without
bump mapping.*

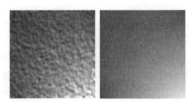

To see how this works, let's take a look at an example. If white text on a black background were applied as a bump map, the resulting rendering would appear as if the text were embossed. If the bump map is inverted, the text looks engraved, rather than embossed, as shown in Figure 8.37.

Figure 8.37.
The values of the applied bump map affect how the image is rendered.

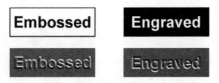

Bump maps give the most astonishing results when they are used in a rendering because they give the highly realistic results. The values of the bump map, when combined with a surface map, make the image look 3D.

Limitations of Surface Mapping

Using surface maps is the way that most animation packages create realistic renderings and animations, but surface mapping does have its limitations. The first of its limitations is that each of the two-dimensional image files used for surface mapping take up disk space. Because the quality of the surface map is directly related to the quality of the image that it is based on, high-resolution, two-dimensional images are desired. Multiple objects with multiple surface maps can significantly increase the amount of hard disk space needed for animation production because most image files take up at least 800KB.

The second limitation is the fact that it is not uncommon to have problems with the seams of the image files that are used for surface mapping, as shown in Figure 8.38. When the image is mapped onto the three-dimensional object, many times there will be a seam that is noticeable in the patterned materials, such as wood or marble. This is a problem caused by the map being too small for the object. It can be corrected by enlarging the map or by reducing the size of the model(s). Both of these two solutions increase the amount of time spent producing the animation, because it requires rendering and re-rendering the image or animation to check the map-to-object proportions.

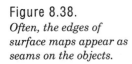

Figure 8.38.
Often, the edges of surface maps appear as seams on the objects.

Procedural Mapping

A time-saving alternative to surface mapping is procedural mapping. *Procedural mapping* is an external process, often an add-on program, that is used to generate surface qualities based on an algorithm rather than on bitmaps. For example, a marble procedural map applied to an object causes the object to be rendered as marble. There are no raster images involved. The algorithm in the procedural map automatically creates the look of marble for the object when the object is rendered.

Procedural mapping is used because it doesn't have the size and seam problems of surface mapping. Because procedural mapping uses external processes (code), it takes up a significantly smaller amount of hard disk space. When procedural mapping is used, there is no need for raster images to create textures. Also, procedural mapping does not have problems with surface seams because each surface texture is uniquely generated through the external process for each object. It must be noted, however, that procedural mapping is very costly because each texture requires a separate procedural map (algorithm). Most often, procedural mapping code must be purchased separately from the animation program or custom-programmed by a capable individual.

The Animation Environment

The final part of all 3D animation packages is the animation environment. The animation portion of the package allows the developer to define the movements and changes that occur within the 3D scene over time. Most often, this requires accessing a particular frame and then moving the objects to the desired positions. This creates a keyframe. The computer then interpolates the frames between the frames.

Keyframe Animation

As you saw in Chapter 7, "2D Animation," keyframe animation allows the user to define the key movements or action of objects in the animation. The computer then generates the intermediate frames, called tweens. 3D animation works on the same premise, but 3D objects are translated rather than manipulating sprites.

The keyframes that are defined can be any number of frames apart, yet they are usually a maximum of thirty frames. The closer together the keyframes are, the more likely the computer will generate the proper movements. If the keyframes are too far apart, generally the movements of the model will not be as the developer intended.

> ### note
>
> Setting up a keyframe animation is not rocket science. But, note that the computer will not always generate exactly what the animator wants in the tweens. Many times, the animator will have to define some of the intermediate frames (making them keyframes), or tween frames, because the computer cannot determine the exact movements that the operator wants in the tweens.

Some packages also allow the user to see the movements of the objects and the frames in which they occur, in a grid formation on the screen. This is usually a secondary screen, which can be called up; that allows the operator to manipulate the movements of the objects without physically moving them in the database. It is very time-consuming to manually move objects in the animator, especially if the animation is quite lengthy. This secondary screen, usually called the keyframe information grid, allows the quick manipulation of the keys of the objects, as shown in Figure 8.39. The keyframe information grid can also be useful when the user wants to loop an animation with the beginning and ending frames being the same. Most keyframe information grids allow the user to copy, move, delete, and slide key positions.

Figure 8.39.
The transformation grid allows easy editing of the keyframes in the animation.

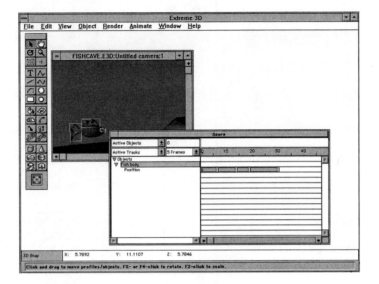

Paths, Translation, and Motion

Defining the movements of the objects in the 3D animation package requires defining the translation (move, rotate, or scale) of the 3D objects in the keyframes.

For example, suppose you wanted to create an animation of a logo spinning 360 degrees over 30 frames so that you could create an animation that can be looped over and over (played continually). After the model has been built and the rendering attributes have been set up, you can define the movements of the animation. In the first frame of the animation, the logo appears in its original position, as shown in Figure 8.40.

To define the rotation over 30 frames, you would access frame 30 in the animation package. Within that frame, you would rotate the logo 360 degrees, as shown in Figure 8.41. In short, you have just created an animation in a starting position in frame 1 and a rotated position in frame 30. Changing the time index would reveal that the animation rotates 360 degrees over 30 frames, as shown in Figure 8.42. All object movements within a 3D animation program are defined and function similarly.

Figure 8.40.
*Setting the originating
positions in the first
frame.*

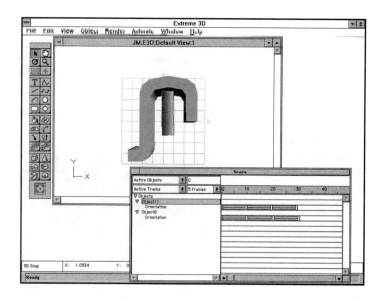

Figure 8.41.
*Setting the destination
location in frame 30.*

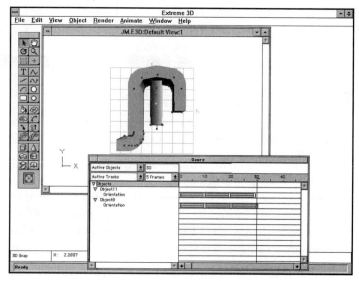

Figure 8.42.
Defining a keyframe at frames 1 and 30 will create the rotating logo.

3D Deformations

One other feature found in many animation programs is called 3D deformation. Akin to 2D deformations, 3D deformations allow you to deform objects in 3D space. As you saw in Chapter 7, you can squish, squash, and morph objects in an animation, as shown in Figure 8.43.

Figure 8.43.
3D deformations allow you to manipulate 3D objects in many different ways.

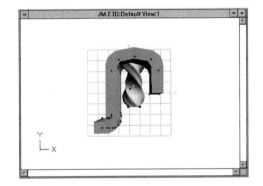

Kinematics, Inverse Kinematics, and Kinesiology

One of the most difficult things to do in the 3D animation process is to create realistic movements of objects over time. As you saw in Chapter 7, much of the realism in an animation is related to how objects move. Whether an object moves at a constant rate or fluctuates can affect the realism of the animation.

Several terms apply to the way various types of objects move. Kinematics deals with the movements of objects over time, whereas kinesiology deals with human motion. The next couple of sections take a look at these two types of time and motion parameters. Often, 3D animation packages will support some type of time and motion tools, although they might not support both of the tools mentioned here.

Kinematics

Kinematics is the simple editing of movements of the objects over time. This includes the slowing down of parts over time as they converge or the speeding up of objects over time as they diverge. It also includes transforming an animation sequence so that all of the parts within the database move at a constant speed or velocity over the duration of the segment.

This type of manipulation can be very useful because it is difficult to get objects to move at fluctuating rates over time when putting together an animation sequence. It is even more difficult to get objects to converge or diverge with a constant speed differentiation over time. Without the use of kinematics, the user has to calculate, or in most instances guess, what distance an object needs to move, over time, to get a consistent fluctuating velocity. By using kinematics, the computer calculates this information automatically making all the objects move at the same speed or making a certain object speed up or slow down.

Inverse Kinematics

Inverse kinematics deals with three-dimensional model systems that move in relation to each other through a hierarchical structure, instead of distance related to time. Inverse kinematics is usually reserved for multiple-sectioned composite models, such as a mechanical assembly. Within a model with several discrete parts, certain parts can be given specifications for degrees of freedom along the X, Y, or Z axis based on definable pivot or junction points. This is useful especially when animating linkages or other similar mechanical assemblies because each of the joints can be given limits to movement, thus making it somewhat representative of the real world.

Kinesiology

Kinesiology is the study of the ranges and motions of the human body. Many of the 3D animation programs that support character animations, and even some that don't, support real-life human movements. Using knowledge about the range of motions of the human body based on kinesiology, the software can automatically include specifications for degrees of freedom and range of motion for objects denoted as human features.

Particle Systems

Environmental conditions, or particle systems, are another fascinating addition to the animation package—one that can make a rendering even more photo-realistic. Particle systems can include things such as fog, sun glares, rain, and snow. These types of rendering additions are usually limited to high-priced animation packages but can be found in some of the lower-priced ones as well.

Summary

In this chapter you took a brief look at the world of 3D animation. Understand that you've only scratched the surface of the things that most of today's 3D animation packages can do. The main portions of any 3D animation package include the modeler, renderer, and animator. The robustness of any 3D animation package is based on the robustness of all three of these items. If you are looking for a 3D package to create photo-realistic animation with, you'll want to closely examine all three parts to make sure it is a good package.

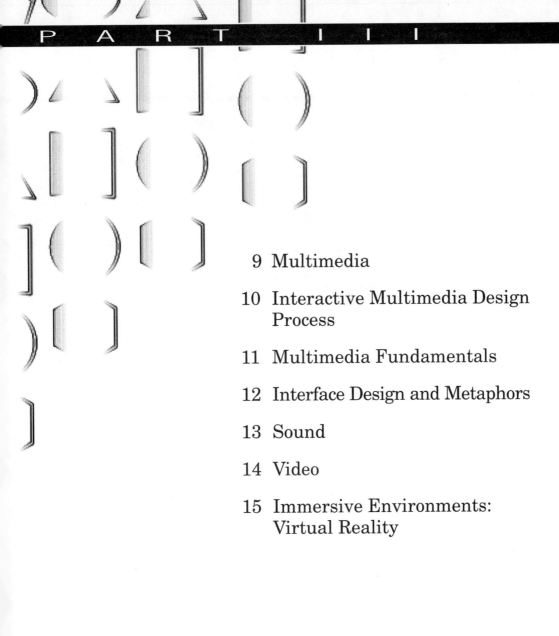

PART III

9 Multimedia

10 Interactive Multimedia Design
Process

11 Multimedia Fundamentals

12 Interface Design and Metaphors

13 Sound

14 Video

15 Immersive Environments:
Virtual Reality

CHAPTER

9

Multimedia

Throughout the previous chapters of this book, you have been reading about the various design concepts related to creating Web pages and the media elements on those pages. From design, color, and typography to animation, you've looked at many of the visual aspects of media element design for the Web. Indeed, the efficiency and effectiveness of communication have increased as a result of the computer and the digital elements that can be used in information delivery.

To many people, the ability to utilize multimedia is not something new. Many people define multimedia as the use of multiple media to deliver information, no matter whether it is a person, a computer, or the Web that is delivering it. Many teachers, professors, and others who have been delivering lectures and presentations for years emphatically exclaim that they've been doing multimedia presentations for years. To them, the use of the computer doesn't make a multimedia presentation.

The real difference that multimedia and interactive multimedia make in communication is not so much in the idea of using multiple media, although this makes the information easier to digest. The real difference is in the method of communication, and it is a function of the computer itself, as shown in Figure 9.1. With today's multimedia, the power is the ability to non-sequentially access and present information, regardless of whether that information is contained within a body of text, a static graphic, or an animation.

Figure 9.1.
The difference between the traditional and modern concept of multimedia is an issue of method, not media.

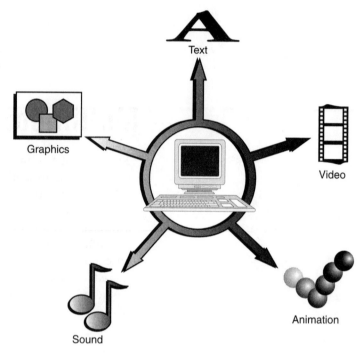

Text

Graphics

Video

Sound

Animation

In this chapter, you will read about multimedia in relationship to the computer, for that is the basis for this book. Those who believe that multimedia can include a lecture that uses transparencies, films, or tape-recorded audio combined with a lecturer's voice (text, graphics, animation, and sound) will inevitably see that this, unfortunately, is not an accepted definition for this chapter. Multimedia is not classified as such simply because a presentation uses multiple media. There is one other pervading factor that classifies a certain presentation as multimedia.

Today, the most widely accepted definition of multimedia is that multimedia is any informational presentation (designed to inform, educate, persuade, or entertain) that includes text, graphics, sound, animation, or video and is displayed or controlled by the computer. In this context, assume that multimedia and interactive multimedia are synonymous. Some classify multimedia as a presentation controlled by the computer and interactive multimedia as a presentation controlled by the user; both are executed on the computer. Nonetheless, today's definition excludes the statements of many individuals who claim to be producing or using multimedia by the default that the presentation uses multiple media.

Note that the traditional definition of multimedia (the lecturer's voice, text, graphics, and so on) coincides with the modern definition in all but one part: the computer. The only difference between the old paradigm and the new is the computer. It is the computer that clarifies and defines what is multimedia by today's standards.

Realizing that I might have offended some people in the previous paragraphs or at least ruffled some feathers a bit, I ask that you stick with this chapter until you see why I (and many others) classify multimedia this way. I realize that I am treading on sacred ground, but I hope you will see that multimedia's advantages are due to the computer and its non-linear and non-sequential nature, not just the digital multimedia media elements that are used.

Linearity

The factor that makes multimedia unique is its non-linear and non-sequential nature. This characteristic is a function of the computer and makes interaction key in communication. To understand the difference between linear and non-linear information distribution, compare two educational settings. The lecture, in which all information is provided in a progression from beginning to end, is an example of linear presentation. Alternatively, a question-and-answer session, in which students ask questions based upon their skill level, is a example of a non-linear presentation of information. The non-linear environment exhibits customized, audience-centered information. The linear environment exhibits information that is presented from beginning to end, usually simple to complex, with a linear progression in between.

Educators and presenters alike have known for a long time that information is much more readily comprehended and accepted when it is tailored to the audience. To do this, they usually use a linear progression from simple to complex. In addition, information is more readily understood when the audience interacts with it.

However, the traditional media used for communication cannot be everything to everyone. Writers and educators alike must cognitively organize and structure information, leading the reader from the simple to the complex. A book may be too difficult or basic for certain individuals, so it is not adequate for them. Traditional communication media, due to linearity, cannot be everything to everyone.

A book or any other static and traditional communication device is linear by default. From our childhood, our paradigm of information reception, the method by which we receive, assimilate, learn, and organize information, is programmed and delivered in a linear fashion. Most humans have difficulty dealing with non-sequential information because it contradicts our direct and programmed way of receiving information.

Linear Thinking: Inherent or Conditioned Behavior?

One of the pursuing questions that overshadows multimedia development and delivery is "Why do humans so resolutely need linear information?" Why must everything be organized, structured, and almost pre-programmed for learning or knowledge transfer to occur? Is it an inherent behavior that information that is received can be encoded only when it is structured? Or is it simply an environmental, conditioned behavior?

As many agree, this natural tendency for structured, linear information is the result of our environment, and it is a conditioned behavior. To understand this, take a good look at the things you do throughout your lifetime.

Everything that surrounds your life is based upon the linear passage of time. Your birthday, your age, your work habits, your study habits, and even your music is based on time and its linear nature. If you look at what you spend most of your time doing, it involves tracking the linear passage of time or the linear arrangement of items. If you are like me, you have a linear, daily schedule that you follow, and you would be less productive without it. Those non-linear things, such as an emergency meeting or unscheduled interruption, are, even in the day-to-day routine, difficult to accommodate at times because your time is planned linearly.

The linearity of our lives, in addition to our methods of receiving information, has significant impact on our lives. Even mundane things are affected by the passage of time. Without the consciousness of time, we become disoriented because we lose the connection with time's linearity, which is unnoticeably ever-present. Have you ever been on vacation and forgotten what day it is? The rest of your week probably feels a little different; it feels like Saturday rather than Friday. One other example is a frequent occurrence for many people: Have you ever forgotten your watch and felt the entire day either crept or flew by? We, as humans, need the linear element of time, and it is a basic premise for many of the things we do. Without it, we become disoriented.

It is amazing that humans become so affected, even programmed, by linearity that we don't recognize its effect in other areas of our lives. From birth, we learn that our second birthday follows the first. The third follows the second. At some point, we become conscious that our linear existence upon this natural earth will end. There is a beginning, a finite end, and a linear path or progression in between.

Linearity and Communication

The linearity that is a result of time is also exhibited in the communication media that we use on a daily basis. From childhood, we become familiar with books, magazines, and other printed materials. Note that the same linearity in which we live is also present in the traditional materials with which we communicate. The book begins on page one. Page two follows page three, and so on, until the end of the book. A book has both a finite beginning and a finite end and a linear progression in between. Is this a coincidence?

To see if it is a coincidence, look even farther back than the printed page. It might be a coincidence that pages in a book follow a linear progression due to replication issues.

What about primitive cave drawings or Egyptian hieroglyphics, as shown in Figure 9.2? Do these elements also present a linear progression? Are they finite, having a beginning and an end? Does the story or information presented run in a linear progression? Studies into these methods of communication do reveal that they too are based upon linearity.

Figure 9.2.
Communication, from its very beginnings, is a linear process.

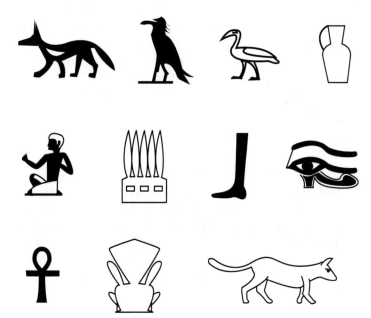

Throughout most of the communication media that humans have used over the span of time, you will find three commonalties: a beginning, an ending, and a linear progression in between, as shown in Figure 9.3. They are linear communication media.

Figure 9.3.
The three commonalties of traditional communication media.

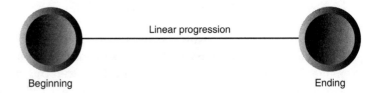

Beginning   Ending

Linear progression

Linearity and Learning

It is no surprise that most students learn best in a structured environment. Understand that structured learning environments are a vital method of receiving instruction. This chapter is in no way meant to belittle the careful planning and implementation of educational materials designed in a linear progression from the simple to the complex. Time has proven that this is an effective method of instruction in many different fields.

However, many of the sources that are used for learning and information presentation, ones that are designed in a linear fashion, have affected the way that learning and thinking occur throughout our lifetime.

From experiences in early childhood, the brain is conformed to acquiring information in an organized and progressive fashion. However, the brain, in many individuals, can be more responsive to non-linear and non-sequential information presentation. Looking at the various learning styles of a range of individuals reveals that, although some thrive on structured learning or information reception, others have significant difficulty decoding and encoding the information in this atmosphere.

The brain is the most complex organ in the human body. It is also one that researchers know little about. For every discovery, there seems to be more that can be learned about this puzzling organ.

Nonetheless, it is known that much of human memory, and therefore learning, is based upon associations either through unconscious events or through purposely imposed constructs such as mnemonic devices. Knowing that associations are developed this way, it is accurate to say that they vary from individual to individual. Associations then are based upon experiences, environment, and instruction of the individual, as shown in Figure 9.4.

Because associations are variable, many are developed in a non-sequential manner. The brain, in the early stages of child development, learns to construct associations non-sequentially. In the first years of child development, so many motor skills, as well as sense-based skills, are developed that development (or association) occurs in a non-sequential order. In effect, the brain first develops the method of non-sequential learning through association.

Figure 9.4.
The brain creates associations via experiences, environment, and instruction.

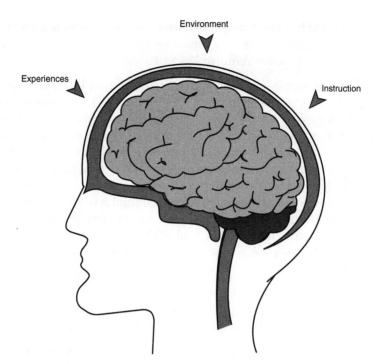

However, soon after developing this non-sequential schema, the brain must be trained to learn in a linear fashion. As you have read, there is a natural order or progression in most everything we encounter. The brain begins to learn progression, sequence, and order, modeling the ways in which communication and other physical aspects function.

As a father with a child just over two years old, I am amazed to see how quickly children are forced to lay aside non-sequential thinking skills to develop linear skills. One of my daughter's first toys was a set of eight colored cups that each fit inside one another. The cups are sized so that only one will fit inside another. If they are properly ordered, they all fit inside one another like a set of measuring cups for cooking.

Children quickly learn order and linear thinking with toys such as these. Many of the development toys on the market are focused at developing linear thinking skills. From a very young age, we become familiar with the constructs of linearity.

Linear Media

The first part of this chapter is devoted to acknowledging that much of our lives surrounds linear thought development. Why? Why require the brain, which begins by developing associations in a non-sequential manner, to learn to create associations in a structured or linear way? The answer is that most of our communication requires linear thought.

For example, children learning to read first learn the alphabet. The alphabet is linear and the characters are ordered in a progression. Letters are assembled linearly to create words. Words are assembled linearly to create paragraphs, pages, and eventually a medium by which communication can occur. Notice the thought conditioning that occurs here. Conditioning the brain to order letters, words, and paragraphs can often condition us to habitually think this way, if the only communication devices we ever encounter are linear devices. When we are not exposed to non-sequential communication tools, linear conditioning leads to conditioned behavior. This is why non-linear thought, which is the basis for interactive multimedia and Web development, is difficult for many people. Conditioned behaviors are a result of repetitive conditioned actions.

Those who have never dealt with a non-linear information environment become disoriented, as in forgetting the day or a watch. So much of our lives revolves around linear thought that non-linear thought becomes foreign, almost strange, to us. All it takes is learning to once again think non-linearly.

Linear conditioning leads to linear thinking. If the only media you ever receive information from are newspapers, books, and other traditional methods, you probably find Web- and CD-ROM-based materials difficult to use or create. This is natural. Most people who are accustomed to linear environments find interactive materials difficult. Structure is a primary attribute of linearity. However, with conscientious practice, you can become a non-linear thinker.

It must be noted that this chapter is not devoted to discrediting linear thought processes. Linear thought processes are what much of our world is based upon. In addition, completely non-sequential interactive environments with no structure at all are disastrous. Trying to make sense of information in such an environment is nigh to impossible. There must be a balance between linear and non-linear processes.

The ability to think both linearly and non-linearly is important when developing interactive materials. In fact, non-linear thinking is one of the most important elements of multimedia and hypermedia. Most often the linear element is needed to develop a logical schema for information to be delivered. However, it is the non-linear element that allows the developer to create unique environments that are both utilitarian and aesthetic, as well as ones that anticipate the entire range of audience needs. Developing multimedia and hypermedia environments effectively requires the ability to think both linearly and non-linearly.

Non-Linear Media and Non-Linear Thinking

The need for non-linear communication media was actually first recognized in the 1930s by Vannevar Bush. He envisioned a hypertext system, predecessor to both multimedia and hypermedia, to link documents on microfilm. His ideas came well before the technology could support his aspirations.

Over time, the technology reached a maturation level that could support Bush's ideas in the mid-1960s. Ted Nelson first defined a hypertext system and then hypermedia during this time period. Hypertext systems are those in which the text content can be searched and cross-linked. Figure 9.5 shows how hypertext works. Note that the content of any page can be linked to any other page. You might say that sounds like the Web you use today. Indeed, the Web includes hypertext, but it also includes a more powerful feature, that of hypermedia.

Figure 9.5.
Hypertext systems allow text across multiple sources (pages) to be cross-linked and searched.

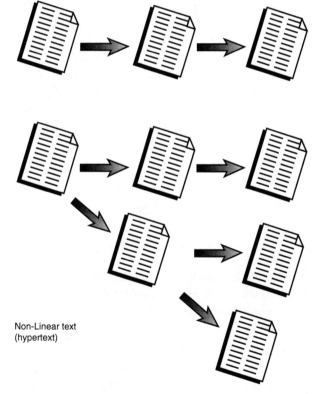

Non-Linear text
(hypertext)

Hypermedia

In 1965, Nelson developed a proposal for a computer communication system that integrated hypertext but also specified that the system include multiple media (multimedia), such as graphics and sound, as shown in Figure 9.6. This communication system had the ability to communicate universally, without regard to platforms, software, and operating systems. This profound proposal defined hypermedia and established what we enjoy as today's World Wide Web.

Figure 9.6.
*Hypermedia utilizes
hypertext and multiple
media.*

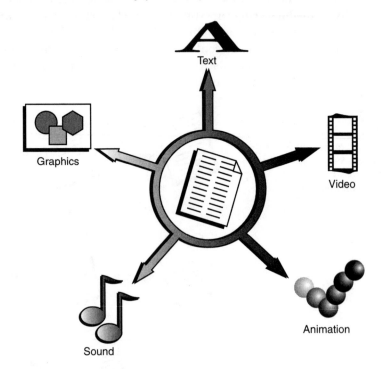

Nelson probably had little idea that his proposal would have such a great effect on the world at large. His original intention was to share physics research collaboratively among researchers. His idea has exploded into the World Wide Web that you know today.

Today, the Web is inundated with information resources, from the small-town newspaper where you grew up to the state of the U.S. government. (See Figure 9.7.) Almost every conceivable institution, business, and individual is quickly becoming a master of Web content.

Figure 9.7.
The Web includes a variety of information sources, from the small-town newspaper to the U.S. government.

Note that you need no degree, license, or legislative body (well, kind of, but I won't discuss that in this book) to publish information on the Web. Therefore, a lot of what the Web offers is noise. So many people thinking in linear terms with little content development experience are rushing to publish on the World Wide Web. The Web overflows with pages that are digital versions of linear communication devices, such as the "digitized book" or "digitized brochure," as shown in Figure 9.8. For every 30 pages that appear on the Web, only 1 page uses a non-linear method of communication, around which the construct of the Web was born. Pasting digitized versions of traditional documents more often than not is waste of Internet resources.

Figure 9.8.
Digitized versions of traditional documents do not provide many advantages over the traditional document itself.

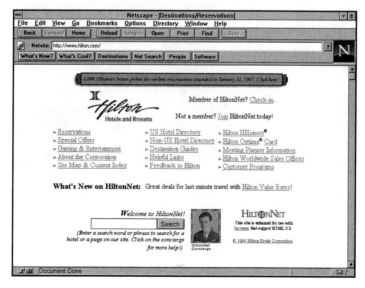

Much like the computer revolution in the desktop publishing world, everyone is now a Web publishing expert. As with the decrease of the would-be desktop publishers, Web content deliverers will also decrease as people begin to understand that the Web is more than multiple media or a new linear communication device.

Media That Support Non-Linear Communication

People are quickly acknowledging that Web development is more than access to a computer, a knowledge of HTML, or the latest multimedia software applications. The Web is an interactive communications beast that is rapidly evolving and ever changing to support what we need it to be.

The biggest difficulty people have is breaking out of linear thinking, due to lifelong conditioning for a linear environment. Breaking this pattern is probably more difficult to do than creating the most complex site or page. People are slowly seeing that computer multimedia and hypermedia often conflict with linear thinking and the traditional paradigm of communication. Non-sequential thinking is required to produce a tool that utilizes any non-sequential schema. Anyone can digitize a traditional document and throw it on the Web. Designing a unique, audience-centered Web site as shown in Figure 9.9 is unequaled.

Figure 9.9.
*Unique non-linear
environments on the Web
will always supersede
linear environments.*

The true Web publisher, who wants to create effective sites, strives to integrate both linear and non-linear structure into his or her Web pages and site. It is surprising that so many of the younger generation can so easily and quickly adapt to the non-sequential environment. As I grew up, this technological advantage (due to a lack of conditioning) was exhibited in the VCR phenomena. My parents always asked me to set the clock on the VCR. They were not accustomed to the nature of the technology. Even today, I am amazed at the technological level of many of the middle-school–aged children. Many of them can surf the Web, as well as create adequate Web pages, with relative ease.

A look at some of the top companies in the U.S. and around the world points to the fact that most Web developers are under the age of 30. I want to purport that this is due predominantly to a lack of linear conditioning, but I have no statistics to support this claim. One thing I do know is that conditioned behaviors are a result of conditioned repetitive actions, which lead to exhibited, repetitive behaviors. As the non-sequential environment becomes more widely used by the younger generation, learning, teaching, and information presentation styles will mimic the conditioned behaviors.

Summary

As you have read in this chapter, successful Web development is a result of a combination of linear and non-linear thinking. Traditional documents digitized for Web publication are no more effective than the traditional document itself. The Web hinges upon interaction and its audience-centered nature. Over the next few years, it will be interesting to see how the genre of the Web will end up. Nonetheless, one thing is for sure: It will be a crossbreed of linear and non-linear communication, as well as multiple media.

10

Interactive Multimedia Design Process

As with the development of any other communication media, there is a defined process that you can follow to create Web documents that communicate effectively . Whenever a document, book, or other published product is created, the people involved painstakingly follow a trial-and-error process.

When creating a document, such as a brochure or flyer, you look at the audience and what you want to communicate. Then you determine how to best fit the content to that audience. If you were writing a book, you would center upon the audience and cater your information to that audience. Web-based delivery is no different. However, with hypermedia and multi-media, you have many more options, many more elements, and often, a wider audience. Adapting the wide variety of media elements such as text, graphics, sound, and video, so that they effectively communicate, can be very challenging.

In this chapter you'll read about a development process that can be used to help you develop a Web site. Web development hinges upon communication. Some-times creating a Web site will be as simple as posting predeveloped pages to your site and making the connecting links so that the pages work properly. On the other hand, you might be responsible for creating the content, generating graphics, and acquiring multimedia elements that support the pages. What happens if the content and the pages are not already developed? How do you go about massaging the content, planning the pages, and developing the site so that it communicates well? How do you develop it so that it pleases the audience? And how do you know that the content is appropriate for Web-based delivery? This chapter focuses on establishing a development process for the delivery of Web content. Much of what you'll read has its roots in educational design and verbal and visual communication principles. The model described in this chapter was originally intended for multimedia development, but it is easily adapted to developing content and pages for a Web site. In fact, this development process can be adapted to the development of almost any communication media.

Suppose your boss comes into your office one day and says, "We'd like for you to spearhead our Web development team. We don't really know what we should put on the site, we just know we need to establish our presence on the Web for our clients." He concludes by saying, "By the way, we have a major conference in a month and would like to showcase our new Web site." What do you do? Where do you start? How do you know where you're going? One thing is for sure, your job (and credibility) is riding upon successfully establishing your company's Web presence.

Never fear, the entire Web development process can be laid out procedurally. There is a step-by-step approach that you can take to successfully develop a Web site, as shown in Figure 10.1. This approach is not necessarily the end-all to developing sites, but it will help you in planning and looking at all of the variables involved in Web site production. Most sites fail due to poor planning and design.

Figure 10.1.
The development process.

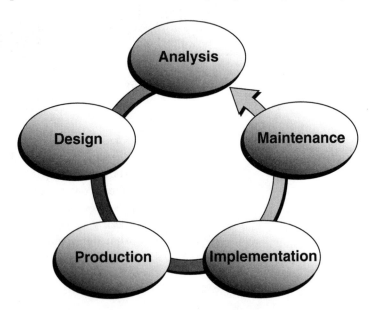

Planning

So what is it that your Web site is really trying to convey? Yep, you guessed it: a message. While reading Chapter 1, "Graphic Design," you were presented with the communication model and the effect of noise in the communication process. Communication is the essence of what a Web site is all about. Whether the goal is to inform, persuade, educate, or entertain, the intent in delivering content via the Web is to present the audience with information and for that information to be comprehended, encoded, and acted upon by the audience.

One of the main goals in planning a Web site is to reduce or completely eliminate the noise that can hinder the communicability of a Web site. If the audience misinterprets what is presented or doesn't understand what is presented, the Web site has failed.

Next question: How do you get your message to be comprehended and encoded by your audience? How do you get the audience to remember or act upon it? Well, the first step is to make your information relevant to your audience, as shown in Figure 10.2. Any content you provide should be audience-centered; it must be relevant and pertinent to them. The content must attract and hold the audience's attention while also completely communicating your message. This is the first law of Web communication.

In addition to relating to the audience, your content should be presented logically. There should be, in any communication medium, a logical progression or thought process that can be identified. Sites that are poorly planned often fail due to illogical arrangement of content. Arrangement of your content should be intuitive—like the audience would expect to see it. Most of this can be solved with ample planning.

With traditional documents, logical order is created in the presentation of paragraphs, sentences, and words, as well as in the flow of the textural passages. With hypermedia, it is a little different because you can arrange pages in a variety of ways and can insert text, graphics, sound, and so on in any way you want. With Web-based media, you must deal with its non-sequential nature. You must be careful that your content follows a logical progression throughout your site and throughout the pages contained within it.

Figure 10.2.
*Communicating with a
Web-based medium.*

By now, you've seen some horrid sites on the Web. They're all over. Dancing elements prancing around your screen, huge graphics that communicate poorly, content that is presented in an awkward fashion—these are things of which you should be leery. Logical progression within your pages will stem from how, and how well, you use graphics and multimedia elements as well as navigation items.

Graphics and other media elements should be only used to enhance, complement, clarify, or complete what you say with words. Many times, people use graphics to fill space, cramming every nook and cranny with something visual. The overall effect of such a page is less than stimulating and often confusing. To help present your site's information in a logical order, graphic design principles should be utilized to help your audience assimilate your information. Graphics that appear on Web pages are generally used for three main purposes. Graphics are used to do the following:

- Enhance, complement, and supplement content that cannot be adequately described or explained with text.
- Present navigational items such as buttons, button bars, and icons to allow the user to navigate your site.
- Aid in creating a visual flow by laying out information through the use of directional, helper, and "filler" graphics.

As you are laying out your pages and making decisions about what the page will include and how the content will be presented, keep in mind that graphics are a vital part of Web page design. Aside from the purposes for graphics, note that graphics should always do the following:

- Graphics used for content purposes should always aid in communication. Graphics used this way should always display something that cannot be adequately communicated with text or add more clarity to the text.
- Graphics should never overshadow or distract the audience from what you are presenting.
- Graphics should contribute to the overall tone of the site. Graphics at a site for business professionals should contribute to a professional tone or look.
- The audience's impression of your graphics will be based not only on what is being shown in the graphic but also on its size, placement, and orientation.
- Graphics displayed on a page must be designed around the audience's browser, platform, and machine.

Lastly, the nature of Web-based information centers around navigability and nonlinearity. You must provide an easy navigation scheme for your site. Being able to dive deeper into a site's information efficiently is important to the audience, as is easily being able to leave a page. Navigation should never overshadow the information being presented. As you're developing your site, be attentive to the issue of navigation. Many users are turned off by the difficulty of navigating through a site that is difficult to use. The audience leaves the site still looking for the answers it came to the site to find. When you begin developing your site, use navigation items such as buttons, icons, and button bars that are obvious, almost exaggerated. Remember: People didn't come just to surf, it's your content they want.

Nontransient Information

The tremendous evolution of computers and computer networks has advanced our ability to communicate. It has also greatly affected the types of media we can use to communicate and how quickly we can make changes to the delivery medium. The next two sections examine the media we use to communicate and take a look at how our choice of media is actually dependent upon the nature of the information.

Prior to the Web, all physical information distribution media (such as books, CDs, and so on) had a relatively stable and nontransient life cycle. Therefore, we could accept the time needed to develop them. For example, textbooks usually contain information that remains relatively stable for a period of six months to a year, so we can accept a three-month cycle to create a book. Information such as this—information that remains stable—can be classified as nontransient information. Nontransient information is information that changes or becomes outdated on a nine- to twelve-month cycle.

Today, most developers deliver nontransient information using static media— media that cannot be changed. This isn't a new revelation. Almost all communication media, including print-based media, CD-ROMs, and laserdisks, fall into this category. Looking at these media, we see that up to this day, stable information could be easily delivered on one of these media. But what if that information suddenly changed? What if we wanted to use one of these media to communicate information that changed on a day-to-day basis? Could we accept that our product is entirely outdated at the time it is released? No, our delivery method must be dynamic, rather than static, for information that rapidly changes.

Transient Information

Today we see an exponential rate of change in the information we deal with on a day-to-day basis. As it relates to computers, the information changes daily (almost hourly). This is the point at which Web development and delivery excels. World Wide Web–based delivery is dynamic. It can be quickly changed or adapted and can support the demands of transient information. It is fluid and can be developed in real time. Transient information is information that has a short life cycle—changing or becoming outdated in nine months or less.

So why bring up the issue of transient and nontransient information? Who cares? As a Web developer, this issue is vitally important because it reveals a trend that is occurring in both industry and education.

Most institutions are beginning to distinguish between transient and nontransient information in the way they distribute it. Institutions are focusing their development efforts based on how quickly the information changes. If the information has a relatively long life cycle, the information supports distribution in a book or on a CD. If the information has a short life cycle, it is distributed via the Web. Many publishers and other traditionally based businesses are focusing on providing information, rather than a physical, tangible product. As the Web develops to the point of supporting full-blown multimedia capabilities (full-screen video, CD-quality audio, and so on), it will be vital for companies to shift their focus from being product producers to information facilitators and providers. Information provision is becoming increasingly more dependent upon the Web as a communication medium because of the increasingly fluid nature of the information.

Content

As they say in the multimedia development field, content is king. Successful Web development is centered on how successfully the content and graphics communicate to the user. There is a precarious balance between these two elements. Poor content can never be dressed up, even with great graphics. The content is still poor. Also, good content can never communicate effectively with poor graphics. Visual appeal is an important aspect of any communication media. The first step in developing a good communication tool is analysis of the content you intend to provide.

To begin looking for the content for your site, the first thing you must have is a general goal, as shown in Figure 10.3. What's your site going to be about? What are you providing to your audience?

Figure 10.3.
Analyzing the content.

Most Web sites are established to inform, persuade, educate, or entertain the audience. Depending on which of these you are trying to do, your site might look a little different. The majority of sites focus on the first of these: informing and persuading. More than likely, if you are developing a site for your company, it will also be categorized as either informing or persuading. Do you want to present information about your company or its products? Are you trying to persuade the audience to buy your product, or are you just presenting information? Establish what you are trying to do at your site and try to state it in a single sentence. This will force you to focus on the main purpose of your site, rather than all the little extras you would like to provide.

Authorship

The next decision you must make concerns authorship of the content. Many times, you will want to provide information at your site that has been developed by someone in the company. Most of the time, a company will own content of this nature. To be honest, most Web sites being developed transform information that already exists, such as an online version of a traditional brochure or another corporate document. Nonetheless, even if you believe your company owns the content, you must still ascertain if the information you want to present via your Web site belongs to the company or not. It is always a good idea to establish this in writing.

In addition to the text provided on your pages, the graphic elements and any multimedia elements are also a concern. Due to the legal aspects of ownership and copyrights, you cannot just throw anything on your Web site. You must consider who owns or who has created any and all items you want to present at your Web site. You also must get permission before using them.

In this respect, creating a Web site is just like creating a book. You wouldn't begin writing a book by simply copying illustrations or text from another book. So it is also with Web content. You must establish who owns the copyright for the material you want to present and obtain the proper permissions to use it.

Copyrights

Copyright is a gray area on the Web, even though the lines defining copyrights in the United States are black and white. Most of the information put on the Web is assumed to be in the public domain. However, many of the graphics, text, and other items are actually copyrighted and could be determined as such in court. The public domain refers to any work that is not protected under copyright (patent or trademark) or media that is not considered a creative work. Items can also be considered public domain if the copyright for the item expires.

So what is a copyright? From the date of creation, any text, graphic, sound, video clip, or animation belongs to and is property of the individual who created it. To use any of these items requires permission from the copyright holder. However, as per the Copyright Act of 1976, an employer who hires a consultant as work-for-hire owns the copyright if it is within the scope of the project. All derivative works, compilations, and reuse of a copyrighted piece, in whole and often in part, require the permission of the author or copyright holder.

So then the most difficult part of obtaining permission for use of a copyrighted item is often determining who holds the copyright. Defining whether or not you are "consulting" with a company is really what determines the authorship, and ultimately the right of copyright of a particular creative work. Really, the outer fringes of the "consultant" definition can get quite gray. In fact, the Supreme Court stated that there is no single rule that determines whether you are a consultant or an employee. In a case of precedence, the Supreme Court established a list of 14 questions that can be used to help determine this issue. It is easier to define what is not consulting than what is. However, it is true that if you are not consulting, the copyright is the property of the company of which you are an employee.

I am not a legal expert. I have no law degree. But there are some simple things that can be used to determine if you are legally considered a consultant or an employee. You are not consulting if

- The person hiring you has the right to control the means and the manner in which the product is created.
- Work performed on the product is conducted at the hiring party's premises, office, or location.
- Work performed on the product is conducted using the hiring party's software, computers, or equipment.
- Work performed on the product is required during work hours set by the hiring party.

Ultimately, deciphering whether or not you are an employee of the hiring party is what determines copyright issues. If you are an employee, all copyrights of creative work generated in the natural course of business belong to the hiring body. No formal documentation is required between an employee and an employer for this to occur. However, a consultant creating something for a company has much more power over the issue of copyrights. For transfer of copyright to occur, the scope of the employment must include a description of this transfer in the contract between the consultant and hiring body.

By definition, there are three rules concerning authorship. An author can be defined as the following:

- The creator of a work.
- The hiring body of the creator of a work, when the work is created in the normal course and scope of employment.
- The hiring body hires an independent contractor by commission or special order.

First and foremost, a copyright is held by the person that created the work. So the first type of author that can hold a copyright is the creator of the work. The only time that this is not true is when the author of a work is hired by a company with the scope of the project including the copyright to the work. It can also be nullified if the individual is hired as a subcontractor, with the scope of the project including the copyright to the work. Both of these cases require the author to sign a work-for-hire agreement. In such an agreement, normally an entire section deals with the scope of the project, defining any and all boundaries and limitations concerning copyrights and use of the work. The work-for-hire agreement also defines other parameters that we will discuss later, such as pricing, deliverables, and tax issues.

So what defines copyrightable works? Well, there are nine different types of commissioned works specified in the Copyright Act of 1976, and they include contributions to collective works, audiovisual works, compilations, supplementary works, translations, instructional text, tests, answer material for tests, and atlases. As a Web developer, you'll most often be faced with the first two of these.

Once a copyright has been established, affixed with a copyright symbol, or registered by the author, the copyright will last for the life of the author plus 50 years. If there are multiple authors, the copyright lasts for the life of the last survivor plus 50 years.

Unauthorized use of copyrighted material can carry significant financial repercussions, regardless of whether the item has been officially copyrighted through the Library of Congress. Anything you create that is deemed a creative work can be copyrighted. This includes graphics you create, text you write, or even Web pages in some cases. To protect your work, you might simply add a copyright signature to it (copyright 1999 John Doe). Under current copyright laws, this protects your work, even if you do not officially copyright it. In legalese, this is known as "Intent to Copyright." To use any item carrying a copyright signature requires permission from the holder of the copyright.

However, on the Web, tracking infringement—who is using what—is a problem. It is very difficult to find or prosecute individuals for copyright infringement. For the most part, the same rules that apply to traditional documents also apply to Web-based documents. Concerning copyrights, you must be cautious of what you use at your site. This includes not only what you create, but also what you use from the public domain.

Whenever you create something for Web distribution, realize that, literally, the whole world has access to your information. In addition, U.S. copyrights do not apply outside the U.S. Do not put information on your site that you want to protect through a copyright. Although copyright laws are established and you could pursue litigation (in the U.S.), it is very difficult to prove or prosecute for copyright infringement. It is also very costly. Many people mistakenly believe that anything on the Web is in the public domain. Nothing could be further from the truth! That's like saying anything you find in a magazine you can reprint or repurpose. Things on the Web are copyrightable, and just because they appear on the Web does not mean they are public domain. Be cautious about what you provide on your Web site.

Before you begin cranking out pages, to protect yourself and your company, verify in writing that you have permission to use the media elements you want to provide. This includes all the media elements: text, graphics, sound, animation, and video. Even some specialized scripting and programming can be copyrightable. Even if everyone says it was developed in-house or says it's okay to use, I would obtain permissions in writing. This is the safest path to follow.

Licenses and Releases

Obtaining permission to use a copyrighted element can be as simple as a permission letter. It might, however, require a license or release. A license is a fee that is paid to use a copyrighted item in another publication.

In the digital publishing arena, licenses are the most common way of obtaining a permission. Most often licenses are required when the media element such as a graphic or sound clip is used in a salable, corporate product. Often the licensing fee is based on the price of the new product that uses the copyrighted item, the level at which the product is distributed (regional, national, international), and the number of copies of the product that are being created. For example, let's say you wanted to use a stock image from ABC Images, Inc., in a brochure you're designing. Let's also say that this brochure is to internationally market your product and that you're going to print 500,000 of them. In this instance, you will pay more to use the image than you would if you were marketing regionally with a small print run of about 1,000. Licensing fees are often subjective and based upon the assumed or perceived value of the item to the licensee.

The second type of permission that can be obtained for copyrighted items is a release. A release is a formal agreement that allows an individual to use a copyrighted item at no charge. A release usually defines specific parameters in which the item can be used.

A release is frequently associated with the development of products for which there is no price or in which the price or distribution is quite small. This often includes Web site development. Although releases are free, there are also restrictions of use associated with them. For example, some releases state that you cannot use the copyrighted element for public display (like a presentation), whereas others might have restrictions specific to the type of media element. For Web development, even for those things that are created in-house, it is always a good idea to at least secure a release before using those items.

Graphics and Media Elements

A final word about protecting your graphics and media elements: Keep your eyes open for emerging technologies designed to help you protect your work. One prime example is a new graphics-encoding technology that embeds copyright information right within the graphic image. However, the copyright information cannot be seen without the aid of special decoder software. As a graphics animal myself, I think that this is something that is a godsend to those of us in the graphics industry. I believe we will be seeing more software innovations like this in the very near future, ones designed to digitally protect creative work.

Audience

One of the most promising aspects of Web development is the ability to customize your site to your audience. All good Web sites are audience-centered. What does your audience expect to see at your site? What will attract them? What will repel them? The whole point in identifying and analyzing the audience is to custom-tailor the Web site around their needs.

Whether you are communicating through a book, a live presentation, or a Web site, it is imperative that you build a profile of your prospective or target users, as shown in Figure 10.4. Target a single population for which you are providing content. What are their ages? What are their backgrounds? What skills do they have? As any good communicator knows, successful communication only occurs when the text, graphics, and any other aid transfers a message from sender to receiver in its entirety. To do this requires knowledge about the audience. A measure of whether communication has occurred successfully can be seen in how much of the message the audience receives, and in the accuracy of their interpretation. Many things contribute to the way the audience receives and interprets your message.

Age

One of the first things that comes to mind as you look at the audience is age. Age greatly affects how you present your content. For example, if the age of your audience is younger than 20 years of age, you might want to use something attention-getting. Also, keeping this age group's attention requires some ingenuity. However, if your audience is older than 20 years of age, something attention-getting might repel, if not offend, the audience. So, age plays a large role in how you present your information.

Background

You must also consider your audience's background when developing your site. For example, a technical discussion on some complex concept might be good for some of your audience members, but are you excluding those who don't have the background needed to assimilate the information you're presenting? Does the audience need to have some prerequisite knowledge before your content makes sense? If so, you might want to either provide links to sites on the Web where your audience can get the prerequisite knowledge or start your content at a lower level.

Figure 10.4.
Audience attributes.

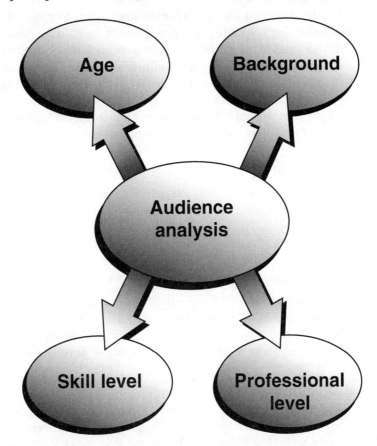

Skill Level

Another consideration is the skill level of your audience. For example, if you are planning to create content that requires a specific plug-in or helper application, will your audience have the skills necessary to find the plug-in or helper and install it? Will the audience need to know how to download files or understand compression programs like Pkware's PKZIP or Aladdin's Stuffit Expander? To you these might seem like simple things, but to an audience member, they can be significant hurdles. Consider the skill level of your audience. If needed, provide links to get plug-ins and helpers and even instructions for installation if you believe your audience needs them. To overcome skill limitations in your audience, use a customer service approach. Provide the audience everything it needs to be able to efficiently and effectively use your site.

Professional Level

Lastly, you must also consider the professional level of the individuals that will be accessing your site. This really has to do with the tone of your site, but it can also be related to age level. Do business professionals make up the predominance of your audience? If so, you'll definitely want to take a reserved approach to both navigability and content presentation. When questioning at what professional level you should shoot, it is always better to err on the side of conservatism than on the avant-garde. Even in sites that are avant-garde (far out, techno-punk, artsy, flamboyant, and so on) attempt to present it with a professional overtone.

Development

To some, the idea of the development system being a variable involved in Web development seems strange; however, I believe it as a very important consideration. More and more corporations are creating Web development groups, rather than having a single individual create all the Web site information. In addition, often the group will contain individuals from several different departments who are often oblivious to the collaborative resources.

The primary aspects of concern for the development system are the applications, platform, tools, and other resources that might be utilized. Looking at these items in a group setting makes everyone aware of the collaborative resources. Figure 10.5 graphically shows the major points of development system analysis.

Applications

As you begin planning a Web site, you really need nothing more than a simple text editor and a paint application for graphics. However, you'll find that there are many tools that have been developed that make Web page creation and maintenance more efficient. Heck, each person in your group probably has at least one of them. If you are part of a Web development group, consider discussing the various software applications you have amoung yourselves. Some of the most useful tools for Web development include

- A Web creation tool, such as Microsoft FrontPage, Adobe PageMill, Macromedia Backstage, or Netscape Communicator.
- A raster editor, such as Adobe Photoshop or Fractal Design Painter.
- A vector drawing program, such as Macromedia FreeHand or Adobe Illustrator.

Figure 10.5.
The development system.

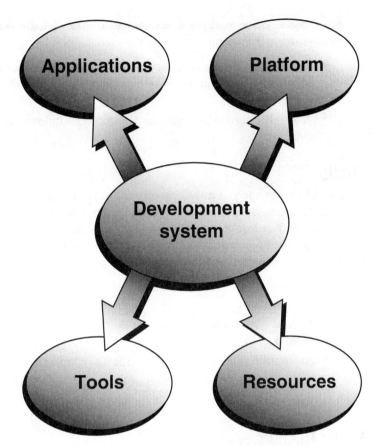

Platform

You will also want to verify the platform(s) on which the Web group will be developing the Web site. It is common to develop a site on a local hard drive or storage device prior to uploading it to the Web server. Some developers prefer UNIX, others Windows, and still others prefer the Macintosh. Any platform will do, but you must be aware of the differences across the various platforms as you begin working. Also, file format differences across platforms must be addressed. Aside from the issues of colors and fonts discussed earlier, PC users will probably want to invest in a utility program that will allow them to read Macintosh disks. Macintosh users should be able to read cross-platform disks, assuming System 7.5 or later is installed.

For those who are working across platforms for Web development, you may want to consider purchasing

- File transfer software, such as Pacific Micro's Mac-In-DOS or MacOpener, to enable cross-platform capability (PC users) and file transfer.
- A graphic converter, such as Hijaak95 (Windows) or Debablizer (Macintosh).

Tools

In addition to specific development applications, you might also need other tools to add special capabilities. For example, if you wanted to add internal multimedia elements, you might consider adding other applications to your list of development tools. If you want to deliver a wide range of multimedia elements through your Web site, you could include the following:

- Authoring software, such as Macromedia Director or Macromedia Authorware.
- Digital video software, such as Adobe Premiere or AutoDesk Animator Studio.
- Animation software, such as Kinetix 3D Studio Max or Rio Topas.
- Audio software, such as Sound Forge or Sound Edit Pro.
- Print software, such as Adobe Acrobat.

Other Resources

Beyond the hardware and software resources you will be using, you must also determine the skills that each of the group members has. Often a Web development group will consist of individuals who have a wide variety of skills. When you are looking at the development system, it is also a good time to discuss the skills that each person has and how each one will contribute to the development of the Web site.

Delivery

Earlier you analyzed the audience and considered what it would be looking for at your site. Now you must also take a look at the hardware that the audience will use to access your site. This is the most frequently overlooked part of the development process.

The main concerns in the delivery system are what type of network access the users have, what platform they are using, and the typical machine configuration they will be using. (See Figure 10.6.)

Figure 10.6.
The delivery system.

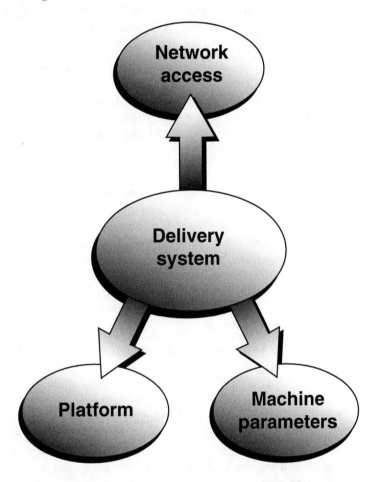

Network Access

The most important aspect of the user's delivery system is his or her connection to the Internet. As you are planning to deliver specific elements to your audience, you need to consider from where your users will be logging onto the Internet.

Is your audience predominantly composed of users logging in from home using a dial-up connection? If so, you will want to choose carefully how much and how many multimedia elements you deliver, due to the amount of time these elements take to download via a modem. If you are focusing on corporate or education users, you might be able to include larger graphics, animation, or video if users have fast network connections to the Internet.

Aside from multimedia elements, inline graphics can cause the user significant problems. Providing too many inline images can result in frustration for the user and an immediate exit of your site. If your audience is mostly dial-up users, consider providing a lightweight site that they can quickly and easily access. Your content plan should reflect any limitations that your audience will have.

Platform

In the first chapter, you looked at how the operating system affects the pages that are loaded into the browser. You read how both fonts and color change from platform to platform. One of the things you will invariably do is create a profile of the typical user's machine. Much like creating a profile of the audience for content guidelines, a profile of the user's machine will help you create content that will be effectively displayed on the user's machine. Undoubtedly, it will keep you from creating what cannot be effectively utilized by your audience.

Machine Parameters

Last, but not least, are the individualized parameters of the user's machine. This is more than just the platform or network connection. You must consider the various aspects of the user's computer so that you will know what type of multimedia he or she can utilize. Does the user have a sound card? Will his or her computer play downloaded video? Does the computer have enough RAM to support multimedia plug-ins such as Shockwave, VRML, or QuickTimeVR? Discuss these types of questions with the development team members. Try to put together a typical audience member's computer configuration, much like the audience profile.

Function

So you have analyzed all the variables—now what? After looking at the content, audience, development, and delivery systems, you must now summarize the information you have. Up to this point, you've been defining the parameters under which communication should occur. At the beginning of this process, you developed a general goal in a single sentence. Now you must take that goal and create objectives and an abstract to summarize and describe your site. The objectives and the abstract should give more description to your overall goal. To do a functional analysis, you will need to document your goal, create objectives, and create an abstract that describes the site you will be creating. (See Figure 10.7.)

Figure 10.7.
Functional analysis.

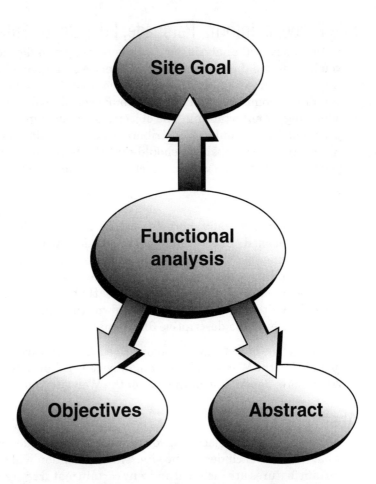

Through the functional analysis, written documentation of the information found during analysis is vitally important. That's why the functional analysis is really nothing more than a conclusionary document describing the things that the group has found. Consider that you, or one of your group members, might not always be involved with Web development. Some might move on to other jobs, become ill, or for some other reason be removed from the Web development group. Documenting the parameters for your site helps any newcomers to your group. It also helps keep everyone on track with the original purpose of the site. The document becomes an abbreviated summary that can be used to quickly brief a new member on the focus and purpose of the Web site you're creating. It can also be used to explain to your boss or a client what the Web site is about and what it will communicate.

Site Purpose: Inform, Persuade, Educate, or Entertain?

In the functional analysis, you will be refining and developing the information you have found during analysis into concise statements that describe your site. As you are creating objectives and the abstract, make sure that both items culminate, complete, and support your overall goal of informing, persuading, educating, or entertaining. The objectives should supplement, yet complement, your goal. They should all contribute to accomplishing the main goal of the site. Alternatively, the abstract should give the background necessary to establish your rationale for the way in which you plan to create your Web site.

Objectives

Objectives are generally short statements that define the way the overall goal will be accomplished. Each statement might deal with a specific area. A sample objective may be "The Web site's product area will inform the reader of our current and new product lines." Also, the objectives can be used to not only describe a feature but also indicate how that feature will be executed, such as "The Web site's product area will inform the reader of our current and new product lines using descriptive 3D animations that the user can download."

Typically, the objectives will deal with each of the various aspects that are to be included in the Web site. There might be fewer than 10 objectives or as many as 20 or more, depending on the size of the Web site you are planning.

Abstract

After defining the objectives, you definitely want to describe your rationale for what has been included in the site. This description will generally describe why certain features are included and why certain features are not included. All of the information is based on the conclusions made from the analysis performed by the Web design group.

The abstract should be written with sufficient length that an outside individual could read the document to get a description of the site, as well as the rational for its existence. Use the parameters that you found during the analysis as your basis for the decisions made.

Design

Graphics and graphic design play a large role in the communicability of a site, as shown in Figure 10.8. The graphical layout of the pages, as well as the graphics themselves, will largely contribute to the audience's opinion of your site in addition to the site's communicative value.

Figure 10.8.
Evaluation of your site begins with the graphics.

The Look

Designing appealing, graphical pages is not rocket science. Indeed, the biggest difficulty is in developing an artist's eye. To develop an artist's eye simply requires training yourself so that you can tell what looks good and what looks bad.

At this point, simply realize that the graphical content of a page should contribute to the content that is being provided. Don't use graphics to just take up space. Often, graphics can be used to set the mood as well as the tone for a site. A simple comparison of a corporate site to a site for kids reveals how graphics contribute in this domain. Graphics play an important role in setting the tone of a site, as shown in Figure 10.9.

Graphics also help in the aesthetic dimension by providing visual appeal. Static text becomes much more interesting as you add related graphics to a page, as shown in Figure 10.10. The content of the page also becomes clearer because you can visually describe what is being communicated with text. Images communicate much quicker than text and much more vividly as well.

Figure 10.9.
Graphics set the mood of the site.

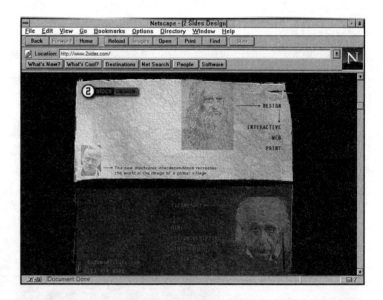

Figure 10.10.
The power of graphical communication.

Metaphor

In the multimedia world, a common buzzword commonly creeps up as you begin discussing multimedia and hypermedia. The buzzword is *metaphor*. A metaphor is a theme, motif, or storyline that attempts to familiarize the audience with something new, using association. Metaphors are intended to decrease user apprehension when presented with a new environment by drawing on past knowledge.

One of the most difficult items to tackle when dealing with communication tools is the comfort level of the user. How do you get the user comfortable with navigating or using a new informational environment such as a Web site? How do you get the navigation issues out of the way so they can get to what they really came for (your content)?

This is what a metaphor attempts to do. By drawing on your previous experience, a metaphor attempts to link something the user is familiar with to the workings of a new informational environment. For example, you might create a Web site that works like a book—which would be blasé, but nonetheless it is a metaphor. By using a book metaphor for your pages, you would assume that the user could more quickly and easily begin navigating your site. Using the book metaphor means that users don't have to learn how to navigate the site. They use it just like a book—something they assumably already know how to use. This is the primary goal of a metaphor: to get the user past navigational issues and environment control so that he or she can get to your content quickly and easily.

Many metaphors have been used. Figure 10.11 shows an example of a digital device metaphor. Note that this site uses an interface analogous to a hand-held device. The developers are assuming that you are comfortable with and can use such a device. Therefore, using the site draws upon your past experience and makes using the site easier with which to become familiar.

Figure 10.11.
An example of
a metaphor.

As you begin considering how the user will navigate your site, consider using a metaphor to draw on the user's past knowledge. When you use a metaphor, your site will be successful and aid the user in overcoming the new environment. (See Figure 10.12.) If a metaphor is designed with the user's knowledge and skills in mind, it can be fun, both in design and execution.

Figure 10.12.
Using a metaphor to draw upon past knowledge and skills.

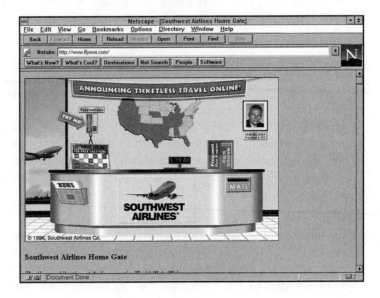

If you decide to use a metaphor, make sure it is somewhat obvious to your audience. Use something that is relevant. If the metaphor you use is too abstract, it will become counterproductive. The best metaphors are ones with which the audience quickly associates.

Interface Design

In addition to a metaphor is the interface itself. The interface that you present to the user is the communication channel between the user and the content of the site. The interface contains all the navigation controls for the site, as shown in Figure 10.13.

An interface is the point of interaction between the computer and the user. It must provide for input and output from both parties. It is also the point of communication and interaction whereby the user interacts with the computer and vice versa.

Often, the interface is part of the metaphor; there can be overlap between the two. The metaphor is the association, and the interface is the place of physical interaction, as shown in Figure 10.14. As you proceed through this book, you will invariably see many sites that sport good and bad examples of metaphors and interfaces.

Figure 10.13.
The interface presents the navigational controls for the site.

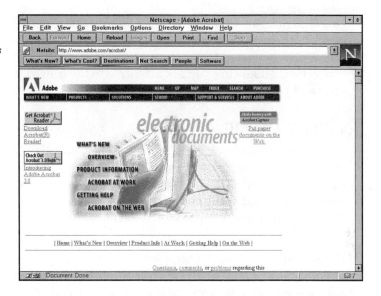

Figure 10.14.
The interface: a point of interaction.

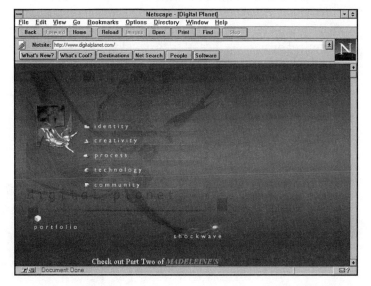

Functionality

Developing the interface and a metaphor for the information at your site might be the most difficult part of creating a good Web site. The biggest problems with most interfaces is that they are unnatural and difficult to use or they have little relevance to the audience. When you are developing your site, approach interface design in a utilitarian way. Look at the various functions you must support (from your objectives) and design buttons, icons, and button bars based on those functions.

One final note about interfaces and metaphors is that there should be consistency between the two. I have seen Web sites and multimedia CD-ROMs that lose the connection between the metaphor and the interface. In some, there is no connection. Make sure you are attentive to the consistency between your metaphor and your interface.

Technical Design

After you have addressed the content and graphical issues, you begin laying out the technical structure for your Web site. When Web sites are conceived, often they are designed with shortsighted vision. Often times, the site is developed on a small scale, and then the site quickly mushrooms into a very large site almost overnight. When this happens, the technical design of a site can be either a help or a hindrance.

Developing a technical plan for your site is really a continuation of all the planning you have done. At this point, you should have the various areas of your site defined and a good idea of the branches and pages in each area. You should have the various graphics and multimedia elements you want to include identified, complete with releases or licenses secured or in process. The focus of technical design, as it relates to developing the site's pages and media elements, is to develop a visual, hierarchical structure for your pages. To do this often requires some basic sketches of how your site will be laid out. The main concerns in technical design are the site layout, the server structure, and the actual directories and files, as shown in Figure 10.15.

Figure 10.15.
The aspects of technical design.

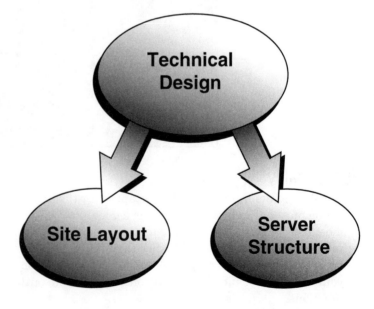

Site Layout

How often do you leave for a trip without a map? I rarely do. I am a person who hates to wander aimlessly, hoping I'll find my destination. Oh sure, there are times my wife and I just go on a short vacation without predetermining where we're going, but time is not an issue on trips like that. Most often when I travel, at least on business, I don't have time to waste. I cannot leave anything to chance when I'm on a time schedule. I must reach a destination accurately, and in a timely manner.

Creating a Web site is much like a business trip. You've done your homework, and you know where you want to go. Now all you need is a map to lay out the physical pages and structure for your site. You could just start cranking pages and leave the arrangement to chance, but why would you? Not taking a map can leave you aimlessly wandering, hoping you'll hit your destination.

Now that you know what your site will contain, as far as the content is concerned, you need to develop a site map. Although the site map is usually a sketch, Figure 10.16 shows a Web site that uses the map in its pages. A site map shows all the various pages at your site and is most often a sketch. The site map lays out all the links from one page to the next as well as the various media elements that will be a part of the pages. The site map becomes an invaluable tool as you start creating the pages and uploading them to your Web server.

Figure 10.16.
Creating a site map.

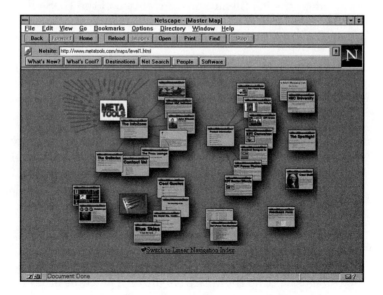

Server Structure: Directories and Files

In addition to being an aid for page development, the site map also shows you the relative and absolute file structure for your server. This will become very important as your site grows, and as you begin adding more content and pages to your site. Just like the abstract and the objectives, the site map is a living document. As you expand your site, your map, abstract, and objectives also expand.

One of the things you need to focus on when developing a site map is how you will set up the file structure on your server. You will want to create a structure that is logical and easy to manage. For example, all the pages for a particular area will probably reside in the same folder or directory on the server. Subsequent divisions of each area may have their own directories. Try to group your files logically so that managing your site is not a memory exercise. As you add pages and content to your site, make sure you also frequently update your map. I hate using a highway map or a site map that's not up-to-date. You will too, so make sure you update!

In addition to developing a logical directory structure, you will want to adopt some type of file naming convention for your HTML and other files that are on the server. If you are working in an environment that supports long filenames, use it to your advantage. However, if there are PC users in your group, you might have to adopt the 8.3 filenaming convention of the DOS environment.

Production

As you've seen, there is a lot of work and planning put into the site before a single page is ever created. It might seem like a lot of up-front work, and it is. Successful sites don't just happen. There is a tremendous amount of planning involved in creating any good communication medium.

The production phase is where everything seems to come together. If you are working as a freelance Web consultant or as part of a development group, it is here that you will see most of the physical work emerge. Time spent planning is not wasted. The planning that goes into Web site development is a long-term investment that will pay off after the site is completed.

Putting Together the Site

Most of the work performed during production will be performed offline. In fact, I suggest setting the entire site up on a machine other than the server as you are working. This ensures that your work is left untouched by any other personnel. Secondly, it gives you full control of what you're creating and saves the unveiling of the site until you are ready.

During production, it is vitally important that you back up your work. Make sure that as you are developing your site you store incremental versions of both your HTML files and any other media elements that you are incorporating.

Managing Production

If you are working in a group setting, communication and coordination between group members will be vitally important. Someone will be ultimately responsible for seeing that work is being completed on the various elements for the Web site. If this is you, make a frequent habit of reviewing the work that is being done by others. Secure accurate deadlines of when elements will be completed and ready for inclusion in the Web site pages.

During production, remember to test the pages and site frequently as it is being completed. Remember the discussion concerning browsers and platforms. Test the pages using the hardware and software that the target audience will be using. Test, retest, and test again to ensure that the pages appear as intended.

Client or Corporate Check-Offs

If you are working as a freelance Web consultant, you will definitely want to establish a system of client check-offs or approvals. Basically, this gives the client the opportunity to review the work that is being done, rather than getting surprised at the end of the project. As a consultant, using written approvals also gives you documentation that the client signed off on what you were doing. You run into no end of trouble if you do not use a system of approvals with your clientele.

Implementation

After all the pages have been completed offline, the last part of setting up the site is moving it to the server. Some of the software mentioned earlier, such as Microsoft FrontPage, offers a very easy way to upload the pages. If you manually upload the pages to your server using FTP, you will undoubtedly have to do some fine-tuning. Regardless, you will again want to test all the pages and elements rigorously to ensure that the site works as intended once it has been uploaded.

Maintenance

Because the Web is a fluid medium, there will be updates and maintenance that will occur over time. The hardest part—just planning and getting your site online—is over. If you've followed the planning steps presented in this chapter, you should find that managing your site is easy. You will find, no doubt, that your Web site will be a continually evolving creature and, as long as you continually adapt your objectives, abstract, site map, and pages concurrently, you'll find that managing your site will be a much easier task.

Critical Points

The development process presented here should be used as a guide and not the law concerning Web development. Time or budget restraints might require eliminating certain steps to see that the site is produced in a timely manner. The most important planning aspects of the development process are

- Audience analysis
- Content analysis
- Delivery system
- Interface design
- Site map

Summary

In this chapter you have taken an extensive look at development process for Web. Beginning with an analysis of the content, the developer reviews all the necessary items to be included in the Web site, including all text, graphics, sound, animation, and video. Prior to delivering these elements over the Web, the developer must secure licenses or releases for their use. As you read, you must be cautious of what you place on the Web, both as a provider and developer. By analyzing the audience, you are able to establish an audience profile that describes the audience's age, background, and skills so that content can be audience-centered. There is a relationship and correlation between analyzing the content and audience, and successful Web communication media. You also looked at the development and delivery systems to determine collaborative capabilities and developmental constraints. Concluding the analysis is the documentation of the site goal, objectives, and abstract that describes, defines, and validates the site and its content.

Following analysis is production, where most of the physical product is created. Most sites are developed offline and include client check-offs for work that is done. During the production process, frequent testing should be done to ensure the operability of the site with the target browser, platform, and machine. Implementing the created site requires uploading the site pages and materials to the server, with ample testing of the finished product. Finally, site diagrams, along with the goal, objectives, and abstract, should be updated as frequently as the site itself. Maintaining up-to-date documentation ensures manageability.

11

Multimedia Fundamentals

In Chapter 9, "Multimedia," you read that good multimedia and hypermedia products have a balance between linearity and non-linearity. Remember that linearity most often applies to the way the structure or logical flow of the content is presented to your audience. The non-sequential element allows the reader to choose the level or depth at which he wants to begin assimilating your information. In essence, the non-linearity allows the user to choose when and where he wants to go.

In Chapter 10, "Interactive Multimedia Design Process," you were presented with a model for creating multimedia and hypermedia materials. The entire development process usually involves many individuals with a variety of backgrounds. A single project may involve an Internet specialist, an information design specialist, a media designer, a technical manager, and any range of other individuals.

No matter how many individuals are involved with multimedia and hypermedia development, three predominant areas of knowledge are usually represented: education or communication, visual science, and computer science. Each of these knowledge areas needs to be represented to effectively create hypermedia or multimedia.

In this chapter, you will read about the various knowledge areas related to the development of multimedia and hypermedia. In addition, you will take a look at the contributions that individuals representing these knowledge areas can make to a group setting.

To conclude this chapter, you will also read about some of the various concerns surrounding the Web browser as well as other Internet resources that can be used in hypermedia. Remember that the Web is designed to be a multiprotocol, universal communication media. Things such as e-mail, FTP, and Gopher, as well as other services, may be useful in the sites and pages you develop.

As you saw in earlier chapters, pages often look different when viewed on different browsers and different platforms. In the section on browsers, you'll take a look at how the browser functions and how it can display content from the Web.

The Multimedia Knowledge Base

As the complexity of communications media has increased, so have the number and range of skills required to produce and create those communications media. The development of each media element, text, graphics, sound, animation and video requires a skill in itself. In multimedia and hypermedia, where any range of these media elements can be involved, the number of people required to create a communication device can become quite significant.

The entire multimedia and hypermedia knowledge base can be summed up by saying that there are three predominant knowledge bases involved: education and communication, visual science, and computer science. Each of these areas significantly impacts the effectiveness of a multimedia or hypermedia tool.

Most unsuccessful communication devices are a result of a missing key person in one of these primary areas. The importance of representative individuals in each of these primary areas cannot be highlighted enough. As you will see in the discussions, all three contributions are vitally important.

As shown in Figure 11.1, the combination of education, visual science, and computer science provides the knowledge base for interactive multimedia development. It is the overlap of these knowledge areas that allows the various software tools you use on a daily basis to be effective.

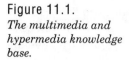

Figure 11.1.
The multimedia and hypermedia knowledge base.

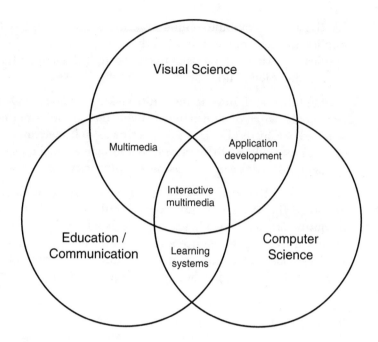

A careful examination of these three areas reveals the significant aspects that they contribute to interactive media and hypermedia development. Note that education includes the principles involved in instructional design, effective communication, and the pedagogical concerns of the transfer of knowledge. Visual science contributes the knowledge necessary to create effective graphics and other visual media elements. Visual science is also what provides the capability to determine where graphics should be used and when they are most effective. Computer science is the knowledge necessary to understand the many hardware and software issues related to Web development, such as networking, programming, and the functions of the browser.

One of the things you'll note about Figure 11.1 is that the combination of any two of the various knowledge bases creates a tool very similar to interactive multimedia. For example, the combination of visual science with education and communication creates multimedia. Remember that by the strict definition of multimedia, there is no interactivity. The presentation is controlled by the computer, so there is no programming involved.

Figure 11.1 shows that the combination of education and computer science yields a learning system. A learning system is generally a system designed to provide and manage instruction. Most of these learning systems use few, if any, graphics. Most are menu- and text-based programs that are akin to a command-line interface. Most graphics that are included are quite crude and significantly lower in quality than what you find on the Web.

Lastly, if you combine computer science and visual science, you derive the application development area. In this area, the main focus is to develop software applications that can be used to create digital documents. In software development, education is unrelated.

As you have read, interactive multimedia includes a wide range of communication media, which includes hypermedia, but as you've noticed, hypermedia is not denoted in Figure 11.1. However, in this model, specific points can be established on the outer edges of the interactive multimedia portion to denote the various types of tools that can be considered interactive multimedia.

In Figure 11.2, you see the knowledge base model with specific points labeled, denoting the variety of interactive multimedia that are a result of certain amounts of each knowledge area. Note that hypermedia requires a lot of experience in visual science and computer science and less in education. This, however, does not negate the need for educational principles within Web content. The level to which a particular site requires educational principles will vary.

Figure 11.2.
Tool and knowledge relationships.

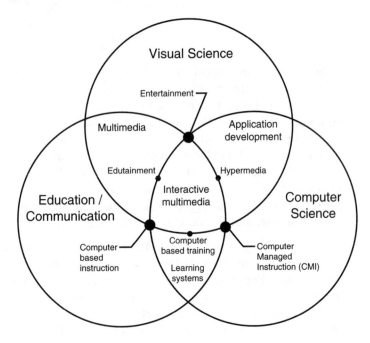

The Development Team

A trend that is occurring within many corporations and businesses is the use of multiple individuals to develop and maintain a company's Web content. With the variety of content and range of media, as well as the tremendous size of some corporate Web sites, creating and managing a business Web site usually requires more than a single individual.

Often, the creation of a Web development team is a natural outgrowth of the development process and the knowledge bases that are involved. A group often consists of a manager, graphics guru, content specialist (usually someone with an education background), information architect, and a programmer. As you can see, even the smallest of groups should contain these key people. In addition, other specialists may be needed as the content requires. For example, if you want to include audio or video at your site, you might need a digital musician or videographer to assist the Web development group. Regardless of the content-related specialists, the knowledge areas of education and communication, visual science, and computer science should be present to create an effective site.

Developing the Content

The primary concern of the content specialist or individual with an education and communication background is the development of the content. Often, this individual is required to write the text and develop the schema for presenting the information. Understand that regardless of whether you strive to educate, persuade, or entertain, there must be schemata or logical flow to the content. There should be a linear flow within the materials so that users with no previous knowledge or background can be guided through the information by the site. This is where linearity becomes important.

Probably one of the hardest things to do as a content developer for the Web is to make assumptions about your audience. Much of the way that materials are designed is focused around the assumptions you make concerning the audience (see Chapter 10). Because the Web is a global medium, the assumptions you make must be rather broad. When strict assumptions are made, you can over-generalize an audience and consequentially exclude them from effectively using the materials at your site.

Developing Supporting Materials

As the content is developed, the person familiar with visual science often assists by not only creating the visual content elements but also suggesting ways in which graphics and other media elements can be effectively used. More often than not, people outside the graphics area have some ideas concerning the use of graphics but usually need assistance in determining application issues such as placement, size, and photo-realism. The task of the visual specialist is to assist in this area.

Networking Concerns

Aside from developing code, the individual with the computer science background has the important task of handling the important issue of bandwidth. Often, this individual can determine the feasibility of delivering certain amounts of content over the Web, specifically graphics and other media elements. The apparent task of the computer science guru is to program the HTML pages, yet most individuals with a computer science background have other valuable knowledge that directly applies to Web development.

The Significance of the Browser

Fundamental to the World Wide Web is the browser software itself. HTML pages have little relevance without a browser to display them. Marc Andreesson probably had no idea that Mosaic, the first Web browser, would have the impact that it did. He probably wouldn't have just given it away had he known. However, his giving it away is part of the reason the Web developed so rapidly. Many browsers quickly followed on the heels of Mosaic, but Mosaic predominantly ruled supreme for quite a while. Today, the two biggest players in the browser market are Netscape Communications and Microsoft. Their two browsers look a little different from the Mosaic of yesterday. Over time, many new and exciting features were added to the basic Mosaic look and function, but all the current browsers still basically function in the same manner.

Browser software is a software program that allows the user to view Web-based documents. All browsers retrieve semantically described information from remote computers and then compose the text, graphics, and multimedia elements on the user's machine. The browser is the fundamental element for viewing hypermedia documents.

As you flip from one site to another, you'll see that your browser is quite busy. How does the whole thing work? Each and every Web site has an address, or Uniform Resource Locator (URL). A URL is the specific address of a Web site or Web resource. Much like your home mailing address, the URL is unique to the site. Clicking links or using bookmarks causes the browser to attempt to access the site's address or URL.

When you simply surf the Web, you really don't have to know too much about URLs. That is what is nice about the Web. You can just click items in the page to go where you want to go, rather than enter information with the keyboard. Many times, you might know the address (URL), so you can also enter it by typing in the browser's address field, as shown in Figure 11.3.

Figure 11.3.
Using the browser's
address field.

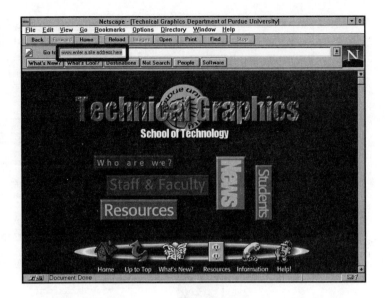

Keep in mind that to enter an address into the browser's address field, you must enter it exactly as you see it. Web addresses are case-sensitive, and browsers don't like extra characters such as backslashes (\), foreslashes (/), or spaces. A site at www.somesite.com is a different site from www.Somesite.com.

As you surf the Web, keep in mind that it is not unusual for a Web site's pages to get shuffled around. If you enter a Web address and get an error—Page not Found— try accessing another part of the site first. For example, if you tried to access a page with http://www.somesite.com/home/page.html and could not access it, try http://www.somesite.com/home/. If that still doesn't work, try http://www.somesite/. Frequently, trying modifications of an address in this fashion will help you find what you are looking for.

Browser Implications

The browser is a relatively small piece of software, but it is quite diverse in the various types of data that it can read. This small piece of software gives you access to a large domain of data. All browsers use the idea of a singular interface that can handle multiple data types, such as pages that combine both text and graphics. The browser also handles various protocols such as WWW, Gopher, and FTP, which is part of the Web's multiprotocol specification.

How does the whole intertwined mass of computing power, the Internet and Web, work? Begin by taking an external look at what happens as you surf the Internet.

When you access any site, the browser requests information from the remote site, downloads the data, and then arranges and displays that data in the work area of the browser, as shown in Figure 11.4. To better understand how the browser is used to surf through pages, look at a graphical representation of a simple Web site.

Figure 11.4.
The work area of the browser.

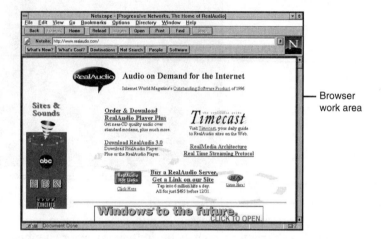

Browser work area

Figure 11.5 shows the contents of the Web site `mysite.com`. Notice the main page of the site, labeled A. This is where you want the audience to start when they visit the site. This page is typically called the home page, or splash page. A home, or splash, page is the main, or first, page that is loaded from a site. Most developers usually list a table of contents for the site on this page. This can be done either through a bulleted list or a graphic that denotes the various areas of information found at the site. Clicking the text or graphics takes you to the information for that area.

As you look at Figure 11.5, keep in mind that the site shown here is quite small. Many corporate sites can grow to contain more than a thousand pages with a complex and intertwined series of links between them, not to mention all the graphics and elements associated with the pages. For example, Adobe's Web site has more than 10,000 pages.

The second thing you might have noticed about Figure 11.5 is the relationship of the pages to one another. The lines drawn from page to page show the hyperlinks or hotlinks from one page to the next. A link, hotlink, or hyperlink is an area on a Web page that, when clicked, takes you to another site or page. This is how you navigate through the information at the site. It is also what makes the Web different from other services available on the Internet.

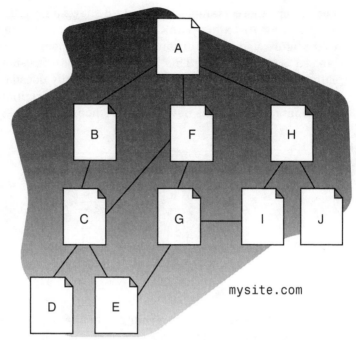

mysite.com

The lines connecting the pages in Figure 11.5 show the hyperlinks within the site. These links are called intrasite links—the internal links within the site. An intrasite link is a hotlink that is referenced to other pages within the current Web site or on the current Web server. Clicking the intrasite hyperlink takes you from one page to another in the site. In the graphic, you see that from page F, you can jump to page C or page G. However, this graphic not only shows you what links are, but it also shows what is meant by non-linear and non-sequential information. Throughout the site, you have a choice of what you view and where you go.

Note that even though the example from Figure 11.5 is relatively simple, it shows the basic concepts of site development. In the figure, note that the main links from the home page (page A) lead to the subordinate pages. These subordinate pages are generally grouped in a logical arrangement. If this were a corporate Web site, page B might be Products, F might be History, and H might be Customer Services. Web sites are usually set up so that the deeper you go into a Web site's pages, the more specific the information. Also, subordinate pages are usually related in some way. In Figure 11.5, all the pages that you can get to from page B (C, D, and E) probably relate to the same type of information—Products.

Look at one more example. Figure 11.6 shows a graphical representation of an external link. An external link is a hotlink that jumps to a page at a different site. In the figure, you see the original site plus another site somewhere in cyberspace, labeled `anothersite.com`. This site could actually reside anywhere geographically—across town or across the world. It really doesn't matter as long as it is properly connected to the Internet. Note that the original site added an external link from page H to this new Web site's home page.

Figure 11.6.

A graphical representation of two Web sites.

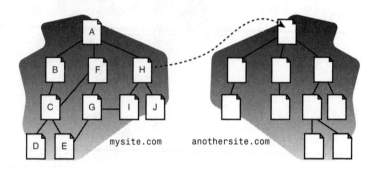

It is better to create links from your site to another site's home page rather than some page deeper in the site's structure. The names of pages inside a site's structure often change; creating a link directly to them might not work after a period of time. However, it is likely that the site's home page will not change (in name). This is more a matter of netiquette and logic than anything else.

In Figure 11.5, you saw that an intrasite link jumps within a single site. Figure 11.6 added an external link to another site. Clicking the external link jumps to the new site's home page (`anothersite.com`).

You have a very simplistic view of the Web in the previous examples. The Web itself is composed of thousands of Web servers that can each contain several different Web sites, several thousand pages, and millions of intrasite and external links.

How the Browser Functions

In the previous section, you saw how the Web is set up. What do you actually see in the browser as you surf? How are links to remote sites represented? A page that is loaded into a browser can contain several items that can be used to navigate the particular site. Aside from content, navigation is a key issue in a hypermedia environment. Most sites are designed so that you can delve deeper into an information thread by clicking blue, text-based links, as shown in Figure 11.7. These links texturally represent another site or page, and clicking the link takes you to that site or page.

Figure 11.7.
Clicking a hypertext link takes you to another site or page.

In addition to text-based links, you can use graphics as links. Often, graphics are used for buttons, button bars, and icons to help you navigate through the site, as shown in Figure 11.8.

Figure 11.8.
Graphics can be used to represent links.

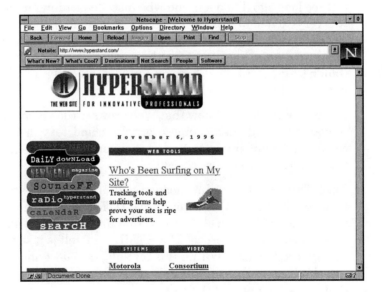

Although what you see in the browser's work area is the display of pages, the browser itself is very busy behind the scenes downloading and storing information to your hard drive as you surf the Web. In any browser are specific settings that you adjust to change the way your browser behaves. In the next couple of sections, you'll take a look at the various parts of the browser and how they affect the pages you view from the Web.

Preferences

As you use your browser, you might want to adjust several specific preferences or settings. In most instances, you'll want to establish the news and e-mail preferences as well as information such as proxy servers.

In addition to these services, you might want to set your browser so that it does not automatically load inline images. If you turn this option off, the browser substitutes a small icon for graphics, instead of taking the time to download and display them. Usually, when I am at home with a 14.4Kbps modem, I turn off inline images so that pages download more quickly. In my office at the university, where our network is directly connected to the Internet, I leave inline images turned on. Depending upon how you connect to the Web, changing this preference can decrease your surfing time when you are looking for something specific or when you're in a hurry.

The Cache

Not too long ago, I had a friend who installed a browser on his computer, and he was very excited to surf the Web and see what all the talk was about. He was very satisfied with his Web connection and the vast array of information at his fingertips. Soon, he noticed that he was running out of hard drive space, and he couldn't figure out why. Knowing he had recently installed a browser was an indicator of the problem.

You probably already know that Web browsers download the HTML code from a remote site, and then compose graphics and text in real time on the client computer. To understand what was happening to my friend's computer, examine this activity a little more closely.

The HTML code that is downloaded contains tags, or descriptions of what should be shown in the browser's work area. HTML is really nothing more than a text-based code description of the items that are on the page and how those items are to be laid out on the screen. The HTML file itself is just a simple text file and is usually pretty small. Within this text file, tags describe the browser text that is to be laid out on the page. The file might also include references to graphic files that are to be a part of the page.

When you access a Web page, the browser first downloads the HTML code to the local hard drive to see what needs to be done. The file is stored in a special location called the *cache* (pronounced "cash"). The browser cache is a special location, usually a folder or directory, on the user's hard drive where HTML files, graphics, and resource files are stored during the browser work session.

After downloading the HTML file, the browser downloads and saves the graphics that are needed for the Web page. These graphics are also stored in the cache. Each time you access a new Web page or site, HTML files and their associated graphic and media files are saved in the cache. Unfortunately, browsers don't automatically empty the files that are in the cache. With my friend's computer, the accumulation of the files in the cache folder was eating up his hard drive.

Although the cache folder does have a tendency to get quite large at times, it does have a good quality. Look at an example to see why the cache is advantageous.

Pick a site that you visit frequently. The first time you visit it, the site's HTML code and graphics are stored in your cache directory. On subsequent visits to the same site, the HTML file is again loaded from the site. However, the graphics are loaded from the cache instead of from the Web site, making the page load more quickly. Without a cache folder, you have to wait for the HTML code and graphics to download each time you visit the site. The cache holds residual data to allow the browser to work faster and decrease wait times. The first place the browser checks for graphics and resource files is the cache. If it does not find the items it needs in the cache, it downloads them from the site.

Undoubtedly, you will want to keep an eye on the number (and size) of the files in your cache directory, as my friend does now. Most browsers allow you to empty the cache within the browser (via the preferences), but I find it much easier to do it from the operating system. The cache folder for most browsers is found in the same location as the browser-executable file. Deleting all the files in the cache will clean it and not cause any problems for the browser.

Note that many of the newer versions of Web browsers do a better job of managing the cache area, often requiring the user to manage the resources.

Plug-Ins

Probably one of the biggest improvements and advancements in the last two years is the addition of plug-ins for Web browsers. Even in the early days of HTML, it was obvious that HTML alone couldn't support the wide variety of features and media elements that visitors wanted to use and distribute on the Web. As a derivative of the Standard Generalized Markup Language (SGML), a precursory coding scheme used for general electronic publishing, HTML is predominantly focused around static Web documents—text and graphics. It does not directly support multimedia element execution in a document; it doesn't know how to view the element.

Prior to plug-ins, users who wanted to distribute video, sound, or other non-traditional Web items had to let the user download it and view it with an external application called a helper application. With the addition of the multimedia integration tags, browsers can now tap into the multimedia resources that were once limited to CD-ROMs using plug-ins. The browser is multimedia-enabled by the plug-in.

You can think of a plug-in as an add-on program that acts as a interpreter for multimedia elements distributed over the Web. The plug-in interprets and executes the sound, video, or program, which allows the user to listen, watch, or interact with the multimedia element right within the browser.

Today, several hundred plug-ins exist for Web browsers. Some of the most widely known plug-ins include Shockwave, RealAudio, QuickTime, Video for Windows, and VRML. Appendix A, "Graphics, Animation, and Multimedia Tools," contains a listing of some of today's most widely used plug-ins. Each plug-in is a separate program that executes when a respective media element is accessed through the browser, such as the RealAudio Player shown in Figure 11.9.

Figure 11.9.
Plug-ins for multimedia elements.

Acquiring and installing plug-ins is pretty easy. Once users download the plug-in, most use a professional setup program to install the files for it. Unfortunately, not all plug-ins support all platforms. If you access a page that requires a plug-in that you do not have, the page will load, but you will not be able to view the multimedia element.

One note about plug-ins is that when you install them, it is a good idea to store them in a common folder. Most browsers include a folder called `Plug-ins` in the directory where the browser executable file is located. This is where you should install your plug-ins.

Scripting

In addition to the various plug-in capabilities, many browsers support custom scripting languages that allow a Web page to contain special functions. Most scripting languages allow a developer to extend the capabilities of the browser by utilizing all the characteristic capabilities of a programming language, such as variables, if-then statements, goto statements, and a wide variety of other characteristics.

Embedded Programs

In 1995, Sun Microsystems introduced a revolutionary new concept to the Web world. Through the use of a new application programming language called Java, small applications (called applets) could be created and embedded into Web pages. Java is an object-oriented programming language used to create executable applications that are commonly distributed over the Internet. When the user accesses the Web page, the application is downloaded and executed. Originally intended as a new programming language for electronic devices such as household consumer devices, Java has turned the possibilities in cyberspace upside-down.

Many people see Java as making a tremendous impact in the software industry, and indeed it has. In addition to small trinkets and nifty animated effects, Java offers the capability to create entire online programs that are only downloaded to your machine as needed (rather than installing them permanently on your computer), a definite paradigm shift. The biggest limitation today is that to view Java programs, you must have a Java-enabled browser. Almost anything can be done with Java's robust capabilities. (See Figure 11.10.)

Figure 11.10.
Java programs via the Web.

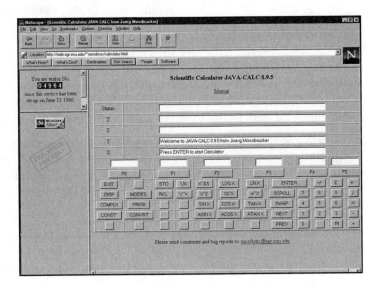

Helper Applications

Last but not least are helper applications. Originally, helper applications were designed to aid Web surfers in viewing almost any digital file that could be passed over the Internet. Today, helper applications are quickly being replaced by internal browser plug-ins.

How does a helper application work? A *helper application* is just that—an external application that helps the browser view almost any type of digital file found on the Internet. From shareware applications to commercial applications such as Microsoft Word, almost any application can be set up as a helper application. When the user commands the browser to download or access a file, the browser checks its list of MIME file types to see what to do. MIME, or Multipurpose Internet Mail Extensions, is a definition scheme that associates a specific file extension with an application.

When the browser checks the MIME file types list, it looks for the three-letter extension of the file in the list. Once it finds the extension, the list tells it what to do with the file. The file types list can tell the browser to save the file or open it with an external application (a helper). For example, TIFF files, a type of bitmap graphic file, cannot be directly opened by some browsers. Most browsers can only open GIF or JPEG images, so a helper application is required to open TIFF images from the Net. In this case, you need to create a MIME setting that tells Netscape to open files with the extension .TIF using another application on your machine—a commercial product such as Microsoft Imager or Adobe Photoshop or a shareware product such as JASC Paint Shop Pro.

In times past, the only way to open a digital video clip such as a QuickTime or Video for Windows file, or a sound clip such as a MIDI file, was through a MIME definition and a helper application. The use of helper applications is basically being replaced with browser plug-ins. It is much nicer to be able to view a media element directly in the browser instead of opening another application.

You might still need to use some helper applications as you surf the Web. MIME definitions are established within the browser and set up just like e-mail and news preferences. This process requires defining a three-letter extension and then telling the browser to use a specific application to open the associated media element.

Assuming it can be downloaded from the Net, any file type can be set up using MIME types, although plug-ins are often the best way to open files that are foreign to the browser. All you need to know is the extension and an application that you want to use to open the file.

Other Internet Resources

Although this book predominantly focuses on media elements for the Web, you must also be aware of many other communication methods and services. Some of these services might not be available to you; it depends upon your service provider or Net hookup. Most services provide access to news, e-mail, and the Web. To use FTP and Telnet, you must simply have the application software and connection to the Internet.

E-Mail

If you send about five letters through the U.S. mail system, you quickly appreciate the cost of e-mail ($0), not to mention speed. E-mail is probably the oldest use of the Internet. Early days of the Internet revolved around e-mail. Today, e-mail is as common as snail mail (regular U.S. post office mail). Electronic mail, or *e-mail*, is the capability to send electronic messages and attached files to remote users via the Internet.

Sending e-mail using your browser is quite easy, but you must have a valid e-mail account. Most browsers allow you to receive and send e-mail right from the browser, as shown in Figure 11.11. E-mail is a vital communication medium due to cost and speed.

Figure 11.11.
Using Mail in Netscape Navigator.

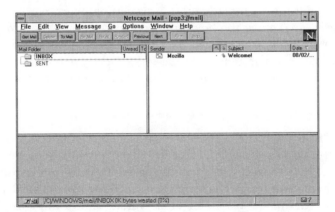

News

Do you ever wish you could talk to people about a specific computer software problem? Using newsgroups allows you to do just that. A newsgroup is an electronic message board where you can post messages, read messages, and exchange files.

Today, there are approximately 10,000 newsgroups concerning subjects from computer vendors to fans of the Goo Goo Dolls. Anything you want to talk about or read about can be found in the Internet's newsgroups. (See Figure 11.12.)

Figure 11.12.
Using News within the browser.

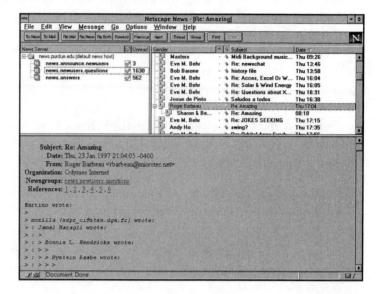

In addition to e-mail, most browsers support newsgroups right within the browser. To use the newsgroups, you must tell the browser where your news server is located. Browsers that support news allow you to establish this information through the preferences. Once you tell the browser where to find the news server, you can choose which newsgroups you want to subscribe to.

FTP

FTP, or File Transfer Protocol, is a set of standards for the transmission of files across the Internet. FTP was one of the first methods for distributing information over the Internet. The whole purpose of the Internet is to distribute files and data to remote users. FTP is a program that allows you to send files (upload) or retrieve files (download) from an FTP server, as shown in Figure 11.13.

Most FTP servers are private, secure servers, meaning that you must have an account—a login and a password—to gain access to the server. Depending on your account setup, you might only be able to read files or you might have full read-write access. You need to talk to the system administrator of the FTP site to gain access, if it is a private FTP server. For most public servers, where you can download shareware and freeware programs, you can use anonymous for the login and guest for the password. This scheme often provides read-only access, allowing you to download but not upload.

Figure 11.13.
Using File Transfer Protocol (FTP).

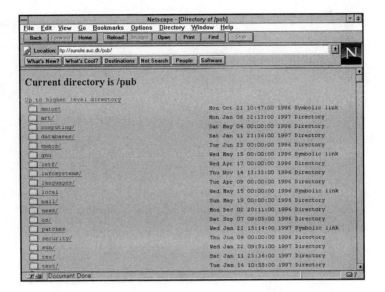

Most browsers can access FTP sites, assuming you have a login and password. To access an FTP site, you simply need the address of the site. Remember that Web communication was designed to support multiple protocols, and FTP is one of them. An FTP address is entered into the browser's address field in the form of ftp.somesite.com. Notice that the www is replaced by ftp, denoting an FTP server.

Gopher

Gopher was an early, pre-Mosaic Internet tool. Before using the graphics and text-based browsers you enjoy today, many people wanted an easier way to search for information on the Internet. Seeing the need, a group of students and professors from the University of Minnesota created a menu-based Internet browsing tool called Gopher, shown in Figure 11.14. Gopher is a menu- and text-based Internet browsing program that can be used to download files and information from remote computers.

When Gopher was created and conceived, it was a striking innovation, but today, Gopher servers are becoming less common. Most Web browsers support Gopher menus. Much like an FTP address, a Gopher address exchanges the www of a regular Web address with gopher. A sample Gopher address looks like gopher.somesite.com.

Figure 11.14.
Using Gopher.

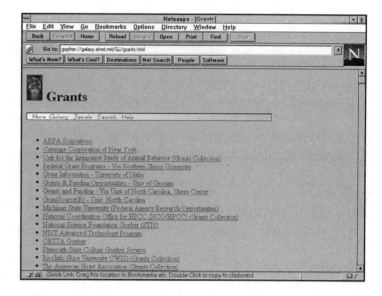

Telnet

Another Internet service is Telnet. Telnet is an application that allows you to connect to and use a remote computer and its applications. Using a Telnet program allows you to connect and use a remote computer as if you were actually sitting at its terminal. At Purdue, we use Telnet to link to an online referencing system for our libraries. Using Telnet, I can link to a remote computer some four or five hundred yards from my office and use it as if I were right there. (See Figure 11.15.)

Figure 11.15.
Using Telnet to connect to a remote computer.

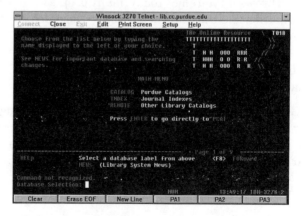

The biggest problem with Telnet is that each remote computer behaves a little differently. Some computers might use UNIX or some other operating system, and the applications running on the remote system can be different as well. Telnet applications must be set up to run a specific way for each machine that you connect to. In addition, the appearance of the Telnet application's interface changes depending on the machine to which you connect.

Summary

In this chapter, you took a look at the fundamentals of multimedia and hypermedia. Concerning development, you read that there are three primary knowledge bases involved in the development process: education and communication, visual science, and computer science. You also read about the most fundamental element in Web delivery, the browser. You read how the browser functions both in what displays onscreen and in what happens behind the scenes. Concluding this chapter was a description of some of the other services that can be used in delivering materials over the Web. Keep in mind that the World Wide Web was designed to be a multiprotocol environment and will support these other services such as FTP, news, and Gopher. Many people frequently use these services to deliver information.

12

Interface Design and Metaphors

Undoubtedly as you surf the Web, you see good sites and poor sites. Unfortunately, the poor sites generally outnumber the good sites. In most instances, the poor sites are weak in one of three areas: content, graphics, or navigation. In previous chapters, you read about the balance between content and graphics. Poor content cannot be dressed up and poor graphics are aesthetically numbing, making communication occur more slowly.

The third typical weakness, navigation, is one that occurs as frequently as poor content or graphics. A site that is difficult to navigate is usually due to a lack of planning or logical flow within the site. The screen is littered with text and graphics elements that make it difficult to tell where you can go in the site. Sometimes difficulty in navigation can come from overuse of text, as shown in Figure 12.1.

Figure 12.1.
Overuse of text-based
navigation can make a
site hard to navigate.

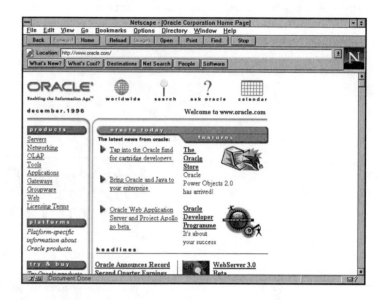

Indeed, being able to choose where you want to go is important, so there must be some way of determining how to navigate a site's pages. Often the arrangement of pages and cluttered screen elements makes it difficult to determine how to navigate a site.

Many of the design elements that surround a Web page are contingent upon the content and the audience for which the content is intended. An artistic page might have little relevance to an audience of a professional nature. Pages often integrate animated elements, graphics, or sounds that have little to do with the content provided on the page. For your message to be accurately communicated and interpreted by your audience, you must have consistency among the elements on your pages as well as the elements that appear across your various pages.

In this chapter, you will read about interface design. Interface design is in itself a complex area of study. Much research has been conducted to determine the effective qualities of good interfaces. In this chapter, you will read about those qualities and how to implement good human-computer interface design principles within your pages. You will also take a look at many examples of good interface designs on the Web.

Interface Development

The method of interacting with any device, whether it is a cellular phone or a Web page, occurs through an interface. An interface is the point of interaction between the user and the device. With the cellular phone, the interface usually includes the buttons representing numbers as well as other buttons for functions such as memory recall and clear. In addition, the cellular phone might have an LCD panel that displays the numbers or functions you enter. The interface on a cellular phone is called a physical interface because you physically interact with it.

When you deal with tangible devices that must be manufactured, the arrangement and placement of items on the interface are limited by the confines of manufacturing. Certain designs and arrangements cannot be manufactured either due to feasibility or cost issues. With multimedia and hypermedia interfaces, manufacturability is not an issue, so there are really no limits due to manufacturability. The only limitations you have are the amount of screen area and the bandwidth limitations of the Web.

On the Web, you can design interfaces in any fashion. Buttons, graphics, and other elements can be anywhere you want them. You'll notice that the good pages you have seen follow some principles to make the interface easier to use and more aesthetically pleasing.

With information devices, such as interactive CD-ROMs or the Web, you must keep in mind the basic premise for which the device was created. The individuals who use your information device probably won't focus on your buttons, your great artistic talent, or other related visual design issues, although all these things contribute to what visitors do want: your content or information. No matter how good the content or graphics, if the audience cannot get to your content or if it is blocked by noise (see Chapter 1, "Graphic Design"), those features do little good. Providing access is how the interface, the means by which your audience interacts with your information, is vitally important. The effectiveness of your interface design determines the speed with which your audience becomes familiar with navigating your environment as well as how comfortable they are using your environment.

In interface design, you need to be concerned with many things:

- Consistency—The elements displayed on your various pages must help the user become comfortable with the look and the feel of the information device.

- Efficiency—The content, design, and navigation elements should assist the user in efficiently finding the information for which they came looking.

- Control—The user must remain in constant control of the information device.

- Clarity—The interface elements themselves, such as buttons and other metaphorical devices, should be clear to the intended audience.

- Practicality—The site's page elements should be designed with the limitations of color depth, browsers, and bandwidth in mind.
- Visual appeal—The pages and site should provide more than a hypertext-based environment. Pages with high amounts of content in text form and few, if any, graphics require more time for the visitor to assimilate the information.

Web Page Elements

Chapter 1 presented the communication model around which the entire Web development and delivery process focuses. Every interface element you create on your pages should contribute to communication, design, or navigation. Just pasting elements on a page for no reason at all distracts and confuses your users.

Three types of elements appear on any Web page: content elements, design elements, and navigation elements. Figure 12.2 shows a page that exhibits all three types of elements.

Figure 12.2.
All page elements are for content, design, or navigation.

The first type of elements you'll find in any Web page are those that present or enhance the content. In Figure 12.2, the inline graphics and the text following are designed to present the user with information. The way the elements are arranged, as well as the thin line between the two columns of information, is focused toward design. Notice the bar to the left of the screen; this is the navigation tool that is used to navigate the site. If you check out this site, you'll see that this bar appears throughout the site, always allowing the audience to easily navigate it.

Take a look at another Web page to distinguish between content, design, and navigation elements. In Figure 12.3, can you identify which elements are content, design, and navigation related?

Figure 12.3.
Determine whether items in the page are content, design, or navigation related.

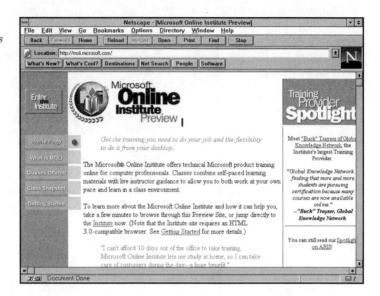

In Figure 12.3, notice that the center text as well as the logo at the top are content related—giving information about the institute. The design elements include the bar on the left of the screen as well as the Training Provider Spotlight bar. What you really want to notice are the buttons that appear over the bar on the left of the screen. These are navigation items. Through the entire site, the pages include the same buttons in the same place on each page. Notice that the navigation items are easy to find and well placed on the page. This is the first issue of interface design—designing for consistency.

Designing for Consistency

If you visit the sites shown in the previous figures, you'll see that all the pages are designed with the same look and feel. Remember that one of the things you can do to build consistency in your Web pages is to use consistent design elements from page to page. (See Chapter 1.) Even more important than including design elements, you should strive to present your navigation elements in the same place with the same look on every page.

A common practice for providing navigation items is to use bars of buttons to represent links. Presenting your navigation items along one side of a page, usually the left side, makes it much easier for your audience to navigate your site.

One alternative to using graphic buttons for links is to use an HTML list to present the pages of your site. As shown in Figure 12.4, you can use any number of list items to represent pages or areas of your site. However, as you'll see in the figure, using too many text items can make the list hard to read.

Figure 12.4.
Using HTML lists to
represent portions of
links within your site.

One of the most common practices on the Web is to use a single inline image as an image map in a page, as shown in Figure 12.5. With an image map, you can define regions for the image that are linked to a specific location in your site or to an external site.

The biggest problem with using image maps is the size of the graphic file. Because an image map generally covers the entire screen, the bitmap file can become quite large, making modem users wait for the image to download. Be cautious of using a single bitmap image as your interface. If you do use them, make sure the size is less than 400 by 300 pixels, as shown in Figure 12.6. This size should keep the file under 100KB, which allows modem users to view the file in about one minute.

A final alternative for creating navigation items is to use frames to divide your screen. Often developers who use frames designate a certain portion of the screen for a menu, as shown in Figure 12.7. When the user clicks an item in the menu, other frames in the document are updated with content. Although frames are a nice feature, realize that they are a browser convention. Certain browsers cannot display frames documents. In addition, there has been discussion that frames will no longer be supported in the next versions of some browsers. Keep this in mind if you decide to use frames to divide your pages.

Figure 12.5.
Using image maps to represent your site's links.

Figure 12.6.
Using smaller image maps makes it more efficient for modem users to download.

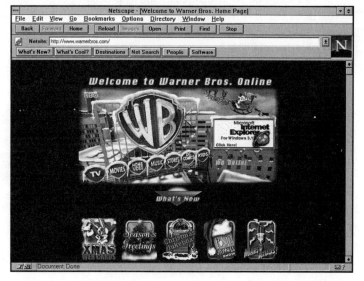

Figure 12.7.
*Using frames to create a
menu structure.*

Of all the ways to present your navigation items, probably the most frequently
used method is the button bar shown in Figure 12.8. The button bar is usually a
small rendition of an image map that appears to have several buttons within it.
As you can see in the figure, the top of the page has a horizontal bar, which
includes small buttons that can be used to navigate the site. A bar designed this
way takes some time to download. Note that this bar would load quicker and
require less HTML programming if each button were separated into a single
inline image, rather than inserted as an image map.

Figure 12.8.
*Using horizontal button
bars for navigation
items.*

The Special Case: The Home Page

In general, you find that developers of sites strive to make every page look the same in design and navigability. The best sites use a consistent look and feel to help the user become comfortable with the site. This lets the user go directly to the information without being hindered by the rest of the environment. On one page in particular, most developers break this rule of thumb: the home, or splash, page.

The home, or splash, page is the first page of a site. Of all your pages, the splash page is vitally important because it sets the tone and the first impression of your site and pages. What you really want to do is capture the essence of your site in that first page. Often, this is achieved with rich graphics and slick designs, as shown in Figure 12.9.

Figure 12.9.
The home page, or first page of your site, should capture your audience's attention.

Much of what you put on your splash page depends on your audience and your site's purpose. As you read in Chapter 10, "Interactive Multimedia Design Process," it is important that you look at these two variables to determine the purpose and your intended audience. Once you examine these goals, you'll know what is applicable for your splash page.

As you develop your splash page, keep in mind the amount of money and effort that goes into advertising every year. Companies spend a lot of money to examine their audience and determine how best to attract them. Your splash page should have this same purpose: attract your audience and make them want to delve into your information. A key is knowing who your audience is.

One of the things that the splash page should do is introduce your site. Often the splash page is used to show an overview of the site's structure, as shown in Figure 12.10. This structure gives the users a quick opportunity to go directly to where they want to go. Once they get past your home page, then you should use consistent navigation and design elements throughout the rest of your site. Your splash page may have an entirely different look from that of the rest of your pages. That's okay as long as all the other pages use the same design and navigation element look and placement.

Figure 12.10.
Placing a site overview on your home page using graphic elements.

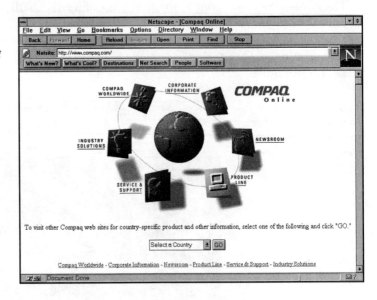

For an alternative to home pages that are distinct from the rest of your pages, you can also create a nice home page that is not necessarily distinct from your other pages, as shown in Figure 12.11.

You can use many different types of elements to represent your site through a home page. Most often, you want to ensure that you have at least an overview of your site so that the user can easily find his or her way around. In addition to an overview of your site's content on your home page, you may also want to include the following features:

- A logo or other company or individual representation quickly identifies a page as belonging to a particular site. Sometimes, links lead users outside your site. The absence of the logo signals that the user has left your pages. In addition, as any marketing person knows, the more a user sees your logo, the better. Web pages give you an ideal opportunity to use this marketing tactic.

Figure 12.11.
*The first page of the site
doesn't have to be a home
page by the strictest of
definitions.*

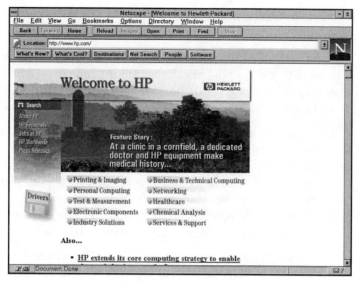

- An address and phone number are a nice addition to a Web page, particularly if you are a vendor or company. Frequently, people visit the site of software manufacturers to get the latest updates and other information. If your consumer base uses the Web, definitely put your phone number and address on the page.

- If you have an e-mail address, make sure you add an anchor within your pages so that people can easily use browser mail programs to send you e-mail. It is frustrating for your users to have to write down your e-mail address and then start their e-mail programs. By putting an e-mail link on your page, they can click it, enter body text, and send it.

- Because there are still many users on the Web with non-graphics browsers (in other words, they can't see your graphics), make sure you put a link on your pages that lets them access graphics-free pages.

- Try to design your home page so that the user does not have to scroll. The nicest home pages are ones in which the developer fits the entire contents onto a single screen.

- You might also want to include a small text line at the bottom of your pages (similar to a footer) that specifies the name and path of the page in your site. This helps users who print out pages identify the page location.

Designing for Efficiency

One of the biggest negative aspects of the Web is the number of poorly designed documents. If traditional written documents followed the pattern of many of these Web documents, communication would be severely limited if it occurred at all.

As with the desktop publishing revolution, people are quickly finding that there is more to Web publishing than cranking code in an ASCII editor or using a page generation program. Efficient Web communication requires that documents be designed in such a way that users can readily access them.

Being able to efficiently extract information from a site has a lot to do with the logical structure of documents. The threads, which are paths through the links of information, must contain some logic to their arrangement. For example, at a corporate site with a products section, you expect to find all the company's products listed under that section. You don't expect to find product X located in the About the Company section. In any Web site, the content and the pages must be arranged in some logical order; it must be linear.

Even though structure exists, you should be certain that there are intrasite links to and from various portions of your site. Figure 12.12 shows a site in which there are no links between the subordinate pages of the site. Because there are no subordinate links, the user must back up through a thread to get to another thread. This lack of links is as detrimental as an illogical structure. To make your site efficient to navigate, you must include a logical Web of links between corresponding pages in your site. Without these links, the pages are nothing more than a digital book. The biggest negative aspect of the Web is the number of poorly designed Web sites.

Figure 12.12.
You must design logical links between corre-sponding pages in your site so that users can efficiently navigate your site.

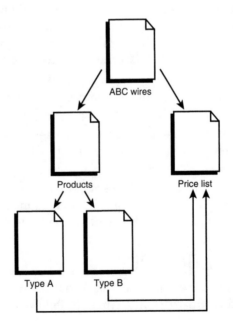

Designing for Control

When the biggest negative aspects of the Web are the number of poorly designed sites or any poorly organized information tools with which users are unfamiliar, the tendency is to be apprehensive and uncomfortable.

More than likely, you have installed software at one time or another. You have probably experienced an installation that goes belly-up and causes the machine to lock up. What was your first reaction to this event? You might have felt uneasy and disoriented and mumbled some expletives. Eventually, you probably had to give the machine a three-finger salute (Ctrl+Alt+Del) or physically turn off the machine. Regardless of your course of action, losing control of the computer environment made you disoriented, uneasy, and more than likely, frustrated.

The same feelings of apprehension occur when the user is not in control of the information being delivered to his computer from the Web. Clicking a button that starts some sporadic special effect or takes them to some unknown site is not something that makes your user comfortable. Waiting seemingly endless periods of time for a graphic or animation to download quite frequently causes feelings of frustration or distaste for the Web.

When you design interfaces, you must strive to let the user have control of the information tool, the browser, at all times. If the user clicks a button, it should do exactly what the user expects. If the button looks like it should lead somewhere, it should. If an item looks like a link, it should be. You must view your user interface, as well as the overall organization of your pages, from the eyes of the user to ascertain whether the design, arrangement, and organization of your interface will make sense to them. If you create items that steal control from the user, your audience probably won't come back.

Designing for Clarity

Have you ever tried to use a telephone where the buttons were too small? Your big, bulky fingers (or long fingernails) are too big for the interface. You probably hit the wrong buttons or too many buttons at one time.

Cluttered Web interfaces or interfaces in which you can't tell what is a link can also be detrimental to a Web site. This idea relates to navigation elements on a Web page. As you saw in Chapter 3, "Typography," text that is too small or the wrong font for the job can make reading passages of text difficult. Similarly, navigation items that are too small, cluttered, or illogical will confuse, frustrate, and repel your audience.

When you design interfaces, you not only want to place your navigation items in a consistent place, but you also want them to be apparent. A page where the user must guess what's a link will distract his attention from the content. You must place navigation items clearly on your pages.

Figure 12.13 shows an example of clear placement of interactive elements. Note that the buttons clearly mark where you can go and it is easy to tell where the link takes you. This page is in color on the Web, which makes the distinction even more clear.

Figure 12.13.
Buttons and interactive elements in a Web page should be clear and noticeable.

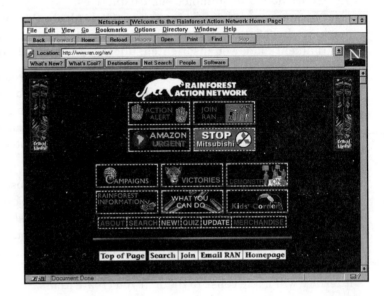

You should also be careful about the abstractions you make on a Web page. Often, designers create a Web page that is truly a work of art, but the page is so abstracted that it is difficult to tell where you are or where you can go. Notice in the figure that the overall look of the page is very artistic, but a closer look reveals that it is difficult to tell where you can go and how you get there.

When you create interfaces and interactive items, be careful of the icons and abstractions you use in your pages. The text, buttons, and other graphics you use should clearly identify what the elements do. When you use graphics and icons to represent pages or threads in your site, also provide a list underneath those graphics so they can be identified, as shown in Figure 12.15.

If you use inline images as shown in Figure 12.14, you can easily insert the text within the graphic. What if the text looks inappropriate? An alternative method to Figure 12.14 is to insert the text links using HTML code. Figure 12.15 shows an image map where the elements of the graphic are represented beneath the image map as hypertext.

Figure 12.14.
Using text beneath icons and abstractions can make navigation easier.

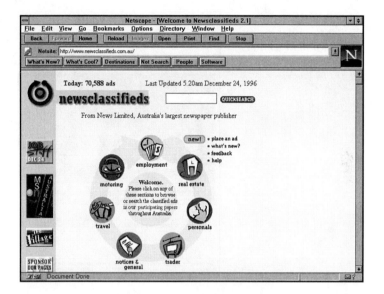

Figure 12.15.
An alternative method of including descriptive text.

Designing for Practicality

As you saw earlier, many home pages use image maps. Image maps can be large graphic images that seem to take forever to download. The image map in Figure 12.16 takes almost a minute to download over a 28.8Kbps modem.

Figure 12.16.
An image map this size requires almost a minute to download over a 28.8Kbps modem.

In the last chapter, you read how the browser accesses pages and downloads all the elements to the user machine prior to displaying them in the browser's work area. Understand that each graphic, animation, and multimedia element requires time to download. For example, a page that contains five images that are each 50KB, plus a small animated logo that is about 30KB, requires close to three minutes to download over a 28.8Kbps modem.

When you design Web pages, you must keep in mind that most of the people connected to the Web use a modem. With a 28.8Kbps modem, it takes approximately one minute to download 100KB of information, which is approximately 2.5KB per second. The greater the number of elements on your page, the longer your audience must wait. You must design your interfaces with as few elements as possible. The best case scenario is to have the interface elements weigh in at less than 20KB. That leaves ample room for the rest of your content elements on each page.

Designing for Visual Appeal

The last concern in developing Web interfaces is the issue of visual appeal. Again, visual appeal is often a subjective evaluation. What looks good to you might not look good to someone else. However, there is a general level at which most people agree that the graphics, design, and the overall interface are visually appealing. Figure 12.17 shows an example of a page that most people agree is visually appealing.

Figure 12.17.
A Web page that most people agree is visually appealing.

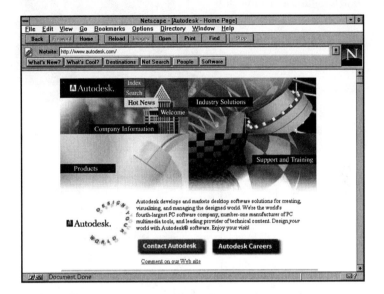

When you design Web pages, you want to strive for graphic elements and an interface design that appeal to your audience but also complement your content. Much of the audience's opinion is based upon what they expect to see. If they expect to see a lot of graphics and see very little, they'll probably be less than impressed. If your audience expects to see a lot of text-based information and a few graphics, give them what they want!

Everything you do hinges upon the audience. Audience analysis is critical when you begin actual work on the pages at your site. If you don't know who your audience is, how can you tailor the information to them?

Examples of Good Interface Design

As you look at Web pages, you find that certain pages appeal to your tastes due to the various elements on the page. In this final section, take a look at the pages presented and notice the things that are highlighted as positives and negatives. Basically, I provide commentary on what I believe to be the strengths and weaknesses of each page:

- At first glance, Figure 12.18 looks rather blasé. Not a lot of graphics are used, but the text is formatted quite nicely. The column to the left makes navigation easy, and all the pages follow a consistent format. Although it could use some content graphics, I'd give this one a thumbs up.

Figure 12.18.
More graphics are needed, but the presentation is clean and the site is consistent—thumbs up!

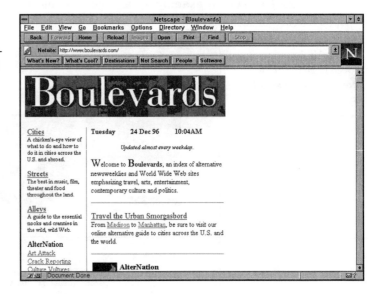

• Figure 12.19 shows a Web page that has a typical problem, information overload. When you first look at this page, it takes a while to understand where to start. Presenting too much information on a page cognitively overloads your audience.

Figure 12.19.
Overall, this site has too many hotlinks, which makes the content and information seem disorganized.

- Figure 12.20 shows a site that connotes the subject of the content very well in the look of the page. Notice the use of the framed menu. The entire site uses the dark theme to replicate the tone of the movie. (If you saw the movie, you know what I mean.) In any case, I found some very interesting things at this site.

Figure 12.20.

Using the graphics and dark background helps to set the tone at this site representative of the movie.

- Figure 12.21 shows another site that overloads the user. The number of list items to the right of the screen is somewhat difficult to read. In addition, the table in the left portion of the screen needs spacing around the graphic. Overall, the screen looks cluttered and hard to read.

- Figure 12.22 shows a better magazine home page. The options are a little easier to read and the elements have more space, which makes them more visually appealing. If you view this on the Web, you'll see that it also highlights the Christmas season by using the traditional green and red colors.

- Navigating the site shown in Figure 12.23 was pretty easy. The bulleted items along the right side of the screen make it easy to tell what's at the site. In addition, the quick text descriptions give you an idea of what you see by clicking the links.

Figure 12.21.
Cramming every nook and cranny with a visual element overloads the user.

Figure 12.22.
Spreading out the text links and adding more space between the various elements make this page easier to read.

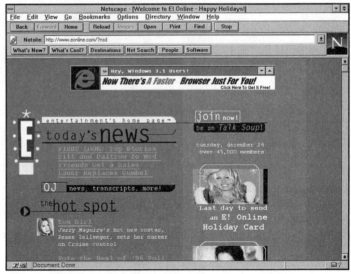

- The interface for the page shown in Figure 12.24 allows you to access a lot of varying degrees of information, but the screen is not cluttered. This page has 16 different hotlinks, but the way it was designed doesn't cause information overload.

Figure 12.23.
*Using graphically
bulleted items makes
navigating a site, as well
as seeing what is there,
much easier.*

Figure 12.24.
*Even with all the links,
this page design is not
cluttered.*

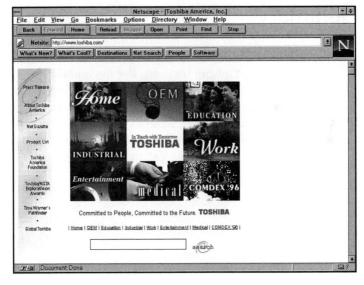

- The page in Figure 12.25 was probably the biggest disappointment of all
  the ones I list. Leading a page with a lot of text is very unappealing.
  However, the graphic at the bottom of the page is quite nice. Be careful
  of using mainly text to introduce your site or pages. You will find that
  using graphics is much more effective.

Figure 12.25.
*A lot of text and white
space make this page less
appealing.*

Summary

In this chapter, you took a look at many of the concerns about designing pages.
Keep in mind that navigating your site should be easy. It is your content that the
audience wants. You can increase the navigability of your site by concentrating
on the main points of concern: consistency, efficiency, control, clarity, practicality, and visual appeal. Throughout this book, you will find many examples of good
Web pages. Take a look at some of the figures in other chapters. What makes
certain pages more effective than others? You will probably find that it concerns
the layout of the page, graphics, and how quickly you can navigate the site.

13

Sound

One of the most important elements in multimedia or hypermedia is sound. Many presentations, both on and independent of the Web, utilize text, graphics, and animation, but few utilize sound to its fullest potential. As you review multimedia CDs, sound is an important part of the sensory experience of multimedia. If you strip a product of its aural attributes, something is noticeably missing.

For example, have you ever watched a movie in which there was no music at all? Most people outside the film industry probably haven't had the opportunity to view raw video clips from a scene of a movie. If you could view them, you would find it considerably less stimulating than the final composite movie. Music added to any media draws both sides of the brain into the occurrence and gives a true multisensory experience.

Music in movies, interactive CD-ROMs, and even Web pages can be used to set the tone, indicate an action, and even aid in remembering bits and pieces of information. Have you ever noticed that the suspenseful parts of a movie stir emotions in the viewer, a lot of which is due to the music? Have you noticed that when you click a graphic button in an interactive CD-ROM, you hear a sound that acknowledges an action took place? You can use music in many ways to set the tone or give feedback to a user.

In addition to these natural uses of music, did you know that music enables humans to remember certain things much easier? For example, how many songs on the radio can you sing? How many advertisement jingles can you remember when you hear the melody or music of the particular jingle?

Music enriches our lives in many ways and can be a useful addition to a seemingly non-aural Web. Currently, not that many Web sites actively use music within the browser. The RealAudio plug-in only recently appeared for Web browsers, and audio is something relatively new on the Web.

Digital audio has been around for quite some time. For many years, recording studios have used digital audio to dub soundtracks through the use of Digital Audio Tapes (DAT) and audio CDs. It is only recently that Web audio was even possible at all.

I purposefully saved the content of these next three chapters for the end of this book. You will find that the use of audio, video, and virtual reality technology is very young in relationship to the Web. Nonetheless, I can guarantee that the use of these technologies will continue to become more widespread over the coming years.

The biggest limitation with today's Web is bandwidth. As you saw in Chapter 5, "Raster-Based Graphics," as well as several other chapters, many of the features you want to use and integrate on the Web are only limited by bandwidth.

Understand that the Web itself is very fast (measured in gigabytes per second). It is the end-user connection that lacks speed. If every user were directly connected to the Internet using a network card and true network connection, bandwidth would not be such an issue. In a direct network connection, users generally can download 100KB of information in about a second or less.

The vast majority of Web surfers connect to the Internet via dial-up access and dial-up connections. With these connections, 100KB of data requires approximately one minute of download time, assuming a 28.8Kbps modem and a server that is not too busy. It is the dial-up users that you must design around. It is their connection that is the lowest common denominator in Web delivery, not the Internet itself. Until the average user can afford and gain access to a high speed connection, developers must deliver content that is feasible (assuming end users are the target audience).

Such are the concerns of Web audio. As with raster graphics, sound files can also be quite large. Audio files are often three times the size of raster graphic files. Because of the amount of data that is required to produce a clean and crisp audio clip, audio files are large digital files. However, you can do many things to an audio file to make it more feasible for distribution on the Web, and in this chapter, you will read about digital audio in general as well as its specific application to the Web. As with graphics, you will find that there are two predominant ways of using sound over the Web.

Understanding the Two Types of Digital Audio

In Chapter 5, you read about the differences between digital and analog data. As with graphics, audio also deals with the conversion of analog sources to digital representations. As you discovered, digital data doesn't mean much to humans. However, when data is presented as waveform (analog) data, our human senses are able to perceive the data.

On the computer, developers basically have two options at their disposal for representing and distributing audio. Much like the choice for graphics (vector or raster), audio can also be represented in one of two ways—as digitally recorded audio or as MIDI. You will find many similarities between vector and raster graphics and MIDI and digital audio.

Digital audio is probably the more common type of audio used on the Web. Digital audio is audio that is sampled and recorded to a digital storage medium such as a disk, CD, or DAT tape through ADC conversion. You may want to review Chapter 5 to familiarize yourself with the sampling process and terms such as sampling rate and bit depth.

Creating digital audio a few years ago required a significant investment in hardware and software, but today, most computers have the capability to easily create digital audio. About two years ago, sound cards emerged with a special chip or processor called a Digital Signal Processor (DSP). The DSP was specially designed to deal with the ADC and DAC conversion of audio.

The first computer that was actually able to deal with digital audio was the Macintosh. Soon after, PCs were given the capability by the vast majority of manufacturers, such as Creative Labs and Turtle Beach, who created add-on sound cards. After flipping a few hardware switches, inserting the card, and installing the card software, you were ready to enjoy digital audio from your previously mute PC. At first, installing sound cards was somewhat difficult, due to configuration problems; most operating systems such as DOS and Windows 3.1 didn't deal with sound cards very effectively. Today, a sound card is standard equipment on most new PCs.

Interface cards with a DSP suddenly gave the developer the ability to sample and manipulate digital audio with little effort. Today, almost any computer with a sound card has the capability to create digitized audio, assuming the machine has a sound card, recording software, and an analog source (such as a microphone, stereo, or boom box).

The second type of audio that can be used on the computer (and the Web) is Musical Instrument Digital Interface (MIDI). MIDI was actually developed and used in the early 1980s by musicians and other audio professionals.

With the emergence of synthesizers, drum machines, and other digital devices, MIDI was developed to allow these various devices to communicate with one another. Using MIDI, a sound played on a synthesizer or other device could be recorded and then used on another machine. You'll find that most MIDI files are used to input music in a computer or other device. MIDI is a generic or universal language whereby various digital audio devices can communicate and share data. MIDI is like networking for musical devices such as synthesizers, drum machines, and sequencers.

Most sound card DSPs not only support digitized audio, but most of the modern cards also support MIDI devices. More often than not, you find that MIDI is integrated right into the DSP, which is nice. Prior to today's direct support of MIDI, older sound cards required add-on cards, or daughter cards, for MIDI support.

A daughter card is simply another interface card that connects to the parent sound card already in the computer. The daughter card extends the capabilities of the parent sound card and helps with certain functions (such as MIDI). Daughter cards are also used for advanced video and animation production. Understand that although most sound cards today support MIDI, many musicians who need advanced capabilities still use daughter cards that provide a wealth of advanced audio processing capabilities.

Digital and MIDI: The Fundamental Difference

The fundamental difference between digital audio and MIDI is the way in which the audio is defined and played back. Although any lengthy discussion of these differences requires an understanding of acoustical physics, the basics are relatively simple.

When you create a digital audio file through the process of sampling, each sample taken from an analog source is described digitally. Each and every pitch and volume characteristic in the audio is descriptively written in the file. A digital audio file is a description of multiple points on the sound curve. These points describe the audio that is playing at specific instances in time, as shown in Figure 13.1. Digital audio files are descriptions of the analog waveform.

Figure 13.1.
Digital audio is a digital description of multiple instances (points) of an analog sound wave.

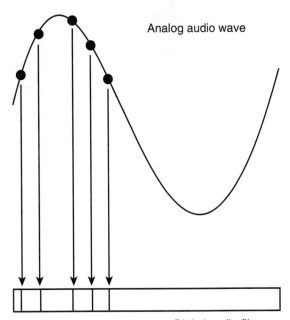

Analog audio wave

Digital audio file

MIDI sound, on the other hand, describes audio much differently. Instead of describing the audio as digitized samples of analog data, at some base level MIDI describes the various notes and instruments that should play at any given time, as shown in Figure 13.2. MIDI files describe a specific instrument, or patch, and the notes it should play over time. The MIDI description can also contain information such as sets of notes that should get louder or softer as well as special effects such as distortion. Each and every instrument in a MIDI sound has information that pertains to it. A MIDI sound file of an orchestra playing Beethoven's Fifth Symphony has detailed information about each and every instrument and how to sequence those instruments.

Figure 13.2.

MIDI describes various instruments and the sounds each instrument plays over time.

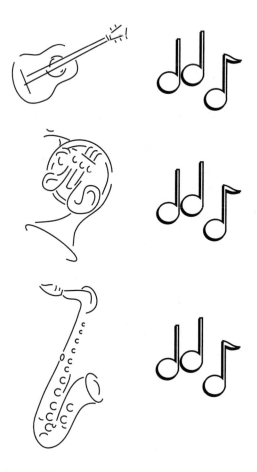

As you'll see in the section "Comparison of Digitized and MIDI Sound," later in this chapter, the differences between digital audio and MIDI are similar to the differences between raster and vector graphics. By the time you finish this chapter, you will understand the significant differences between digital audio and MIDI. Before you read about those differences, take a look at the fundamental differences between digital and analog sound and then the different parameters that are involved with both digital audio and MIDI.

Advantages of a Digital World

The emergence of digital audio is predominantly due to the foresight of companies that saw the tremendous quality differences between analog and digital audio. A frequent problem with analog recordings, such as cassette or video tape, is the degradation that occurs when a recording is dubbed to another medium. This is know as generational degradation.

For example, if you record a live audio presentation to a cassette, the audio probably sounds pretty close to the original live performance. This recording is first generation, so it sounds pretty good. However, if you take that tape recording and dub a copy from it, the copy, or second generation tape, sounds worse that the original. A third generation tape, a copy of the second generation, sounds even worse. An analog copy of an analog source degrades from copy to copy, making the recorded waveforms flatten and consequentially become lower quality, as shown in Figure 13.3.

Figure 13.3.
Analog degradation causes the waveform to flatten due to loss of data.

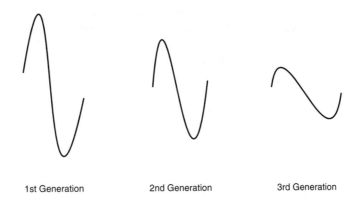

1st Generation   2nd Generation   3rd Generation

The general rule is that any time you dub (copy) an analog source to another analog device of the same quality, the recording loses some quality. This degradation occurs with audio recordings as well as video recordings. Degradation is a physical law that occurs and can only be changed by sampling a higher analog source to a lower analog source.

The lack of degradation is one of the reasons digital recordings are advantageous. Any time an analog recording is made for distribution on cassettes or other media, the best copy that can be made for distribution is a second generation copy. This means that the copy is only half as good as the original live performance.

Digital recordings, on the other hand, do not degrade. Once a digital recording is made, there is no loss of data on subsequent generations of the recording. In essence, once it is digital, copying the recording is like copying any other digital (computer) file. The copy is an exact replica of the original (live) performance.

In addition, digital audio provides one other distinct advantage. Once you create an analog recording and decide that you want to make it better by adding more bass, mids, or highs to the sound, you must make the changes when the original live performance is recorded. You probably have to exaggerate the changes so that you can hear the difference in the second generation copy.

With digital audio, you can perform any number of modifications to the audio once it is digital. You can filter a digital sound file so that the bass, mids, or highs are increased. You can basically manipulate any attribute of the digital representation of the analog waveform.

Due to these two advantages, lack of degradation and the capability to edit a digital track, in the mid-80s many recording companies began using digital devices and audio CDs for recording, editing, and distributing music and other audio clips. With digital devices, degradation was virtually eliminated and editing became a much easier task. With the advent of audio CDs, the highest quality audio possible became a reality. Being able to record 70 minutes of perfectly clear music and audio on a 650MB digital CD revolutionized the music industry and soon revolutionized the computer industry in general.

Digital Audio: Is it Live or...

As you have read, digital audio presents significant advantages over analog sound. Creating digital audio requires that you have three things (see Figure 13.4): a sound card with recording capability (an audio-in or line-in jack), software that allows you to record an analog source, and an analog source such as a microphone, stereo, or boom box. You can digitally sample any device that can play audio and has an audio-out connector.

Figure 13.4.
Things you need to be able to record analog sound.

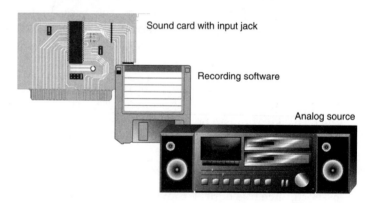

Sound card with input jack

Recording software

Analog source

Before you read about setting up a sound recording environment, you need to look at the three primary variables involved with sound sampling: the sampling rate, bit depth, and mono and stereo sound.

Sampling Rate

As you read in Chapter 5, sampling is the process of converting digital data to analog data. Digital-to-analog conversion is most often a result of hardware, but software is also important.

Sampling an analog source requires converting chunks of analog data to digital representations, as shown in Figure 13.5. The frequency of the chunks is called the sampling rate. The more frequent the chunks, the more representative the digital representation of the analog source.

Figure 13.5.
Sampling requires converting chunks of analog data to digital.

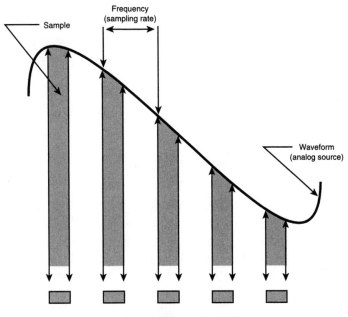

Digitizing audio actually deals with two different frequencies: the frequency at which you convert chunks of data and the frequencies that occur within the analog sound itself. In addition, there is a relationship between the frequencies that occur in the analog source and the frequency with which you take chunks in the digital sampling process. This may sound confusing, but keep in mind that analog audio is composed of frequencies and the digital sampling process also has a frequency called the sampling rate.

The various notes in analog audio are also measured by frequency. Each frequency represents a note or pitch, such as a different note on a piano. Each key on the piano plays a different note, which has a different frequency, as shown in Figure 13.6. The change in frequencies is what your ear detects as different notes.

Figure 13.6.

Each note on the piano represents a different note, which has a frequency (a cycle of a wave form).

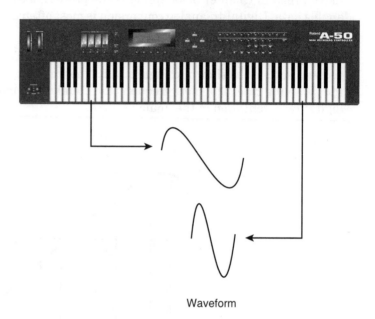

Waveform

Analog frequencies are represented by hertz (Hz) measurements. A hertz is a unit of measurement for the number of cycles per second—how many waveform cycles the sound makes per second, as shown in Figure 13.7. Often frequencies are measured in kilohertz (kHz), which is 1,000 Hertz. For example, a sound measured at 22Hz makes 22 waveform cycles per second, whereas a sound measured at 22kHz makes 22,000 waveform cycles per second! Note that the higher the frequency, the higher the pitch or note that you hear. The lower the frequency, the lower the pitch that you hear.

The highest frequency that the human ear can distinguish is around is 22kHz and the lowest frequency is around 20Hz. Akin to the discussion of visible light in Chapter 2, "Color Theory and Color Models," there are sounds that fall well out of our range of hearing.

For example, elephants are known to emit such low frequencies, well below our limited 20Hz range, that for many years people thought they communicated only by the characteristic "phhhhht" sound they make from their trunks.

Through digital recording, it was discovered that elephants use a very unique and complex language that can only be heard by humans when it is played back at hundreds of times its normal frequency. The waveform cycles so slowly that humans do not perceive it.

Figure 13.7.
*Analog frequency
measurements in hertz
and kilohertz units
represent how many
waveform cycles the
sound makes per second.*

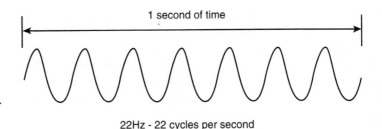

1 second of time

22Hz - 22 cycles per second

22kHz - 22,000 cycles per second

Another example of imperceptible sounds comes from documented studies concerning the communication of dolphins. Dolphins communicate with frequencies that are so high they must be slowed down (decreasing the speed of the waveform) for the human ear to hear.

What does this have to do with digitizing analog audio? You must understand that there is a relationship between analog frequencies and the frequency measurement in the sampling rate. To capture a specific frequency from an analog source, the digital sampling rate must be twice that of the analog frequency. To capture a 22kHz frequency, the digital sampling rate must be 44kHz. This is why most audio software packages have the highest sampling at 44kHz, which is the highest sampling rate that is needed. Recording at a sampling rate over 44kHz records sounds over 22kHz, which are imperceptible to the human ear. Audio CDs sound crystal clear because they are recorded at 44kHz and include the entire range of sound perceptible to the human ear.

Most computer sound packages have three standard sampling rates: 44kHz, 22kHz, and 11kHz. At each of these levels, the perceivable amount of sound is half the sampling rate. For example, at 44kHz, the entire range of sound is digitally captured—half of 44kHz is 22kHz. With a sampling rate of 22kHz, the recorded range is up to 11kHz and with 11kHz, the perceived sounds are up to 5.5kHz.

If you are a close observer, you might be wondering about low frequencies, which I purposefully ignored up to this point in the discussion. Understand that these descriptions of sampling rates (44, 22, and 11kHz) also describe the amount of low tones that are in the digital representation, the ones in the Hz range.

Figure 13.8 shows a waveform presented as a waveform chart, much like many software packages present it. Note that the chart shows a mid-line between the high frequencies, measured in kHz, and the low frequencies, measured in Hz. As the wave goes above the mid-line, your ear perceives high notes. As the wave goes below the mid-line, your ear perceives low notes. Remember that the highest high note is represented by 22kHz and the lowest low note is represented by 20Hz.

Figure 13.8.

A waveform represented on a chart that shows the entire range of humanly perceivable sound.

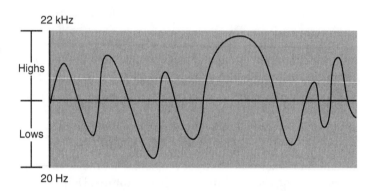

What you must note about the frequency chart is that the description of frequency describes not only the highs, but also the lows included in the digitized sound. For example, in Figure 13.9, the waveform on the chart was sampled at 44kHz. The recorded kilohertz range, based on a 44kHz sample, includes sounds from 1kHz, which is 1,000Hz, to 22kHz. These are the recorded highs. This also means that the lows recorded mirror the highs that are recorded; in other words, the Hz range of 1,000 to 20Hz.

Figure 13.9.

The sampling rate not only describes the recorded highs, but also the recorded lows.

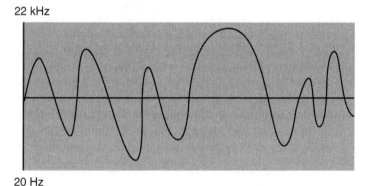

To better understand this, take a look at three examples: one at 44kHz, one at 22kHz, and one at 11kHz, so that you can see that the described range of highs also describes the range of lows.

In Figure 13.10, you see three examples at 44kHz, 22kHz, and 11kHz. As the sampling rate decreases, so does the range of frequencies captured in the audio. Note that the sampling rate not only describes the number of highs that can be sampled, but also the lows. As the sampling rate decreases, the digital representation becomes less representative of the analog source (which is shown in the 44kHz example).

Figure 13.10.

The lower the sampling rate, the lower the quality of the digital representation.

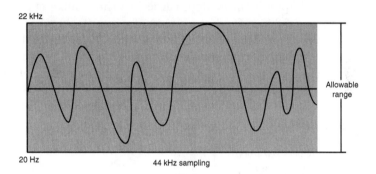

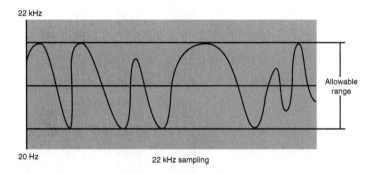

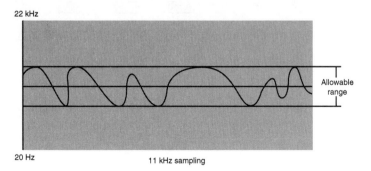

As you can see, the sampling rate affects the representation of the digital sample. The lower the sampling rate, the lower the quality of the digital sound clip. If you listen to the sound clips shown in Figure 13.10, you hear that the 44kHz example sounds clear and crisp, just like being there. The 22kHz sound is lower quality but adequate for playback in multimedia and hypermedia. The final example at 11kHz is noticeably different. It sounds scratchy and has little depth of sound.

Bit Depth

The second attribute of sound is bit depth, or sampling depth. As you remember from Chapter 5, the bit depth describes the number of physical computer bits that can be used to represent a chunk of a sample. Figure 13.11 shows the sampling process. Remember that once the chunk is converted to digital data, it must be written in a digital file. The number of bits that the computer can use to describe the chunk is the bit depth. The higher the bit depth, the more descriptive and representative the digital file.

Figure 13.11.
The description of the digital file is based upon the sampling rate and the bit depth.

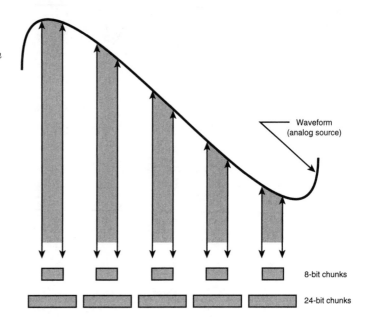

Waveform
(analog source)

8-bit chunks

24-bit chunks

In Chapter 5, you saw that the bit depth of a raster image controls the number of colors that can be used to describe an image. With audio, the number of bits you have available describes the number of various decibels (dB), which are variations not necessarily associated with loudness, that can be used. For example, a audio clip written at 8-bit has 256 different variations from which to describe the samples of the clip. A clip written at 16-bit can use any one of 16.7 million decibel variations to describe the samples of the clip. Keep in mind that a decibel does not automatically measure the loudness of a sound. In this setting, it is more descriptive of pitch than anything else. Realize that CD quality sound is representative of 16-bit quality.

Channels: Monaural and Stereo

One other consideration when dealing with digital audio is the specification of monaural or stereo sound, which is the number of channels of sound. Although I discuss this parameter, realize that most hypermedia and multimedia sound are monaural—a single channel.

Basically, stereo sound means there are differences between what is played in the two speakers, which provides greater depth to the aural experience. Usually, stereo sound describes a sound track that has a left and right component, as shown in Figure 13.12. When the sound is sampled into the computer, dual clips are recorded, one representing the left speaker and one representing the right speaker. A more complex variation also has surround sound, which may have from four to eight different channels in a clip, each designed for a specifically placed speaker.

With monaural sound, often called mono, a singular channel or track is played; both speakers play the same thing. Multimedia and hypermedia use monaural sound because of the tremendous storage requirements of stereo sound clips. Recording or playing back a stereo clip requires twice as much storage space and processing power, as shown graphically in Figure 13.13.

Figure 13.12.
*Stereo sound has both a
left and right component.*

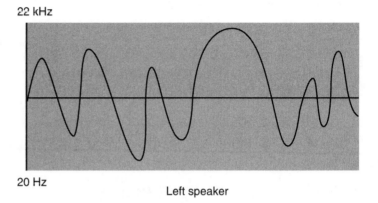

22 kHz

20 Hz

Left speaker

22 kHz

20 Hz

Right speaker

Figure 13.13.
*The comparison of stereo
and mono sound.*

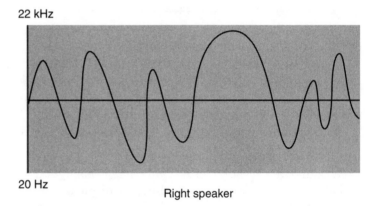

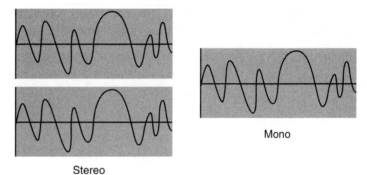

Stereo

Mono

File Sizes

Up to this point, you have seen the three primary determiners for the quality of a sound clip: sampling rate, bit (sampling) depth, and number of channels. Although it is nice to use 16-bit, 44kHz, stereo sound on the Web and in multimedia, realize that this is unrealistic. One minute of a clip with these settings requires approximately 10MB of disk space—completely absurd for hypermedia or multimedia. A quick look at various numbers for different settings will help you understand the effect of these variables on digital file size, as shown in Table 13.1.

Table 13.1. The comparison of stereo and mono sound.

Sampling rate (kHz)	Bit depth	Channels	Disk space for one minute of sound
44	16	Stereo	10.5MB
44	16	Mono	5.2MB
44	8	Stereo	5.2MB
44	8	Mono	2.6MB
22	16	Stereo	5.2MB
22	16	Mono	2.6MB
22	8	Stereo	2.6MB
22	8	Mono	1.3MB
11	16	Stereo	2.6MB
11	16	Mono	1.3MB
11	8	Stereo	1.3MB
11	8	Mono	.6MB

As you can see, the size of digital sound files is dramatically affected by the sampling rate, bit depth, and number of channels. Most often, the sound clips you use in multimedia are 22kHz, 16-bit, mono files. For Web distribution, you might need to drop the bit depth down to 8-bit. You'll read more about considerations for using audio on Web pages later in this chapter.

You can analyze many more aural attributes of sound. You only scratch the surface in this chapter, but the primary concerns with digital audio are sampling rate, bit depth, and number of channels.

Preparing to Sample Audio

Sampling audio on your PC or Mac is a relatively easy task, assuming you have a sound card that can sample audio and an appropriate software package. Most PCs and Macs have some type of system software that allows you to sample audio. If you want something better that allows you to edit and manipulate audio, check out Appendix A, "Graphics, Animation, and Multimedia Tools," for information about sound editors.

The basic scenario for sampling audio is connecting an analog device such as a microphone, tape recorder, or other device to your computer. You'll find that a microphone generally gives you the poorest results, particularly if it came with your machine. If you want to do serious microphone sound recordings, you'll probably need to invest some money in a better microphone than the one that came with your computer.

You'll probably want to record audio using a tape recording or an audio CD, but don't forget about copyright considerations. Make sure you have the right to use any audio that you sample. For more information on copyrights, see Chapter 10, "Interactive Multimedia Design Process."

To sample audio from a device such as a tape recorder or boom box, you need to connect the two devices so that the device is playing through the sound card of the computer. Find the output jack on the back of the sound card to see what type of jack it is. Most often, it is a patch type connector. Figure 13.14 shows an example of the three main types of connectors: 1/4 inch patch, 1/8 inch patch, and the RCA connector.

Figure 13.14.
Various types of audio connectors.

1/4" patch   1/8" patch   RCA-type

Next, look at your tape recorder or whatever device you want to sample from. Look for a line-out connector. If none exists, you can also use a headphone jack. Now all you have to do is get what is usually called a patch cable with the proper connectors for your card and device.

After you get the connection established between your device and card, follow these suggestions for digitizing audio:

- Prior to playing any sound from the device to your computer, make sure the device volume level is on zero. Insert a tape or other media and let it start playing. Then, increase the device volume to 1. This keeps you from overloading or blowing your computer's speakers. If you don't hear sound at a volume level of 1, don't crank it up. Check the operating system's sound levels first.

- Check your settings for the audio levels on the computer. Often, there are separate audio levels for the master volume, line-in, CD, line-out, and any other connections for your sound card. Set the volume of these to 50 percent if possible. Then, you can control the volume using the device's volume adjuster.

- Check in your recording software to see if you can adjust the recording level. If your software has monitor level indicators (see Figure 13.15), as the audio plays through the card you see the LEDs light up. You want the audio volume level to average at the lowest yellow. If the audio peaks in the red as it is playing, that's okay. Generally, you want the average volume level to be close to the lowest yellow level.

Figure 13.15.
Monitor level indicators.

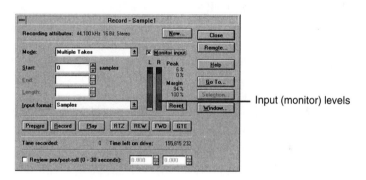

Input (monitor) levels

- As you sample audio, you are able to record only as much audio as you have disk space or memory. Some audio packages allow you to record only in RAM memory. Others write the recording audio directly to the hard disk. Prior to buying any package, make sure it can record audio directly to the hard disk. If it cannot, you'll only be able to record a couple of minutes worth of audio at a time.

- Strive to sample your audio at the highest quality possible—44kHz, 16-bit, stereo. This gives you a high quality digital source from which you can down-sample to 22kHz, 8-bit, mono. Having a digital source file at the highest quality allows you to manipulate it by adjusting the lows or highs.

- Use the lowest quality sound needed in your hypermedia and multimedia products. More than likely, the highest quality you can use is 22kHz, 8-bit, monaural sound clips.

MIDI Audio

For most people, MIDI audio is akin to black magic. Most people don't understand how it works, much less how to create it. In this section, you'll take a brief look at MIDI. You won't read all about it because it is not as widely used as digital audio on the Web—mainly because most people don't understand it. However, it is important that you have a basic understanding of how MIDI files work.

You can think of MIDI as sort of a PostScript description for music. PostScript describes drawings as objects or vector descriptions rather than as individual pixels. MIDI describes the elements of musical performance, such as the musical instruments that can be heard, rather than describe them as bit streams of information. As with PostScript, MIDI is device-independent and has no bit depth or sampling rate.

Synthesized Sound

The whole premise of MIDI sound is based upon the concept of synthesis. Synthesis simply refers to the way in which a waveform is generated. With digital audio, the waveform is described bit-by-bit in relation to time. With MIDI, the MIDI processor is capable of generating the wave based upon a description of the note that should play and the instrument that should be used to play it. This is why MIDI is similar to PostScript. A MIDI file doesn't describe the wave in relation to the bits that describe the wave; it actually generates the wave based on pitch and instrument descriptions.

Synthesis also refers to one other element concerning the wave that is generated. Not only can a MIDI chip generate a sound wave, but it can also manipulate that sound wave over time. Using filters, the sound can be emphasized, de-emphasized, or distorted.

The advantages to MIDI are many. Because of the way a MIDI file describes its data, MIDI files are significantly smaller than digital audio files. Similar to the huge differences between vector and bitmap files, a MIDI representation of a digital audio file may be 1/10 the size of the digital audio file—a definite advantage both in storage and delivery.

A second advantage to MIDI files is that they are malleable. MIDI sound clips can be constructed an instrument at a time. If you create a MIDI file of Beethoven's Fifth Symphony, you can add each instrument definition and the representative notes for that instrument one at a time to the file. The final composite (of all the defined instruments) could be played, edited, and rearranged at any time. Each instrument in the piece is a discrete object.

With all the apparent advantages of MIDI files, there is one significant flaw. A MIDI file can use more than 128 different instruments to play a series of pitches or notes. As the MIDI format became more widely used, there was no standardization of what numbers (1-128) represented what instruments. Consequently, a musician could define an entire piece of music to use the acoustic piano, but figuring out what instrument number to use was a problem because there was no standardization. Instrument number 1 might be the right one on one machine, but it might be instrument 75 on another machine, which might use a different sound card. This is the biggest problem in using MIDI sounds.

The General MIDI Mode was added to the MIDI specification to solve this problem. Most sound cards manufactured today use the General MIDI specification, which allows MIDI sounds created using specific instruments to play consistently across machines with different sound cards.

File Formats and Conversion

As you begin to work with audio files, you will find many digital audio formats but only one MIDI file type. Concerning digitized audio, most packages allow the conversion of files from one format to another, whereas others only allow you to work with a specified format. If you want to purchase a sound editor, look for the file formats described in this section to make sure the editor supports them. On the Web, the most widely used formats are .WAV, .AU, and .AIFF.

File Formats

As with graphic files, there are many file formats on the Web that you can use to distribute your audio files. More than likely, your choice of format will depend upon the platform on which you are generating it. Keep in mind that the Web is a worldwide medium and that platform-specific file formats can set a limit on your audience.

Digital audio file formats for the Web include the following:

- Audio Interchange File Format (AIFF) is predominantly used on Macintosh and Silicon Graphics machines. This format supports various sampling rates, bit depths, and multiple channels.

- Sun Audio (AU) is used predominantly by UNIX users on workstations. This format is special in that it writes its data differently from the other sound formats, but it is usually prone to background noise and external sounds.

- System 7 Sound files (SND) are used predominately for sounds associated with the Macintosh operating system.

- SoundBlaster Vocal files (VOC) are an older sound format originally introduced by Creative Labs' SoundBlaster sound cards.
- Windows Waveform files (WAV) were originally designed for Windows system sounds but are now widely used across the Internet.

Compression Technologies

Due to the tremendous size of digital audio files, many of the file formats are not feasible to deliver directly over the Web. In reality, the only files that are currently used directly within browsers are MIDI files and special streaming audio files, due to Web bandwidth limitations.

If you want to distribute digital sound files, you should compress the files, using external file compression programs, such as Pkware'S PKZIP or Aladdin's Stuffit Deluxe, and allow your audience to download the files apart from the Web browser. The current Web bandwidth cannot support direct distribution or integration of raw digital audio files (WAV, AIFF, or AU).

To integrate audio directly into your pages, you use a streaming technology.

Streaming

One of the latest advances in Web technology centers on the principle of streaming. Understanding the concept of streaming is pretty easy, but its impact is quickly increasing.

In Chapter 11, "Multimedia Fundamentals," you read that before any media element can be viewed in the browser, it must be completely downloaded from the Web. Then, you can view it in the browser. In Chapter 5, you learned about the exceptions to the rule, which are interlaced GIF files and progressive JPEG images. Streaming audio files (and video files) are another exception to the rule.

A streaming audio or video file works similarly to a progressive image, which is displayed gradually as it is downloaded. A streamable audio file is one in which the browser can immediately begin play back, even though the entire file has not downloaded. Once a streamed piece is downloaded, the file can begin playing. In essence, the file is played directly from the Web, within the browser, as it downloads.

Several new technologies allow audio and video data to be streamed and played back simultaneously from the Web. Appendix A lists several of the latest streaming technologies that you can use with these media. However, streaming technology is relatively young and still limited by bandwidth. Most audio files are of relatively low quality—about 11kHz, 8-bit, mono files. You'll find that some tout a higher quality, but it is still dependent upon the speed of the network connection.

In addition to the quality and bandwidth issues, most of the audio (and video) streaming technologies require that you use special server software. More often than not, a server aimed at delivering audio or video is not able to provide any other services. The server software that is installed for delivering audio and video often requires that the server be dedicated to only the task of delivering audio and video.

A few streaming technologies, particularly one that was just introduced by Macromedia, don't require a dedicated server or special server software. Nonetheless, all the streaming technologies require that the client's browser have a plug-in to view the media element. This requirement will probably not change in the coming months. If you decide to use streaming technologies, make sure that your home page acknowledges that certain plug-ins are required to view the site. Keep your site audience-centered.

Comparison of Digitized and MIDI Sound

As you look at distributing sound clips over the Web, keep in mind the fundamental differences between digital audio and MIDI in creation, playback, and delivery, as shown in Table 13.2.

Table 13.2. The comparison of digital audio and MIDI audio.

Function	Digital audio	MIDI audio
Creation	Requires sampling, which creates a bit-by-bit representation of the waveform. Click and record. Requires large amounts of disk space. Difficult to edit distinct elements.	Requires MIDI; creates a description of the sound, based upon notes and instruments. Requires knowledge of MIDI synthesis. Requires small amounts of disk space. Easy to edit discrete elements.

continues

Table 13.2. continued

Function	Digital audio	MIDI audio
Playback	Requires a lot of memory. Sounds the same on every computer. May sound poor.	Requires little memory. Sound depends upon the sound card. Very clear sound.
Delivery	May require server software. Requires client software.	No server software needed. No client software required.

Summary

In this chapter, you looked at the various concerns surrounding the use of digital audio and MIDI audio. Due to the size of digital audio files, much of the current applied research focuses at designing a way to deliver high quality audio over the network. No doubt, pulling this off will require both ingenious software solutions as well as an increase in speed of the end-user Web connection.

14

Video

As with all the other high-density files delivered over the Web, video files are also limited by bandwidth restrictions. Today, the Web has a somewhat small road compared to the data that we want to push over it. Many research efforts are attempting to reduce the size of the data we're pushing (through compression technologies) as well as increase the size of our roads (making the Internet data channels wider). We still have a long way to go to reach full-screen video distribution capability.

Video files, much more than animation files, severely tax the Web. With animation files, all you need to supply is the video information. With audio files, all you have to push over the Net is the sound, but with video files, you must deliver both audio and video—not to mention the fact that the video and audio must be coordinated. Again, designing around the limitation is your biggest task.

No matter how big or how small the animation or video, the biggest difficulty with Web distribution is the bandwidth issue; in other words, how wide and how fast is the pipe that's feeding your machine? To understand why it's an issue, you have to look inside the digital animation and video files to understand why the pipe limits what can be delivered efficiently and effectively. The most difficult media element to distribute over the Web is video because of the density of most video files as well as the delicate timing that must occur between the audio and video portion.

Image Size, Frame Number, and Bit Depth

The same concern of file size that applies to static graphics and animations also applies to video. Everything that is delivered via the Web is primarily an issue of file size: how long it is going to take the user to download the page, graphic, sound, animation, or video clip. No matter what you download, much more than a couple hundred kilobytes will probably leave you wishing you hadn't started.

With animations and video, the limitation presents a significant problem. As you saw in Chapter 6, "Fundamentals of Animation," animations are nothing more than a series of singular images sewn together whose contents change over time. Each additional image or frame adds to the file weight (or wait, whichever way you want to view it). The larger the file, the larger the weight (wait), no matter how you access the Web.

With uncompressed video, adding audio approximately doubles the file size. Remember that a 1MB (1,000KB) video, animation, or graphic file takes around ten minutes to download for your dial-up access users with a 28.8Kbps modem. Your first concern is the size of the file, but what affects that size? As you saw with bitmap graphics, size is contingent upon image resolution, image size, and image bit depth. When you looked at animation elements, compilations of multiple raster images, you saw that size was contingent upon image size and number of frames because the bit depth and dots per inch (dpi) are generally 8-bit and 72 dpi.

With video, three things affect the digital file size: the image size, the number of frames, and the bit depth of the images, as shown in Figure 14.1.

The image size is the biggest contributor to the size of the animation or video file. With Web animation or video, you always use a very small portion of the screen. Surfers don't expect Web animations and video to be much more than 160×120. Why? Look at what you know about the graphics you've created so far. The same principles that apply to animation also apply to video.

Figure 14.1.
*What affects animation
and video file size?*

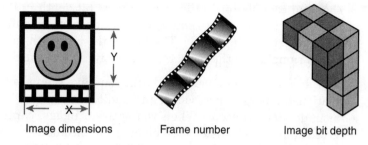

Image dimensions   Frame number   Image bit depth

A single GIF image at 640×480, even at 256 colors, is approximately 100KB. Multiply that by 50 frames and you've just overshot your Web size allotment by 4900KB. The animations or video you deliver must be small, less than or equal to 160×120. In Chapter 6, you saw the standard sizes for animations. To refresh your memory of the general relationship of sizes, take a look at Figure 14.2.

Figure 14.2.
*Relationship of sizes
compared to a 640×480
window.*

The second contributing factor to video file size is the number of frames. The number of frames is the number of singular images in the file. This number can be a significant contributor if no compression is used in the particular digital file format. Most animations delivered over the Web are less than 200 frames at 160×120, and most video with audio is less than 100 frames at 160×120. Using these numbers as a rule of thumb allows you to hit the respective 200KB or 100KB file size parameter.

With video frames, you must also consider the rate at which those frames play back. The rates are significantly less than what you might see on a television or in a video studio. Frame rates in these instances are usually 30 frames per second (fps) at 60 fields per second, but with Web video? Hardly! Web video, which might play sporadically at the low end, usually ranges from 5 to 15 frames per second. Remember that you must work within your capable means.

The final contributor to file size is image bit depth in the animation or video. Remember that bit depth simply describes how much data is allotted to describe a single instance in the file. The higher the bit depth, the more descriptive the digital sample and the more representative it is of the original analog source.

Over and over throughout this book, you have seen the term bit depth and its relationship to graphics, video, and audio. Bit depth is an important and often misunderstood concept. When you scan an image, capture video, or digitally record audio, you transfer the element from the analog world to the digital world. As with the other media elements, digitizing video requires a process known as sampling.

The video sampling process occurs in small pieces, as with any other element. Take an analog chunk, digitally convert it, and digitally describe it. Take another chunk, convert it, digitally describe it down, and so on. The frequency with which you take these chunks is called the sampling rate. The more frequent the chunks, the higher the sampling rate and the better the digital representation of the analog source.

Once you have a chunk, you must describe it digitally. The more digital bits you can use to describe each chunk, the more the final digital representation looks or sounds like the original analog source. The higher the bit depth and the sampling rate, the more representative the digital image, sound, or video clip is of its analog counterpart.

You're only as strong as your weakest link. A high sampling rate with a low bit depth gives you more frequent samples but a poor description of those samples. A high bit depth and a low sampling rate give very detailed descriptions of infrequent samples. The best-case scenario is to sample at your highest capability, with the highest bit depth and sampling rate, and then digitally resample the element to the desired deliverable size.

When applying this rule of thumb to graphics, it means working on raster images in 24-bit mode and then reducing the bit depth to 8-bit before posting them on the Web. As it relates to audio, it means that you sample your audio at the highest quality, 44kHz/16-bit/stereo, and then reduce the quality to that which is applicable to Web distribution (22kHz/8-bit/mono). With Web animation, it means you output your animation from a two-dimensional or three-dimensional package at a large frame size and high quality bit depth and then reduce its quality for distribution. For Web video, it means that you sample video at the highest quality sampling rate and bit depth and then decrease the quality to include it on the Web. Table 14.1 shows the various media elements, the variables that affect file size, and the appropriate settings for sampling (creation) and delivery (Web).

Table 14.1. The various attributes of media elements.

Element	Attributes	Sample	Delivery
Raster graphics	Image dpi	72	72
	Image size	True-size	True-size
	Image bit depth	24-bit	8-bit
Audio	Sampling rate	44kHz	22 or 11kHz
	Bit depth	16-bit	8-bit
	Channels	Stereo	Mono
Animation	Image size	Highest	160×120 or less
	Bit depth	24-bit	8-bit
	Frame number	200	200 or less
	Frame rate	5-15 fps	5-15 fps
Video	Image size	Highest	160×120 or less
	Bit depth	24-bit	Depends upon compression
	Frame number	100	100 or less
	Frame rate	5-15 fps	5-15 fps

The maximum bit depth for an animation or video file, as well as the size and frame rate, often depends upon the compression algorithm that is used within the file format, as shown in Table 14.1. Some algorithms allow higher bit depths, which in turn give you better visual results upon playback. Others restrict you to a particular bit depth per certain circumstances. In the section "Compression Technologies" later in this chapter, you'll see how compression affects these variables as well as the file size.

Animation Versus Video

Through the separation of video and animation into different chapters, you'll note the implication that animation and video are somehow different. In fact, in the minds of most people, they are different. Definitions across the board vary, so take a look at why many people perceive and describe video and animation as two different media elements.

Generally, the most distinct difference is that animation is painstakingly created, either via a three-dimensional model or two-dimensional painting and keying techniques. Video, on the other hand, is captured via a still camera, recorder, or other device and then manipulated. Most often, animations require greater time input behind the computer. Broadcast quality video generally takes more time setting up the particular shot, determining lighting, camera angles, and a variety of other related issues. More time is spent behind the computer with animation, and more time is spent in the recording studio or on the set with video.

In addition to the differences in creation, the term digital video usually connotes that there is sound involved within the particular file, whereas animation may or may not have sound. With animation, it usually depends on your chosen file flavor. For example, animations stored in AutoDesk's FLC ("flic") format do not have audio, but an animation in MOV, AVI, or MPG may have audio. You'll examine these various formats later in this chapter. Simply note that when discussing animation and video with someone else, it may be a good idea to clarify what you mean when you say "animation" and "video." To many people, there is a difference between the two.

Generating Video Clips

Creating your own digital video movies is definitely not rocket science, but you need three fundamental things. As with digitizing audio, you need a video board capable of sampling video (and audio), recording software, and an analog source such as a VCR or camcorder, as shown in Figure 14.3. Realize that these elements are really only the basics. To create extremely complex videos and high-powered special effects, you need to spend thousands of dollars. Realistically, the Web is far from able to deliver such fantastic creations. Keep in mind that most Web video clips are small, thumbnail-size movies that don't require a lot of money to create.

Figure 14.3.
Basic equipment to create digital video clips.

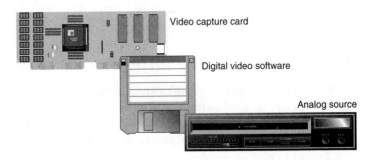

Video capture card

Digital video software

Analog source

The basic setup for capturing video is connecting the analog source to the video sampling card. This allows the software to capture frames of the video and audio and then write it to the hard disk. One thing to keep in mind (and one thing I forgot to mention) is that you need a lot of disk space. Digital video work requires a tremendous amount of disk storage because of the huge data requirements of raw images and sound. For somewhat serious capturing, you might want to pick up an extra hard drive. It doesn't take long to eat up a couple hundred megabytes of disk space when recording.

Most PCs don't come with video capture boards. When shopping for a capture board, you want to look at two primary things: the capture rate (how quickly the board can capture frames) and the types of connecting jacks on the board itself. These are your two primary considerations if you want to capture some simple video for Web distribution.

As you will remember, the frame rate for devices such as a VCR or camcorder run at about 30 frames per second. Most digital video is less, about 15 frames per second. You want to verify that the capture board can truly capture 15 frames per second. Many capture boards give you rates that are significantly slower, meaning that your resulting digital file appears jerky. Considering the realistic delivery speed of the Web, even with streaming technologies, 15 frames per second is more than adequate.

Your second concern with digital capture boards is that the boards have the same connectors as your analog device (VCR, camcorder, and so on). In general, most U.S. devices have one of two connectors, an RCA-type or S-video, as shown in Figure 14.4. The highest quality capture occurs with the S-video connection. In addition, the S-video connection feeds both audio and video at the same time, so you need only one cable.

Figure 14.4.
U.S. video connectors.

RCA-type   S-video

Although I could discuss many more aspects of capturing high-quality video, the primary concerns are frame rate and connectors. If you want more serious digital video production, many books can assist you in creating digital video for delivery through other communications channels. For Web delivery, however, you don't need a full digital video suite with A/B roll capability. A digital video sample created with little investment and resources looks the same as the one created with a high-powered editing suite because of what can be feasibly delivered over the Web.

Compression Technologies

Most animation and video files use compression to help reduce file size. Animation files are often stored in a digital video movie format to help reduce the size of the file. You can put almost anything into one of the digital video file formats, including animations generated from 2D or 3D packages, raster images, and rasterized vector images.

As you found with JPEG images in Chapter 5, "Raster-Based Graphics," some image data is discarded to help maintain smaller file sizes. The data that is discarded is either redundant or acceptably lost. Remember that lossy compression schemes, which are used in the JPEG format, lose a certain amount of data to attain smaller digital file sizes. Lossless compression, on the other hand, doesn't lose any data. When a lossless file is uncompressed, it creates an exact replica of the original file.

As with JPEG images, digital video files are almost always compressed for distribution, but it depends upon how you integrate videos and animations within your pages. If you choose to use an animation or video directly embedded in the HTML code of your pages (via the <EMBED> tag or <A> tag—a hotlinked file), you will probably use one of the compressed digital video formats. When in this form, the animation can be viewed with the aid of a plug-in or a helper application.

Alternatively, animations included in pages as sequential images, such as GIF animations or Java-based animations, do not use these compression formats. They are stored as multiple GIF images rather than as a single file and are directly "playable" by the browser itself. No additional plug-ins or helper applications are needed.

In the compression schemes you saw with JPEG images, the compression works by examining the colors in the image and then choosing colors or data that can be acceptably lost. The redundant colors (data) in the image allow compression to occur. The compressibility of any image is based upon the amount of similarity of the colors in the image. However, the compression that occurs within the digital video formats occurs over a range of images in the video rather than within a single image.

All compression techniques use an algorithm called a compressor/decompressor or codec. The amount that a particular image compresses with a particular codec, its compressibility, is called the compression ratio, a ratio of sizes before and after compression. Compression ratios range from 2:1 to 200:1 and describe the codec's affect on a particular image.

Each digital video format is argumentatively different. Each gives different (but similar) visual results, and each gives different compression ratios. Which is the best? It depends on whom you ask, but the most prevalent formats on the Web are AVI, QuickTime, and MPEG. Viewers for various platforms are available on many sites.

Viewing the digital video formats requires one of two things: a plug-in capable of viewing the particular format or a helper application that can be used to view the format apart from the Web browser. Many plug-ins are emerging for more formats than just AVI, QuickTime, and MPEG. Take a look in Appendix A, "Graphics, Animation, and Multimedia Tools," for information on the latest digital video plug-ins, helper applications for viewing digital video files, and applications for generating digital video.

Video for Windows

Video for Windows, or AVI files, was designed to distribute video in the Windows environment. The advantage to using Video for Windows files is the ease with which they can be distributed and utilized on Windows 3.1, Windows 3.11, Windows 95, and Windows NT machines. Microsoft's Media Player automatically recognizes video segments saved in AVI format. In addition, there are ways to either directly view or convert AVI files for use on other platforms.

The AVI format allows a couple of different codecs to compress the file, even though it is an AVI file. People who view the file do not know that it is compressed with a particular codec. If you create video and save it in the AVI format out of a package such as Adobe Premiere, the codec you choose can affect the quality of displayed output, as shown in Figure 14.5.

Figure 14.5.
Various codecs produce different qualities of video images.

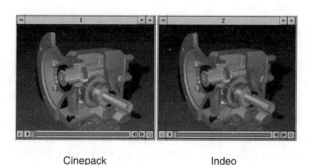

Cinepack   Indeo

The two primary codecs for AVI files are Cinepak and Indeo. In general, Cinepak is better at compressing animations and video that are predominantly composed of solid colors, whereas Indeo is better at recorded video with a large range of colors. Both schemes are lossy and drop certain amounts of detail, but each function is better at certain tasks. If you use a product such as Premiere to save animation or video, you can easily set the save routine to output in your chosen codec, as shown in Figure 14.6.

Figure 14.6.
Using a specific codec at save time.

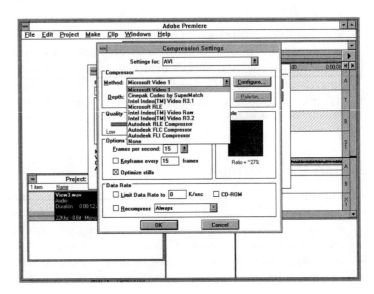

QuickTime

Apple's QuickTime format, the first format available for desktop users, is very similar to Video for Windows. If I were to guess that any particular format was most used on the Web, my answer would be QuickTime chiefly because it is the oldest format of the three.

The real differences in file size and playback quality are difficult to distinguish for general users, but I'm sure the technicians at either company could lay it out and explain why AVI or QuickTime is better. Like many people, I am tired of the Mac versus PC religious debate. Which should you choose? Are you a Mac user or PC user? Choose the one that fits your audience and your platform.

QuickTime, like Video for Windows, allows you to choose your codec. The most frequently used codecs are Cinepak and Indeo. Remember that you should generally use Cinepak for solid colors and Indeo for recorded video.

MPEG

The newcomer to the heated format battle is MPEG, a pretty slick digital format that has proved to be a pretty good contender in the market. Currently, MPEG-based video machines are appearing everywhere. The biggest problem, as with all newer technologies, is that it is pretty pricey. Encoders for MPEG files, which are the boards that allow you to record and or save digital files, range from $500 to $500,000 in price, but users can play most MPEG files found on the Net without additional hardware.

MPEG, unlike AVI or QuickTime, doesn't have options for assigning codecs when you're saving, but most MPEG-encoding programs give the user the option of saving in either MPEG1 or MPEG2 format. When you encounter MPEG files on the Net, you'll often find that the audio and video portions are separate files, but this habit is decreasing as the availability and pricing of MPEG hardware decreases.

Streaming Versus Helper Applications

One of the most promising means of delivering animation and video over the Web is via plug-ins. Plug-ins such as Apple's QuickTime and Microsoft's Video for Windows add a deeper level of possibility on the Web. These plug-ins, like audio plug-ins, allow data to stream across the Net and play back in real time.

As you read earlier in this chapter, the only way to increase the speed at which files can be delivered over the Web is by either decreasing the size of the files or by increasing the bandwidth of the connection the file must be transferred through. Streaming technologies are an attempt to reduce the size of the file. As you have read, streaming data sends portions of a file to the user's machine that are immediately executed or played. Streaming also accomplishes one other important thing: It compresses the file. Streaming is not just being able to deliver files that are instantly executable. It also implies compression.

With video, the amount of data pushed over the Net is twice as much due to the combination of the audio and video portions of the file. Streaming technologies used today, such as QuickTimeVR, are still in their infancy. When you deliver files using these technologies, you must use a very small window to deliver the video. Even when a small window is used, the audio is often mistimed if it plays at all. This streaming technology needs a lot of development to become widely used, even by users who have fast Internet connections. Many streaming plug-ins for audio and video are still under construction, but in the near future, you'll see many more available.

Although there are plug-ins for Apple's QuickTime and Microsoft's Video for Windows, the most common practice is to deliver animation files to the user with the intent of using helper applications. It is the easiest way. You don't have to make sure the user has a plug-in, and for the most part, you can guarantee that the file will play back as you created it.

If you want to deliver video files from your site, I suggest delivering the files through hotlinks, allowing the user to download the file at his or her leisure. Often, users choose to download video at some off-peak time for viewing later. In this scenario, the file is completely downloaded and then played through a helper application, as shown in Figure 14.7. The only restriction is that the user must have a player or viewer capable of opening the animation or video file once it is on his machine. Due to limited bandwidth, this is probably the best way to distribute video files, and quite possibly animation files, to your audience. If you decide to do this, you need to be aware of some of the commonly used formats for video files.

Figure 14.7.
An example of helper application playback.

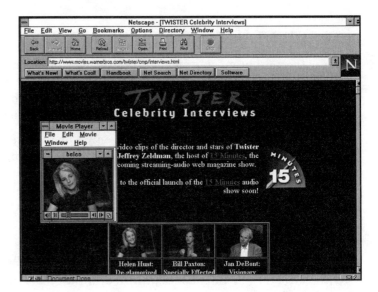

Summary

In this chapter, you have taken a cursory look at video. Indeed, the capability of today's Web limits the amount of video that can be efficiently and effectively delivered. Due to the tremendous requirements of digitized video, you must conscientiously design video elements so that they can be delivered via the Web. Undoubtedly as the Web becomes more supportive of high-bandwidth media elements, you'll see more and more video elements on the Web.

15

Immersive Environments: Virtual Reality

Of the newest technologies found on the Web, and probably the most profound, is one that presents the biggest untapped digital frontier: the use of virtual reality technology on the Web.

As you begin to read this chapter, however, forget all the hype—that picture of photorealistic worlds painted by the media—and look at the base implications of the technology itself. Virtual reality is far from photorealism and total immersion presented to the public at-large. This is predominantly due to the immense overhead of rendering environments such as this in real-time. Although the visual and auditory senses can be fooled, the technology is far from the virtual *holodeck* portrayed in the sci-fi hit *Star Trek: The Next Generation*. In addition, we are only beginning to apply three-dimensional features in the computer media, although movies such as *Lawnmower Man* and *Jurassic Park* tell tales of completely rendered three-dimensional environments and interfaces.

Realize that virtual reality technology, even apart from the Web, is in its infancy. We are just beginning to see its implications in areas from teaching sign language to surgical practices that use it to train interns. Virtual reality has more to do with communication and experiential knowledge than it does with reality or immersion.

As with all of the other media elements discussed throughout this book, the biggest limitation to virtual reality technology on the Web is bandwidth. Over and over, you will see that everything delivered by today's Web is an issue of file size versus bandwidth.

Yet, it should be no surprise that virtual reality on the Web is probably the most demanding of all media elements. Even virtual reality systems that have nothing to do with the Web are laced with hardware and technical issues, and virtual reality continually pushes both hardware and software to the limits. Virtual reality is limited by the current hardware technologies, but it is not all gloom and doom. Many advances have taken place that allow realistic interaction between the natural and digital worlds. Slowly but surely, the virtual reality environment is becoming extremely applicable to many areas of business and education, even with the limitations of current input, output, and processing technologies.

To understand how this wonderful technology is being used, you must first understand that virtual reality technology was developed apart from the Web. It is only as recently as 1995, that virtual environments could be used on the Web at all. In this chapter, you will begin by reading about the developments surrounding virtual reality technology that have taken place outside the Web arena. This is where the technology began; it is developing into something that has dramatic effects in many different areas. Then you will look at virtual environments on the Web, how they are being manipulated, and what the future holds for this new technology.

The Premise of Virtual Reality

Some of the most complex systems that exist in the human body revolve around our natural senses. The physical mechanisms that give us sight and hearing are marvelous in the ways they work. To enable sight, light passes through the lens of the eyes, focusing images on the retinas. The images are received by the rods and cones in our eyes. The perception of color and values is a result of the rods and cones in our eyes.

Other than light values and colors, an important attribute is developed in human beings early in the stages of development: stereoscopic vision. Stereoscopic vision gives us the ability to visually perceive depth and spatial relationships. Because of visual abnormalities, some people cannot perceive depth; they have no stereoscopic vision, or they inaccurately perceive depth—a condition sometimes called astigmatism.

The placement of the eyes in the human skull is what allows most individuals to be able to perceive depth. Because each eye is offset slightly, each receives a slightly different image of the viewed environment. The overlapping area of sight received by each eye creates an area within the field of vision called the stereoscopic field of vision, as shown in Figure 15.1. Although the total visible area of sight, called the field of view or field of vision, is generally 120 degrees, the portion in which we are given depth perception is much smaller.

Figure 15.1.
The field of stereoscopic vision is a result of the overlapping fields of vision of each eye.

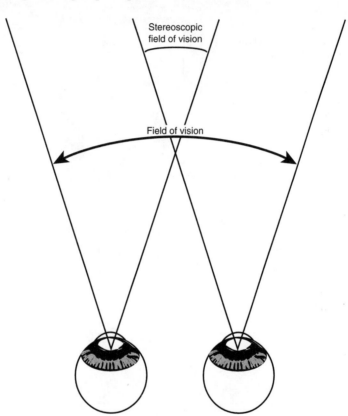

Stereoscopic
field of vision

Field of vision

The images received by each eye, although slightly different, are what create the ability to perceive depth visually. The differing images are sent to the visual cortex within the brain where they are composited, creating a three-dimensional, or stereoscopic, image.

To achieve the effect of stereoscopic vision in VR or other display systems, the knowledge of how the eyes work is used to create separate images that when viewed through special glasses give the effect of stereoscopic vision. To create a stereoscopic image, two images are projected to a screen as a composite image, as shown in Figure 15.2. Generally, one part of the image has a red cast and the other has a blue cast. Using special glasses that have a red lens and a blue lens, each eye sees a different image. The varying images are then composited by the brain's visual cortex, giving the three-dimensional or stereoscopic effect. Consequently, viewing the image without the special glasses makes the image look blurry or out of focus.

Figure 15.2.
Stereoscopic images are
a result of tinted images
viewed through special
glasses.

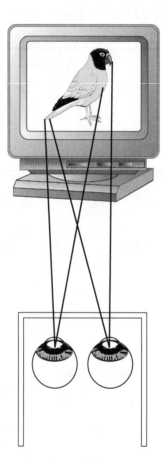

Although stereoscopic vision, the perception of depth, is part of virtual reality, the virtual environment also includes the ability to move about, or "to look or move around," within the virtual environment. In a virtual environment, the user has the ability to position himself anywhere within the environment, because it is three-dimensional. In addition, objects can be moved and manipulated, which also presents a visual change in what the user sees.

As you saw in Chapter 8, "3D Animation," all three-dimensional environments have a viewer, a coordinate system, and objects within the environment. In the virtual reality environment, all three of these items are important.

The first of these elements to become important is the coordinate system, which is based upon X, Y, and Z positioning and orientation. Everything within the 3D database (including the viewer, the user) has a position in space. In addition, everything has an orientation within 3D space, as shown in Figure 15.3. Remember that location means position, whereas orientation deals with rotation around an axis.

Figure 15.3.
All objects, including the viewer, have a location and orientation in the 3D database.

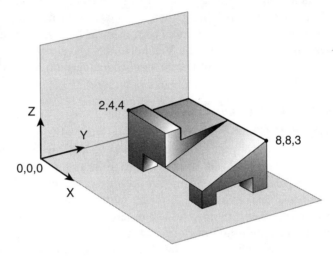

Within the virtual environment, objects can be moved. Yet the most prominent movement occurs as a result of the viewer's movement. As you read, stereoscopic vision is one characteristic of virtual reality systems. However, movement is also an important characteristic. If you viewed a virtual environment on a display screen, the ability to see stereoscopically would be nice, but what is more important is the ability to move around in the environment.

In most virtual environments, to move around in the database—in other words, to change what you are currently looking at—you are given the ability to control the view by changing the viewpoint. In virtual reality systems, moving the viewer changes what is seen in the environment, as shown in Figure 15.4. The left side of Figure 15.4 shows an example of an object in a 3D environment. The right side of Figure 15.4 shows the object being viewed from a different location in the virtual 3D space.

Figure 15.4.
Moving the viewer creates a different view of three-dimensional space.

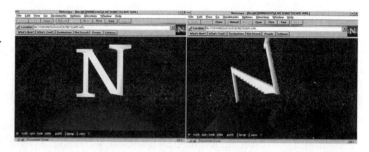

This is not so difficult to understand. As you operate in the real world, to get a different view of something, such as a chair in the middle of a room, you physically move from one side of the room to another. The same principles that apply to our physical world apply to the VR world. By changing the current location of the view, a different view of the three-dimensional environment is obtained.

Virtual Reality Systems

Virtual reality environments apart from the Web are generally very complex and expensive environments. Because of the lack of severe bandwidth limitations, as those found on the Web, the environments can be much more complex, as well as utilize a wider variety of input and output devices. However, creating virtual worlds and being able to interact with them are very expensive ventures. Purchasing the software and the machine alone can cost you well over $10,000. This doesn't include input and output devices such as a head-mounted display, boom-display, control stick, or glove. Because the technology is so new, it can be very expensive to get into virtual reality, apart from that already on the Web.

VRML and the Web

VRML or Virtual Reality Modeling Language (previously called Virtual Reality Markup Language) is a method of describing three-dimensional objects and worlds that can be interactively manipulated and viewed on the Web, as shown in Figure 15.5. Any range of objects can be described with VRML, from a simple three-dimensional logo to a landscape or mechanical design.

As you have read, simply being able to view objects in a 3D scene is not all that different from static bitmap or graphic images. Yet the VRML environment presents much more flexibility. After a VRML file has been downloaded from the Web, a user can manipulate the views of the environment by using special controls in the browser. In general, there are three manipulations that can be performed on an object, as shown in Figure 15.6: pitch, yaw, and roll. Each of these corresponds to the change of an object in relation to one of the three primary axes of X (pitch), Y (yaw), and Z (roll).

Figure 15.5.
Almost anything can be described using the VRML language.

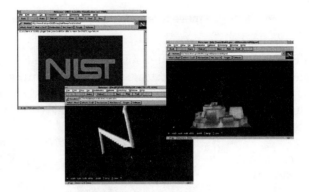

Figure 15.6.
Basic translations of VRML models.

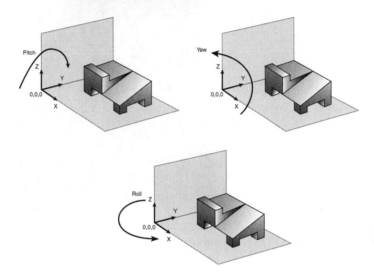

The combination of X, Y, and Z locations with an object's pitch (rotation relative to the X axis), yaw (rotation relative to the Y axis), and roll (rotation relative to the Z axis) completely describes the location and orientation of an object in three-dimensional space. These six degrees of freedom are commonly used to describe the location and orientation of objects in a 3D database through an X,Y,Z location and a P,Y,R orientation.

Other Implications

As you saw in Chapter 8, whenever you have a 3D scene, it must be rendered for screen display. You'll recall the various methods of rendering, which include wireframe, flat, Gouroud, Phong, ray-tracing, and radiosity. In the VRML environment, most objects and models can be rendered with the first three of these techniques. Some more robust files can actually contain surfaces, textures, and lighting as well.

Most VRML environments will display rendered objects. Figure 15.7 shows an example of a VRML file with lighting and surface textures. If you decide to get into VRML, you will probably want to do more reading to learn about lighting and designing 3D models, which is a big part of effective VRML environments.

Figure 15.7.
Most VRML files include rendered objects, and lighting and surface textures.

Summary

In this chapter you have taken a very cursory look at VRML technology. The technology is not very old, and we are just beginning to see the implications of it. Over the next several years, you will undoubtedly see more of it being used on the Web as software becomes smarter and hardware becomes faster.

G LOSSARY

<A> An HTML tag for creating links to other pages or resources; an anchor tag.

<EMBED> An HTML tag for including multimedia elements on Web pages.

<H1> An HTML tag for creating headings of various sizes; importance of heading is denoted by number. 1 is the most important, and 6 is the least important.

<HR> An HTML tag for creating horizontal rules.

<IMG> An HTML tag for including images within a Web page.

<P> A block-level HTML tag that creates a paragraph of text offset from other elements by a carriage return-line feed.

24-bit color Describes an image that can contain up to 16.7 million colors.

2D animation Describes an animation file that has been created using a package where every frame's contents are defined through either vector or bitmap descriptions.

3D Animation Describes an animation file that has been generated from a 3D model or scene.

3D Studio Max A 3D animation package created by Autodesk, Inc.

8-bit color Describes an image that contains up to 256 colors. All colors are described in a matrix called the Color Lookup Table (CLUT).

absorbed light One of the ways color is created. Objects absorb certain portions of the visible spectrum. Colors that are not absorbed are reflected back toward the view, making the object appear colored.

abstract A brief purpose and summary statement describing a Web site.

acetate Clear plastic film used to create traditional cel animation.

achromatic colors Includes hues that have no true color, such as black, white, and gray.

additive colors Color system used to create projected or displayed images via a cathode ray tube.

additive primaries Red, green, and blue.

address field The portion of a browser where a universal resource locator (URL) can be typed.

Adobe A company well known for its raster and vector graphics applications.

Afterburner A filter used to convert image and multimedia files created in Macromedia products to a form that is distributable over the Web.

algorithm A mathematical or logical schemata for solving a problem.

aliasing Characteristic stair-stepped nature of vector lines on a display screen or in an extracted bitmap.

alignment Describes the positioning of text bodies in relationship to other screen elements.

alpha channels A special part of high-resolution files that can contain masking and gamma information.

alphanumeric character A character (letter or number).

ambient light The amount of light present without any other light sources—representative of sunlight, moonlight, and atmospheric light.

analog data Data that is composed of a range of frequency variations; what the human senses are able to perceive.

analog degradation The decay of analog information as a result of copying an analog source to another analog device.

analog source A device used to record or play back analog data such as a VCR or a cassette tape.

analog to digital conversion (ADC) The process of converting analog data to digital data; often performed by a hardware chip or software.

animation The phenomenon caused by quickly viewing changing images giving the perception of movement or change over time.

animator The portion of a 3D animation package that allows the operator to define changes over time.

Animator Studio A 2D animation package created by Autodesk, Inc.

anti-alias halo Discolored pixels that occur around the edges of an object as a result of prior anti-aliasing.

anti-aliasing The process of blurring the edges of an image or object to make it appear smoother.

Apple Manufacturers of the Macintosh computer.

applet A small, self-contained executable application that has been created in the Java language.

application development The process of creating software designed to perform a task.

ASCII text A standard and universal computer text format.

astigmatism The inability or skewed ability to perceive depth.

asymmetrical balance Describes a layout in which there is an unequal amount of visual elements on each side of a page.

atmospheric conditions Naturally occurring phenomenon that changes the colors and values seen in the environment, such as fog, rain, and snow.

AU *See Sun Audio.*

Audio Interchange File Format (AIFF) A digital audio file format predominantly used on Macintosh and Silicon Graphics machines.

author The creator of a work, who holds the right of copyright from the data of creation.

Authorware   An interaction-based authoring program created by Macromedia.

Autodesk FLI and FLC   A digital animation format that uses frame differencing to write the frames in the animation.

avant-garde   Generally viewed as a paradigm shift or something that is out of the ordinary.

AVI   *See Video for Windows.*

Backstage   An HTML page generation and site management tool created by Macromedia.

balance   Refers to the equal or unequal amount of visual elements on a page; described as either symmetrical or asymmetrical.

banding   The visual stripes that can appear in 256-color images as a result of interpolation.

bandwidth   Describes the amount of data that can be pushed over a network connection.

Bézier curves   Special spline curves that have control points that can be moved, thus changing the shape of the curve.

binary compression (BIN)   A standard Internet external compression scheme.

binary data   Data that is described using a series of 0s and 1s; digital data.

bit depth   Determines the number of physical bits that can be used to represent a sample from an analog source.

bitmap   A graphic in which the smallest element is the pixel.

bitmap editor   An application designed to edit bitmap images.

bitmap fonts   Fonts that are described using bitmap images.

bitmap graphics   *See bitmap.*

blending   Merging two or more items to obtain steps in between.

BMP   *See Windows Bitmap.*

bookmark   A browser convention that allows the user to copy URL locations that can be used later to instantly access a Web site.

Boolean operations   Logical operations that are used to create unique objects from a set of lower objects. The three primary operations are union, subtraction, and intersection.

boundary representation (B-rep)   A method of describing the limits and form of a 3D model.

browser   A special application designed to view HTML pages from the WWW.

bump mapping   A special feature of 3D animation programs that allows the user to specify textures through the use of other bitmaps. Depths are generated from grayscale values and applied to an object or a surface.

byte   A series of 8 bits.

cache   A special location on the hard drive where a browser can temporarily store files for future use.

cameras A special view created in 3D animation programs for rendering a 3D scene; a perspective view.

cathode ray tube A tube that allows images to be projected from special guns to create displayed images.

cel A single frame from an animation; previously described as a traditionally generated animation frame because each frame was created on a celluloid or acetate substance.

cel animation Traditional method of creating animations in which each frame was hand-drawn and painted on a celluloid or acetate substance.

channels Special saved selections (raster editor); a track of music in an audio program (mono versus stereo).

chroma keying A special compositing feature that allows one clip to substitute for a special color in the second clip.

clip-art Pregenerated and generally public domain graphics that can be used in derivative works.

codec Acronym for compressor/decompression, generally used to describe the code that performs compression and decompression.

collective works Works that are based upon a collection of other unique works, such as a set of books previously not bundled together.

color The visual phenomenon that occurs as a result of absorption or projection of visible light.

color cycling An animation effect in which colors are substituted in an image, such as cycling from red to blue.

Color Lookup Table (CLUT) The color matrix used in 8-bit images. Each color in the CLUT has a number, and each pixel in the image is associated with one number from the CLUT.

color schemes Sequences of color that are known to look visually pleasing when used together in images.

color shifting An unappealing visual affect in which colors shift from proper to inappropriate colors; generally occurs when the computer has to interpolate colors.

color space The method of theoretically defining all of the colors that can be replicated or generated by a specific device.

color wheel A circular arrangement of all the colors for a particular device.

command-line interface An operating environment in which commands are typed, one line at a time.

communication The process of sending a message through a communication channel. The message must be received and interpreted correctly for communication to occur.

Compact Disc Read-Only Memory (CD-ROM) A computer storage medium in which digital data is stored on a plastic-coated silver platter. CD-ROMs can contain from 550 to 650 megabytes.

compilations A copyrightable work in which major portions of various works are used together to create a new work such as combining songs from various artists to create a greatest hits CD.

complementary Colors that occur across the color wheel from one another such as blue and orange, red and green, and purple and yellow. Most color-blindness problems occur with complementary colors.

compositing The effect of merging two media elements into one media element.

compression The process of reducing digital file size by either deleting unneeded data or substituting for redundant data.

compression ratio A description of a codec's effectiveness. Obtained by comparing bits before and after compression.

consistency Describes recurring elements that appear across multiple pages of a Web site.

content The media elements used to convey a message; it also includes the message being conveyed.

contrast A description of the value differences between adjacent items or colors.

cool colors Colors that tend to recede in a graphic, such as green, blue, and violet.

copyright The method of protecting creative works in the United States.

CYMK Describes the colors used in four-color process printing.

CYMK color model The conceptual color space used to describe the gamut of colors for printed output.

daughter card An add-on computer interface card that connects to an existing card within the computer, rather than to the computer's main system board.

Debablizer A program for the Macintosh platform that is used to convert graphic, sound, and digital video files.

decibels A measure of frequency variations that are not necessarily associated with loudness.

deformation Refers to a object that is deformed.

derivative works A work that is partially based upon another work, such as reusing a graphic in another publication.

Design Painter A raster-editing application.

device dependent A media element that has a fixed resolution; designed for output on a specific device.

device independent A media element that does not have a fixed resolution; can be adjusted for output on any device.

device resolution Describes the number of dots per inch for a specific device.

dial-up access Internet access in which a user uses a modem to dial into a remote computer. All Web materials are downloaded to the remote computer and then through the modem. It is the slowest type of network connection.

dial-up connection Internet access in which a user uses a modem to dial into a computer. All materials are downloaded directly from the Internet through the modem.

digital audio An audio file that describes a waveform bit by bit as it occurs over time.

Digital Audio Tape (DAT) A digital recording and playback device used in the music industry.

digital data *See binary data.*

Digital to analog conversion (DAC) The process of converting digital data to analog data so that it can be interpreted by humans.

direct network connection A network connection in which the user's machine is connected to the network through a network interface card. This is the fastest type of network connection.

Director A time-based authoring program created by Macromedia.

dithering The process of scattering pixels during interpolation to overcome banding.

dots per inch (dpi) A measurement of the number of displayable or printable dots per square inch

DSP Digital Signal Processor A special processor found on most sound cards that allows the sound card to process audio functions and commands.

dub A slang term for copying a medium.

dynamic Describes animated graphics, as opposed to static or unmoving graphics.

edutainment Software with an educational purpose that is entertaining as well.

electromagnetic spectrum The range of waveforms that occur in the environment.

e-mail Electronic mail; the capability to send text messages and other digital files across the Internet.

embedded programs Self-contained applications that can be included in a Web page.

executable application A stand-alone program most often designed to do a specific task. Requires no other programs to execute.

Explorer A Web browser created by Microsoft.

external file compression Compression that occurs independent of any particular type of digital data.

external link A link in a Web page that leads outside the current site.

eyeflow The direction in which a user's eyes are drawn or directed across a page.

farcle A sharp and intense flash of reflected lights, similar to a starburst.

field of vision The range or cone of vision.

file size The size of a digital file.

File Transfer Protocol (FTP) An Internet service designed to distribute and retrieve files across the Internet.

filter A special add-on program that allows the user to create a special effect or perform some special function.

flat shading Rendering in which the scene or model is represented by wires and flat polygonal colors.

FLI *See Autodesk FLI and FLC.*

font *See typefont.*

four-color process Color printing technology that utilizes cyan, yellow, magenta, and black inks to create full color reproductions.

fps Frames per second.

frame A single instance in time in an animation: one cel.

frame number The total number of frames in a digital animation or video.

frame rate *See fps.*

FreeHand A vector-illustration program created by Macromedia.

frequency A method of describing a particular sound; measured in Hertz.

frequency variations The fundamental basis for analog data, composed of waves.

FrontPage An HTML generator and site management tool created by Microsoft.

gamut Describes the entire range of something, such as gamut of colors—the entire range of colors.

General MIDI Mode The specification that states the standard MIDI channel and instrument numbers.

generation Used to describe a hierarchy of copies in analog dubbing.

GIF 89a A special GIF file that can contain transparency data.

Gopher A text- and menu-based Internet search program.

Gouroud A rendering technique in which polygonal faces are rendered using surface normals—no shades and shadows, though.

graphic A visual representation.

Graphic Interchange Format (GIF) A special file format developed by CompuServe that can contain 256-color data as well as transparency information.

grayscale The scale of values from black to white.

handles Small square boxes used in vector illustration programs to represent points.

helper application An external application used to aid the browser in viewing certain types of files.

hertz A measure of waveform cycles per second.

hexadecimal color A base-16 mathematical scheme used to define colors for a Web browser.

hierarchical linking The ability to link one object to another so that changes to one object also affect the linked object.

HLS Hue, light, and saturation.

HLS color model A color model used to describe a gamut of colors by hue, light, and saturation.

home page The primary or beginning page at a Web site.

horizontal space The width of the letter M in a font.

hotlinks A text, graphic, or other media element that when clicked takes the user to a different site or page.

hue A characteristic of color that distinguishes it from other colors; the name of a color such as red, blue, and green.

human-computer interface An area of study that focuses on the development of effective interface design.

hyperlink *See hotlinks.*

hypermedia Media that includes text, graphics, sound, animation, and video, and is not confined to a single medium.

hypertext Text that is non-linear and non-sequential.

Hypertext Markup Language (HTML) The scripting language used to describe the contents of Web pages; a derivative of the SGML language.

icons Graphics representations or abstractions.

Illustrator A vector illustration program created by Adobe.

image bit depth *See bit depth.*

image maps Special graphics that can be used in Web pages that are divided into regions; each region can be hotlinked to a different site or page.

image resolution A description of an image's dpi.

image size A description of an image's physical size in pixels.

in-betweens Frames that occur in between the key actions or movements in an animation.

indexed *See 8-bit color.*

inline image An image inserted into a Web page using the <A> tag.

interactive multimedia Any combination of text, graphics, sound, animation, and video that is controlled by the user and displayed by a computer.

interface The point of interaction between a user and a computer.

Interlaced GIF A GIF file that is stored so that it can be downloaded and displayed one chunk at a time.

internal file compression File compression that occurs as a result of the data in a particular file format.

Internet A collection of interconnected computers to allow the sharing of data and interaction of people around the world.

interpolate To derive something based on other dependent variables.

interpreter Generally, a program that executes many lines of code one line at a time.

intersection A basic Boolean operation in which the overlapping area or volume of two objects becomes residual and all remaining area, non-shared, is deleted.

intrasite link A link that jumps you to another page in the current site.

Inverse Kinematics The study of interrelationships between mechanical objects and their movements over time.

Java A platform-independent, object-oriented programming language.

JavaScript A scripting language that is a simplified derivative of the Java programming language.

Joint Pictures Experts Group (JPEG) A graphic image file format that uses lossy compression and can contain image data up to 24bits.

keyframe A frame in an animation in which a key action or change is taking place.

kilohertz (kHz) 1,000 hertz.

kinematics The study of the relationship of movement as it relates to mechanical objects.

kinesiology The study of the relationship of movement as it related to the human body.

layering The capability of a graphics application to store objects distinctly and separately.

leading The spacing between multiple lines of text.

Lepel ZivWelch compression (LZW) Lossless compression scheme most often used in the TIFF file format.

letter spacing The spacing between letters of a font.

license A permission to use a copyrighted item in which a fee is paid based upon various parameters for use.

light source An object that emits light.

linear Pertaining to progression or straight movement.

lossless Compression programs in which no data is lost; the uncompressed file creates an exact replica of the original.

lossy Compression scheme in which certain amounts of data are sacrificed for higher compression ratios.

Macintosh PICT Native Macintosh metafile format that can house both vector and raster information.

Macromedia A company specializing in interactive multimedia and graphics applications.

mapped Pertaining to 8-bit color mapping.

metaphor A construct used to familiarize an audience with an information tool based upon past experience.

modeler The portion of a 3D animation package that is used to create or import modeling data.

monaurel Describes a single channel digital audio file.

monochromatic An image using only tints and shades of a single hue.

monospaced fonts Fonts in which there is no letter spacing variations from character to character.

morph The ability to smoothly interpolate between two or more images.

Mosaic   The first Web browser, introduced by Marc Andreesen.

Motion Picture Experts Group (MPG)   A digital video format commonly found on the Web.

MOV   *See QuickTime.*

MPEG   *See Motion Picture Experts Group.*

MPG   *See Motion Picture Experts Group.*

multimedia   Any combination of text, graphics, sound, animation, and video displayed and controlled by the computer.

Multiple Master   A special type of vector font.

multiprotocol   The capability to utilize and communicate using various network protocols.

Multipurpose Internet Mail Extension (MIME)   The method of associating Internet file types with specific extensions with applications that can open them.

Munsell color model   A color model that strives to describe all the colors that occur in nature. .

Musical Instrument Device Interface (MIDI)   A method of digitally describing audio using instrument and note descriptions.

Navigator   A Web browser created by Netscape Communications.

negative space   Describes white space, or areas without visual elements, on a Web page.

newsgroup   An Internet bulletin board composed of groups of individuals who discuss specific topics; an electronic bulletin board.

noise   Anything that disrupts a message from being received or interpreted.

non-disclosure statement   A legal document that protects an idea.

non-linear   Pertaining to non-sequential, non-progressive, or non-traditional media.

non-transient information   Information that remains stable or accurate over a period of nine months to one year.

Non-Uniform Rational B-Splines (NURBS)   A parametric modeling environment in which surface points can be easily edited; allows very complex organic surfaces and objects.

onion skinning   A carry-over technique from traditional cel animation in which the contents of adjacent frames are composited to enable comparisons of motion.

opacity   Describes the visual solidness of surfaces; transparent is the opposite of opaque.

operating system   The environment and commands used to perform basic computing operations.

origin   In relation to the 3D coordinate system, the origin is the location 0,0,0.

orthographic view   A view in which the viewer's line of sight is perpendicular to one full side of an object.

PageMill An HTML generator and site management program created by Adobe.

palette *See Color Lookup Table (CLUT).*

palletized *See 8-bit color.*

paradigm A way of thinking or a personal view of something.

particle systems A special function within a 3D animation program that allows the animator to create effects like rain, snow, and tornadoes.

path of motion The path on which animated objects travel; defined by keyframe positioning and orientation.

persistence of vision The visual phenomenon that cause the eyes and brain to perceive an image even after it has been removed from sight.

perspective A pictorial drawing in which the lines in the scene tend to converge to the horizon.

phong A rendering engine that is able to generate smooth surfaces and calculate highlights and shadows based on lights positioned in the environment.

Photoshop A raster-editing application created by Adobe.

PICT *See Macintosh PICT.*

pitch A single note or tone; various pitches (notes) have various frequencies.

pixels (picture element) The smallest element of a bitmap image, computer monitor, or television display.

pixels per inch (ppi) The number of pixels per square inch; ppi equals dpi.

platform *See operating system.*

plug-ins Add-on programs that extend the capability of a Web browser by allowing it to view a wide range of files, such as animations, digital videos, or multimedia elements.

point size Describes the size of a font in points.

points A unit of measurement for lines and text; 72 points equals 1 inch.

polygonal mesh Describes a surface model that uses polygons, most often triangles, to define the surface of a model.

Portable Network Graphics (PNG) A new graphics format designed to unify the formats used on the Web. Boasts all of the features of both JPEG and GIF in a single format.

positive space Describes an area on a Web page that contains visual elements such as text or graphics.

PostScript A page description language developed by Adobe that is used by most vector drawing programs.

Premiere A digital video editing program created by Adobe.

primary color The main colors of any given color system; all other colors in the system are derived from the primary colors.

procedural mapping A method of adding surface textures to 3D objects through the use of algorithms.

progressive JPEG A special type of JPEG image that allows the browser to begin viewing the image prior to its being fully downloaded.

public domain Media elements or works that can be freely used, without a license or release.

QuickTime (MOV) A digital video format, created by Apple, which was originally designed for use on the Macintosh.

radiant light A light source in which light is projected in all directions with no decrease in intensity.

radiosity The most photo-realistic type of 3D rendering; takes into consideration all light within a scene.

Random Access Memory (RAM) The main memory of the computer, which is used to temporarily store data.

raster-based graphics See bitmap.

ray-tracing A rendering technique that traces light rays within a scene; it does not calculate scattered light rays.

RCA-type A typical cable connector used with digital video and digital audio.

reflected light See additive colors.

reflectivity An object property that describes its shininess and how much of the scene is reflected in the surface.

release A permission to use a copyrighted item without payment or fees; often, usage has certain limitations.

remapping Pertains to changing the color palette of an image.

renderer The part of the 3D animation program that generates a raster image or animation.

rendering engine Special code that uses the 3D scene to create a flat raster image; includes wireframe, flat, Gouroud, phong, ray-tracing, and radiosity.

resolution A term generally used to describe the photo-realism of an image; describes the ratio of image resolution to image size.

RGB (Red, Green, Blue) Describes the primary colors used to create color on CRT devices.

RGB color See 24-bit color.

RGB color model Theoretical color space used to describe the range of colors available on a computer monitor.

rhodopsin Chemical found in the human eye that allows the perception of color.

rods The special color-sensitive cells within the retinal surfaces.

roll Relates to rotation around the Z-axis.

Run Length Encoding See Windows Bitmap.

S-Video A video cable connector commonly found on U.S. devices.

sampling The process of converting analog data to digital data.

sampling rate The frequency with which samples or chunks are taken from an analog source.

sans serif Typefonts without feet and tails.

saturation Describes the purity of a color—how much of a color is in a hue.

scan lines Describes the horizontal lines of pixels in a computer monitor.

serif The small feet and tails that occur on some fonts to make them easier to read.

serif fonts Fonts with feet and tails.

shade Areas or surfaces that are opposite the light source.

shadows Areas or surfaces that are blocked from a light source by another feature or object.

Shockwave A plug-in created by Macromedia for viewing multimedia and vector elements on the Web.

Simple Text The standard Macintosh ASCII text editor.

SIT A compressed file created by Aladdin's Stuffit Deluxe.

site A Web site; a server designed to distribute HTML documents.

site map A planning tool for charting the contents of a Web site.

SND *See System 7 Sound Files (SND).*

solid model A model that has theoretical volume and engineering properties.

Sound Blaster Vocal Files (VOC) A digital audio format designed by Creative Labs.

spatial Relating to 3D coordinate space or space relationships.

spectrum The colors that compose visible light: red, orange, yellow, green, blue, indigo, and violet.

splash page *See home page.*

spline A curve with weighted control points.

spotlight A directed light source.

sprite An element or object in a 2D animation program.

Standard Generalized Markup Language (SGML) An advanced markup language that is commonly used for electronic encyclopedias or dictionaries.

static Pertains to images that do not change or are not animated.

stereo A multiple-channel digital audio file.

stereoscopic field of vision The area created by the overlapping cone of vision from each eye; field in which depth is perceived.

stereoscopic vision The ability to perceive depth.

storyboard A thumbnail representation, often used for planning an animation, multimedia, or hypermedia products.

streaming The process of delivering small chunks of a digital file over the Internet for instant execution.

Stuffit Expander A compression program used on the Macintosh platform.

subtraction   One of the basic Boolean operations; the volume or area of one object is subtracted from the volume or area of another.

subtractive colors   Method of producing colors on a white page by applying hues.

subtractive primaries   Cyan, yellow, magenta, black; describes the primary colors used to create printed color.

Sun Audio (AU)   Audio format predominantly used on the UNIX operating system.

surface mapping   The process of applying qualities to 3D objects so that they look realistic.

surface model   A model composed of surfaces with no volume characteristics.

symmetrical balance   Describes a layout in which there is an equal amount of visual elements on each side of a page.

synthesis   The ability to create a waveform (analog data).

System 7 Sound Files (SND) Standard Macintosh system sound format.

system palette   The color palette or Color Lookup Table associated with a 256-color environment.

Tagged   Image   File   Format (TIFF)   A raster graphic file format that was designed to contain high-resolution image data for print purposes.

text editor   A program designed to edit plain ASCII text files.

TIFF   *See Tagged Image File Format (TIFF).*

tiles   Bitmaps that are used as repeating segments over the background of a browser; a tiled background.

tint   Adding white to any hue.

tone   The overall manner in which a site is presented.

Topas   A 3D animation package created by Rio.

transient information   Information that is rapidly changing—generally changes within nine months or less.

translation   A basic manipulation of an object; includes move, rotate, and scale.

translucent   The ability of light to pass through a surface.

transparency   The ability to see through an object.

triad   A color scheme using three colors that are equally spaced from one another on the color wheel.

True Color   *See 24-bit color.*

TrueType   A typical type of vector font.

tweens   *See in-betweens.*

typeface   *See typefont.*

typefont   A unique set of characters that have similar characteristics; examples include Helvetica, Geneva, and Times.

typography   The study of type and its various characteristics.

union   A basic Boolean operation in which the overlapping volume or area between two objects is joined (or welded) to create a single object.

Uniform Resource Locator (URL) The unique naming address scheme used on the Web.

value Pertaining to the lightness or darkness of a color. Adding black to a hue creates a shade; adding white to a hue creates a tint.

VBScript A Web-based scripting language.

VDOLive One of the newer digital video streaming formats.

vector fonts Fonts that are described using vector descriptions.

vector-based graphics Graphics in which the smaller drawing elements are points, lines, and arcs.

Video for Windows (AVI) A common digital video format created for use on the Windows platform.

Virtual Reality Modeling Language (VRML) A markup language designed to deliver 3D environment descriptions for viewing on the Web.

visible light The small portion of the electromagnetic spectrum that humans can perceive.

visual appeal Describes the artistic or aesthetic qualities of an image or page.

VOC *See Sound Blaster Vocal Files (VOC).*

warm color Color that tends to come toward the view; includes colors such as red, yellow, and orange.

WAV *See Windows Waveform Files (WAV).*

weight (of a font) The thickness of the lines that compose the font.

white space *See negative space.*

Windows Bitmap (BMP) Raster format created by Microsoft for bitmap images.

Windows Waveform Files (WAV) The standard Windows digital audio format.

wireframe model A model composed of connecting lines and points with no surfaces.

wireframe rendering A rendering in which the lines of the object are rendered but no surfaces are rendered.

WordPad The Windows 95 and Windows NT ASCII text editor.

World Wide Web (WWW) A portion of the Internet devoted to delivering HTML pages and hypermedia content.

Yahoo! A Web index site that contains thousands of Web links categorized by topic (http://www.yahoo.com).

yaw Rotation around the Y-axis.

ZIP A compressed file created by Pkware's PKZIP program.

A

Graphics, Animation, and Multimedia Tools

As you've noticed throughout this book, there are very few references to specific tools (unless a tool affects the content being presented). This appendix shows a variety of the tools that can be used to generate various media elements as well as create entire pages and sites. Whenever possible, a Web site address is also included so that you can find out more information about the particular software.

Commercial software products are those that you can purchase from a vendor or through retail locations. The tools presented here are the ones that are most widely used throughout the industry. You'll find that in most states, it is cheaper to order through mail-order houses than it is to purchase the software through a retail chain.

Graphics Tools

Adobe Illustrator

Description: One of the most widely used vector-based drawing programs.

`http://www.adobe.com`

Adobe Photoshop

Description: One of the most widely used raster-based editing programs.

`http://www.adobe.com`

CorelDRAW! 6

Description: Predominantly a vector-based drawing program but also includes a raster editor (Corel PhotoPaint).

`http://www.corel.com`

Corel PhotoPaint

Description: One of the most widely used raster-editing applications.

`http://www.corel.com`

Deneba Software's Canvas

Description: A combination vector- and raster-based drawing program.

`http://www.deneba.com`

Equilibrium Software's Debabelizer

Description: File format conversion program.

`http://www.equil.com`

Fractal Design Expression

Description: Vector-based drawing program.

`http://www.fractal.com`

Fractal Design Painter

Description: Raster-based drawing program.

`http://www.fractal.com`

JASC, Inc.'s Paint Shop Pro

Description: Raster-based drawing program.

`http://www.jasc.com`

Macromedia FreeHand

Description: Vector-based drawing program.

`http://www.macromedia.com`

Quarterdeck Corp.'s Hijaak Pro

Description: Raster image editor and conversion program. Supports the widest variety of file formats and excels at conversion from one format to another.

`http://www.quarterdeck.com`

Ron Scott's QFX

Description: A combo raster/vector program.

`http://www.qfx.com`

Specular Collage

Description: Raster-based program.

`http://www.specular.com`

Other Graphics Tools

Metatools Kai's Power Goo

Description: Raster image editor and special effects generator.

`http://www.metatools.com`

Metatools Kai's Power Tools

Description: Add-on plug-ins for Photoshop and Painter.

`http://www.metatools.com`

Alien Skin Software's The Black Box

Description: Add-on plug-ins for special effects in Photoshop.

`http://www.alienskin.com`

Strata MediaPaint

Description: Raster-based special effects.

`http://www.strata3d.com`

Animation Tools

3*D EYE TriSpectives

Description: 3D rendering and animation package.

http://www.eye.com

Astound WebMotion

Description: Java and 2D animation creation.

http://www.golddisk.com

auto*des*sys formZ

Description: 3D rendering and animation package.

http://www.formz.com/

Caligari TrueSpace2

Description: 3D rendering and animation package.

http://www.caligari.com

Electric Image

Description: 3D rendering and animation package.

http://www.electricimage.com

Fractal Design Ray Dream Designer

Description: 3D rendering and animation package.

http://www.fractal.com

FutureWave Software's FutureSplash Animator 1.0

Description: Vector-based 2D animation package.

http://www.futurewave.com

Kinetix Animator Studio

Description: 2D rendering and animation package.

http://www.ktx.com

Kinetix 3D Studio

Description: 3D rendering and animation package.

http://www.ktx.com

Kinetix 3D Studio Max

Description: One of the most widely used 3D rendering and animation packages.

http://www.ktx.com

Macromedia Director

Description: Time-based authoring tool (also capable of 2D animation).

http://www.macromedia.com

Metatools Bryce2

Description: 3D rendering package.

http://www.metatools.com

Newtek's LightWave 3D

Description: 3D rendering and animation software.

http://www.newtek.com

SoftImage

Description: 3D rendering and animation package.

http://www.softimage.com/Softimage/

Specular Infinit-D

Description: 3D rendering and animation package.

http://www.specular.com

Strata Studio Pro

Description: 3D rendering and animation package.

http://www.strata3d.com

Sound Tools

Macromedia SoundEdit 16

Description: Mac-based sound editing tool.

http://www.macromedia.com

Macromedia Sound Forge

Description: PC-based sound editing tool.

http://www.macromedia.com

Video Tools

Adobe Premiere

Description: Video editing program.

http://www.adobe.com

Denim Software's Illuminaire

Description: Video editing program.

http://www.denimsoftware.com

Strata VideoShop

Description: Video editing program.

http://www.strata3d.com

Authoring Tools

Astound

Description: Multimedia presentation package.

http://www.golddisk.com

Aimtech Jamba

Description: Java authoring tool.

http://www.aimtech.com

Aimtech IconAuthor

Description: Authoring tool.

http://www.aimtech.com

Allen Communication's Quest

Description: Authoring tool.

http://www.allencomm.com

Macromedia Authorware

Description: Authoring tool.

http://www.macromedia.com

Macromedia Director

Description: Time-based authoring tool (also capable of 2D animation).

http://www.macromedia.com

mFactory's mTropolis

Description: Authoring tool.

http://www.mfactory.com

Oracle Media Objects

Description: Authoring tool.

http://www.oracle.com

Quark Immedia

Description: Authoring program.

http://www.quark.com

Strata MediaForge

Description: Authoring program.

http://www.strata3d.com

HTML Editors, Generators, and Site Management Tools

Adobe PageMill

Description: Page generation and site management tool.

http://www.adobe.com

Brooklyn North Software Works HTML Assistant Pro

Description: Page generation tool.

http://www.brooknorth.com

InContext System's InContext Spider

Description: Page generation tool.

http://www.incontext.com

Macromedia Backstage Designer

Description: Page generation and site management tool.

`http://www.macromedia.com`

Microsoft FrontPage 97

Description: Page generation and site management tool.

`http://www.microsoft.com`

NetObjects Fusion

Description: Page generation tool.

`http://www.netobjects.com`

Quarterdeck WebAuthor

Description: Page generation and site management tool.

`http://www.quarterdeck.com`

Sausage Software's Hot Dog Professional

Description: Page generation tool.

`http://www.sausage.com`

SoftQuad's HoTMetaL Pro

Description: Page generation tool.

`http://www.softquad.com`

Browsers

IBM Web Explorer

`http://www.ibm.com`

Microsoft Internet Explorer

`http://www.microsoft.com`

Netscape Communication's Communicator

`http://www.netscape.com`

Netscape Communication's Navigator

`http://www.netscape.com`

Spyglass Mosaic

`http://www.spyglass.com`

INDEX

SYMBOLS

2D (two-dimensional) animation, 145-149, 161-162, 361
animation files, 149
cels, 145, 162-163
effects, 179
 chroma-keying, 180-181
 color cycling, 179-180
 compositing, 180
 deformations, 174-175
 filters, 183
 morphing, 181-183
 rotoscoping, 180
historical perspective, 147-148
integrating, 150
keyframes, 150-151
 bit depth, 154-155
 frame rates, 152
 sizes, 152-154
limitations, 157-158, 161
motion
 acceleration, 169-171
 deceleration, 169-171
 linking multiple paths, 172-174
 paths, 167-169
 rotation, 172
persistence of vision, 145
raster-based, 149
software, 155-158
source images
 clip-art, 179
 cut-outs, 178

sprites, 151
 raster, 165
 static, 163-164
 vector, 165-166
techniques, 175-176
 blending, 177
 onion-skinning, 176
 transparency, 177
vector-based, 149
3*D Eye Software, 380
3D (three-dimensional) animation, 145-149, 185-187, 361
animation files, 149
cels, 145
deformations, 223
environment, 220
 keyframes, 220-221
 particle systems, 224
 paths of motion, 221
historical perspective, 147-148
integrating, 150
inverse kinematics, 224
keyframes, 150-151
 bit depth, 154-155
 frame rates, 152
 sizes, 152-154
kinematics, 223-224
kinesiology, 224
modeling environment, 187
 coordinate space, 188-189
 objects, 188
 viewpoints, 189-191

persistence of vision, 145
procedural mapping, 219
raster-based, 149
rendering engines, 199
   Gouroud, 201-202
   Phong, 202
   ray-tracing, 203-204
   wireframe, 200
rendering environment,
   204-206
   cameras, 206-209
   lighting, 209-212
   object textures, 213-218
software, 155-158
sprites, 151
types, 191
   solid models, 194
   surface models, 192-199
   wireframe models,
     191-192
vector-based, 149
Web limitations, 157, 158
**3D (three-dimensional)
objects, casting shadows
on, 36-39**
3D Studio, 380
3D Studio Max, 361, 381
**8-bit (indexed) images, 114,
361**
**24-bit (true color) images,
114**
256-color images, 121-124

A

\<A\> HTML tag, 361
absorbed light, 361
**abstracts (Web site devel-
opment), 262, 361**
**accelerating motion
(animation), 169-171**
access
   dial-up, 365
   network access, planning,
     259-260
accessing FTP sites, 291
acetate, 361
achromatic colors, 34, 361

**ADC (analog to digital
conversion), 112-113, 362**
additive colors, 28-32, 361
address fields, 361
**adjusting paths of motion,
169**
Adobe, 361
   Illustrator, 378
   PageMill, 383
   Photoshop, 378
   Premiere, 382
   Web site, 378, 382
Afterburner, 95, 361
**AIFF (Audio Interchange
File Format), 337, 362**
Aimtech software, 382
algorithms, 361
aliasing, 87-88, 361
Alien Skin Software, 379
alignment, 362
Allen Communication, 382
alpha channels, 362
**alphanumeric characters,
362**
ambient light, 37, 210, 362
analog data, 28, 362
   ADC (analog-to-digital
     conversion), 112-113, 362
   degradation, 362
   sources, 362
**analog-to-digital conver-
sion (ADC), 112-113, 362**
analyzing
   audiences
     ages, 254
     backgrounds, 254
     professional levels, 256
     skill levels, 255
   Web site goals, 260-262
animation, 145-149, 362
   2D (two-dimensional),
     161-162, 361
     cels, 162-163
     limitations, 161
     paths of motion,
       167-169
     raster sprites, 165
     static frames, 163-164
     techniques, 176-179
     vector sprites, 165-166

3D (three-dimensional),
   185-187, 361
   modeling environment,
     187-191, 220
   particle systems, 224
   procedural mapping,
     219
   rendering engines,
     199-204
   rendering environment,
     204-218
   solid models, 194
   surface models, 192-199
   wireframe models,
     191-192
animation files, 149
attributes, 345
bump mapping, 363
cels, 145, 364
deformations, 174-175, 223
frames, 367-368
historical perspective,
   147-148
integrating with Web
   pages, 150
keyframes, 150-151,
   220-221
   bit depth, 154-155
   frame rates, 152
   image sizes, 152-154
   static, 163-164
motion, 221
   inverse kinematics, 224
   kinematics, 170,
     223-224
   kinesiology, 170, 224
   paths, 371
onion-skinning, 370
persistence of vision, 145
raster-based, 149
software, 155-158
   3D Studio, 380
   3D Studio Max, 361, 381
   Animator Studio, 362,
     380
   Bryce2, 381
   choosing, 158
   Director, 381
   Electric Image, 380
   formZ, 380

FutureSplash Animator, 380
Infini-D, 381
LightWave 3D, 381
Ray Dream Designer, 380
SoftImage, 381
Studio Pro, 381
Topas, 374
TriSpectives, 380
TrueSpace2, 380
WebMotion, 380
source images
  clip-art, 179
  cut-outs, 178
sprites, 151, 373
  raster sprites, 165
  vector sprites, 165-166
storyboards, 373
techniques, 175-176
  blending, 177
  chroma-keying, 180-181
  color cycling, 179-180
  compositing, 180
  filters, 183
  morphing, 181-183
  onion-skinning, 176
  rotoscoping, 180
  traditional techniques, 150-152
  transparency, 177
vector-based, 149
video, compared, 345-346
viewing, 150
Web limitations, 157-158
Animator Studio, 362, 380
animators, 362
anti-alias halos, 362
anti-aliasing, 88, 129, 362
Apple, 362
applets (Java), 287, 362
applications
developing, 256
development, 362
executable, 366
helper applications, 288, 351-352, 367
Java applets, 287, 362
see also software

ASCII, 362
associating file types, 288
astigmatism, 362
Astound, 382
  WebMotion, 380
asymmetrical balance, 10, 362
atmospheric conditions, 362
AU (Sun Audio) format, 337, 374
audience analysis
  ages, 254
  backgrounds, 254
  professional levels, 256
  skill levels, 255
audio, 317-319
  attributes, 345
  compression, 338
  decibels, 365
  degradation, 322-323
  digital, 319-322, 339-340, 366
    advantages, 322-324
    DAT (Digital Audio Tape), 366
    file sizes, 333
    monaural, 331
    sampling, 324-335
    stereo, 331
  file formats, 337-338
    AIFF, 362
    MIDI, 320-322, 336-340, 370
    VOC, 373
  frequencies, 325-329, 367
  monaural, 369
  pitch, 371
  software
    SoundEdit 16, 381
    SoundForge, 381
  streaming, 338-339
Audio Interchange File Format (AIFF), 337
authoring software
  Astound, 382
  Authorware, 382
  Director, 383
  IconAuthor, 382
  Immedia, 383

Jamba, 382
MediaForge, 383
mTropolis, 383
Oracle Media Objects, 383
Quest, 382
authors, 362
Authorware, 363, 382
Autodesk
  FLC format, 346, 363
  FLI format, 363
avant-garde, 363
AVI format, 349-350, 375

B

B-rep (boundary representation), 363
backgrounds
  colors, choosing, 48
  tiling, 74
Backstage Designer, 363, 384
balance (site design), 10-13, 363
  asymmetrical, 362
  symmetrical, 374
banding, 363
bandwidth, 363
Bézier curves, 363
Bézier points, 80
BIN (binary compression), 363
binary data, 111, 363
bit depth, 344, 363
  animation frames, 154-155
  audio sampling, 330-331
  raster images, 111-116
bitmap editors, 363
bitmap fonts, 70-73, 363
bitmap graphics, *see* **raster graphics**
BlackBox plug-in, 379
blending frames (2D animation), 177, 363
BMP (Windows bitmap) format, 138, 375
bookmarks, 363

Boolean operations, 363
    3D modeling, 197-199
    subtraction, 374
    union, 374
    vector graphics, 93-94
boundary calculations, 194
boundary representation
    (B-rep), 363
Brooklyn North Software,
    383
browsers, 19, 363, 384
    address fields, 361
    applet support, 287
    browser-safe palettes,
        125-126
    cache, 284-285
    colors, 55-58
    effects on site layout, 19-23
    functions, 278-284
    helper applications, 288
    Mosaic, 370
    Navigator, 370
    plug-ins, 285-286
    preference settings, 284
    scripting, 286
Bryce2, 381
bump mapping, 217, 363
bumpiness, 217-218
Bush, Vannevar, 237
bytes, 363

C

cables
    RCA-type connectors, 372
    S-video, 372
cache, 284-285, 363
calculating hexadecimal
    color, 57-58
Caligari software, 380
camera view, 364
cameras (3D animation),
    206-209
Canvas software, 378
capturing video, 346-347
case, design consider-
    ations, 63
case-sensitivity (URLs), 279

casting shadows
    light sources, 36-38
    projection, 39-40
cathode ray tubes, 364
CD-ROMs, 364
cels, 145, 162-163, 364
channels, 364
choosing
    animation software, 158
    color schemes, 45-48
        background colors, 48
        complementary colors,
            46
        limitations, 48-49
        monochromatic colors,
            45
        triadic, 46
    fonts, 75
chroma-keying, 180-181,
    364
Cinepak, 349
clarity (Web page design),
    307-309
clip-art, 179, 364
closed areas (vector
    graphics), 89-90
CLUT (Color Lookup
    Table), 121, 364
codecs, 348-349, 364
Collage software, 379
collective works, 364
color, 27-28, 364
    8-bit, 361
    24-bit, 361
    achromatic, 34, 361
    additive, 28-32, 361
    backgrounds, 48
    browser-safe palettes,
        55-58, 125-126
    CLUT (Color Lookup
        Table), 121, 364
    color cyling, 179-180
    color depth, 118
    color schemes, 364
        choosing, 45-48
        monochromatic, 45
        triadic, 46, 374
    complementary, 365
    contrast, 34, 45
    cool colors, 41-43, 365

electromagnetic spectrum,
    28
grayscale, 367
hexadecimal, 56-58, 367
hue, 33, 368
    lighting effects, 34-40
limitations, 48-49
measuring, 34, 56-58
models, 49
    CYMK, 53-54, 365
    HLS, 49-51, 368
    Munsell, 52, 370
    RGB, 54, 372
monochromatic, 369
palettes, remapping,
    123-124
palettized color, 121-124
perception of
    human physiology,
        44-45
    human vision, 44-45
primary, 371
printing, 31
psychological aspects,
    43-44
saturation, 22, 34, 373
shifting, 364
spectrum, 373
subtractive, 28-31, 374
system palettes, 374
tinting, 374
true-color images, 116-121
values, 22, 33, 375
visible spectrum, 29
visual aspects, 41-43
warm colors, 41-43, 375
wheels, 364
see also light
color blindness, design
    considerations, 44-45
Color Lookup Table
    (CLUT), 121, 364
color space, 364
command-line interface,
    364
commands
    File menu, Export, 97
    Image menu, Image Size,
        134

communication, 364
  linear, 233
  non-linear, supporting,
    237, 240-241
communicative power
  (Web site design), 17-19
Compact Disc, Read-Only
  Memory (CD-ROM), 364
compilations, 364
complementary colors, 46,
  365
compositing, 180, 365
compression, 139-140,
  348-349, 365
  audio, 338
  binary, 363
  codecs, 348
  external, 141-142, 366
  internal, 141, 368
  lossless, 141, 369
  lossy, 140-141, 348, 369
  LZW (Lepel ZivWelch), 369
  ratios, 365
compressor/decompressors
  (codecs), 348, 364
computer fonts, 70
  bitmap, 73
  choosing, 75
  vector, 71-72
connectors (audio), 334
consistency in design,
  15-17, 299-302, 365
Constrain File Size option
  (Photoshop), 134
content (Web sites), 277,
  365
  authorship, 250
  copyrights, 251-253
  developing, 249
  licenses, 253
  media elements, 254
  planning, 277
  releases, 253
contrast 34, 365
converting
  digital data to analog data,
    112-113
  RGB color to hexadecimal
    color, 57-58
cool colors, 41-43, 365

coordinate space (3D
  animation), 188-189
coordinate systems (virtual
  reality), 357
Copyright Act of 1976, 252
copyrights, 251-253, 365
Corel
  CorelDRAW! 6, 378
  Corel PhotoPaint, 378
  Web site, 378
cross-platform issues,
  257-258
cut-outs (2D animation),
  178
CYMK (cyan, yellow,
  magenta, black) color
  model, 53-54, 365
  four-color process printing,
    31

D

DACs (digital-to-analog
  converters), 112, 366
DAT (Digital Audio Tape),
  366
data sampling, 113-114
daughter cards, 320, 365
Debabelizer, 365, 378
decelerating motion
  (animation), 169-171
decibels, 365
defining
  colors
    hexadecimal, 56-58
    HLS, 34
  paths of motion
    begin/end points, 167
    real-time recording, 168
deformations, 174-175, 223,
  365
degradation
  analog data, 362
  audio, 322-323
Deneba Software, 378
Denim Software, 382
depth perception, 355

derivative works, 365
desaturated colors, 22
design (Web sites), 3-5, 263
  avant-garde, 363
  balance, 10-13, 363
    asymmetrical, 362
    symmetrical, 374
  browser issues, 19-23
  clarity, 307-309
  color, 27-28
    achromatic, 34
    additive, 28-32
    backgrounds, 48
    browser-safe palettes,
      125-126
    color schemes, 45-48
    contrast, 34
    hue, 33-40
    limitations, 48-49
    perception of, 44-45
    psychological aspects,
      43-44
    saturation, 34
    subtractive, 28-31
    values, 33
    warm/cool colors, 41-43
  communicative power,
    17-19
  consistency, 15-17,
    299-302, 365
  content, 277, 298-299
  development teams,
    276-277
  efficiency, 305-306
  eyeflow, 5-6, 366
  graphics, 246-247
  icons, 24-25
  impact on audience, 4
  light
    directed, 31-32
    reflected, 28-31
  linearity, 231-232
    communication, 233
    education, 234-235
    linear thinking, 232
    media, 235-236
    non-linear communica-
      tion, 237-241
  media, 229-231

metaphors, 264-266
negative space, 6-9
networking concerns, 278
noise, 370
positive space, 6-9
practicality, 310
splash pages, 303-305
supporting materials, 277
technical design, 268
   directory structure, 270
   site layout, 269
tone, 9
typography, 5-65
   alignment, 69
   case, 63
   choosing, 75
   computer fonts, 70-73
   font weights, 68
   leading, 69
   letter spacing, 68
   point size, 67
   shadows, 73-75
   styling, 64
   typefaces, 65-66
user interfaces, 266-268,
   307
visual appeal, 13-14,
   310-311, 375
Design Painter, 365
developing Web sites,
243-244, 256
applications, 256
audience analysis
   ages, 254
   backgrounds, 254
   professional levels, 256
   skill levels, 255
content, 249, 277
   authorship, 250
   copyrights, 251-253
   graphics, 254
   licenses, 253
   releases, 253
delivery systems, 258-259
   machine parameters,
     260
   network access, 259-260
   platforms, 260
design, 263
   directory structure, 270
   metaphors, 264-266

   site layout, 269
   technical design, 268
   user interfaces, 266-268
development teams,
   276-277
goals, 245-247, 260-262
implementation phase, 271
maintenance, 271-272
networking concerns, 278
nontransient information,
   247-248
platform issues, 257-258
production phase, 270-271
resources, 258
splash pages, 303-305
supporting materials, 277
tools, 258
transient information, 248
development teams,
276-277
developing supporting
   materials, 277
networking concerns, 278
planning content, 277
device dependent color
models, 365
CYMK, 53-54
RGB, 54
device independence, 365
vector graphics, 86
device resolution, 365
dial-up access, 365
digital animation, *see*
animation
digital audio, 319-322,
339-340, 366
advantages, 322-324
DAT, 366
DSPs, 319
MIDI, compared, 321-322,
   339-340
sampling, 324
   bit depth, 330-331
   file sizes, 333
   monaural, 331
   preparation, 334-335
   rates, 325-330
   stereo, 331
Digital Audio Tape (DAT),
366

digital data, 111
Digital Signal Processors
(DSPs), 319, 366
digital to analog conver-
sion (DAC), 112-113, 366
digital video
compression, 348-349
formats
   AVI, 349-350
   MPEG, 350-351
   QuickTime, 350
helper applications,
   351-352
producing, 346-347
streaming, 351-352
direct network connec-
tions, 366
directed light, 28-32
Director, 366, 381-383
directories, designing, 270
dithering, 124, 366
dpi (dots per inch), 84,
105-106, 366
DSPs (Digital Signal
Processors), 319, 366
dubbing, 366
dynamic graphics, 366

E

e-mail, 289, 366
editors
bitmap editors, 363
Simple Text, 373
WordPad, 375
education
linear thinking, 234
linearity, 235
edutainment, 366
efficiency (Web page
design), 305-306
Electric Image, 380
electromagnetic spectrum,
28, 366
electronic mail (e-mail),
289, 366
<EMBED> HTML tag, 361
embedded programs, 366

Equilibrium Software
   Debabelizer, 378
   Web site, 378
executable applications, 366
Export command (File menu), 97
external file compression, 141-142, 366
external links, 282, 366
eyeflow, 366
   defined, 8
   Web site design, 5-6

F

falloff adjustments, 212
farcles, 366
field of vision, 355, 366
   stereoscopic, 373
File menu, Export command, 97
File Transfer Protocol (FTP), 290-291, 367
files
   animation files, 149
   associations, 288
   compression, 139-140
      external, 141-142, 366
      internal, 141, 368
      lossless, 141
      lossy, 140-141
   formats, 135, 337-338
      AIFF, 337, 362
      AU, 337, 374
      AVI, 349-350, 375
      BMP, 138, 375
      GIF, 117, 136-138, 367-368
      JPEG, 117, 136-137, 369, 372
      MPEG, 350-351
      PICT, 138, 369
      PNG, 138-139, 371
      QuickTime, 350, 372
      SND, 337, 374
      TIFF, 138, 374
      VDOLive, 375
      VOC, 338
      WAV, 338, 375

fills, 89-90
filters, 183, 367
   Afterburner, 95, 361
flat shading, 200, 367
flatland raster environments, 129
FLC format, 346, 363
FLI format, 363
flow (Web site design), 5-6
fluorescent light, 211
fonts, 61
   alignment, 69
   case, 63
   choosing, 75
   computer fonts, 70
      bitmap, 73, 363
      vector, 71-72, 370, 375
   cross-platform issues, 22-23
   horizontal space, 68, 368
   leading, 69
   letter spacing, 68
   monospaced, 69, 369
   point sizes, 67, 371
   sans serif, 65-66, 373
   serif, 65-66, 373
   styles, 64
   TrueType, 374
   typefaces, 65-66
   weights, 68, 375
formats (files), 135, 337-338
   AIFF, 337, 362
   AU, 337, 374
   AVI, 349-350, 375
   BMP, 138, 375
   GIF, 117, 136, 367
      GIF 89a, 367
      interlaced, 137-138, 368
      transparency, 136
   JPEG, 117, 136, 369
      progressive, 137-138, 372
   MPEG, 350-351
   PICT, 138, 369
   PNG, 138-139, 371
   QuickTime, 350, 372
   SND, 337, 374
   TIFF, 138, 374
   VDOLive, 375
   VOC, 338
   WAV, 338, 375

formZ, 380
four-color process printing, 31, 367
Fractal Design
   Expression, 378
   Painter, 378
   Ray Dream Designer, 380
   Web site, 378-380
frames (animation keyframes), 150-152, 220-221, 300-343, 367
   bit depth, 154-155
   frame rates, 152, 368
   in-betweens, 151
   sizes, 152-154
   static, 163-164
FreeHand, 367, 379
   rasterizing vector graphics, 97-98
frequency (audio), 325-329, 367
FrontPage, 367, 384
FTP (File Transfer Protocol), 367
   servers, 290
   sites, accessing, 291
FutureSplash Animator 1.0, 380
FutureWave Software, 380

G

gamut, 367
General MIDI Mode, 337, 367
generating video clips, 346-347
generations (analog dubbing), 367
GIF (Graphic Interchange Format), 117, 136, 367
   GIF 89a, 367
   interlaced, 137-138, 368
   transparent, 136
goals of Web site development, 260-262
GoldDisk Web site, 380-382
Gopher, 291, 367

Gouroud rendering, 367
Gouroud shading, 201-202
graphic design, *see* **design**
Graphic Interchange
  Format, *see* **GIF**
graphics
  aliasing, 87-88
  anti-aliasing, 88
  bitmaps, 78, 363
  clip-art, 364
  compression, 139-140
    external, 141-142
    internal, 141
    lossless, 141
    lossy, 140-141
  design issues, 24-25
  dynamic, 366
  formats, 135
    BMP, 138
    GIF, 117, 136-138,
      367-368
    JPEG, 136-138
    PICT, 138
    PNG, 138-139
    TIFF, 138
  icons, 368
  image maps, 300, 368
  image resolution, 368
  inline images, 368
  loading, browser prefer-
    ences, 284
  purpose of, 246-247
  raster, 78, 101-103,
    126-127
    attributes, 345
    bit depth, 111-116
    browser-safe palettes,
      125-126
    device-dependency,
      104-105
    file sizes, 126
    flatland environments,
      129
    layering, 127-135
    palettized color, 121-124
    pixels, 103-104
    resolution, 105-109
    scaling, 107-115
    sizing, 109-110, 127-135
    true-color, 116-121

  resolution, 84-86, 368
  software
    BlackBox, 379
    Canvas, 378
    Collage, 379
    CorelDRAW! 6, 378
    Debabelizer, 378
    Fractal Design Expres-
      sion, 378
    Fractal Design Painter,
      378
    FreeHand, 379
    Hijaak Pro, 379
    Illustrator, 368, 378
    Kai's Power Goo, 379
    Kai's Power Tools, 379
    MediaPaint, 379
    Paint Shop Pro, 378
    PhotoPaint, 378
    Photoshop, 378
    QFX, 379
  static, 373
  vector, 77-82
    advantages, 86-87
    Boolean operations,
      93-94
    closed areas, 89-90
    compared to raster-
      based, 80-83
    device independence, 86
    disadvantages, 87-88
    fills, 89-90
    grouping, 91-92
    joining elements, 92
    points, 80
    rasterizing, 97-99
    ungrouping, 92
    Web displays, 95-96
    see also animation
grayscale, 367
grouping vector graphics,
  91-92
GUIs (graphical user
  interfaces), 295-296
  clarity, 307-309
  designing, 266-268
    consistency, 299-302
    efficiency, 305-306
    practicality, 310
    visual appeal, 310-311

  developing, 296-298
  navigation, 295-296
    button bars, 302
    frames, 300
    image maps, 300
  sample pages, 311-315
  user controls, 307

H

<H1> HTML tag, 361
handles, 367
hardware, 258-259
  audio connectors, 334
  daughter cards, 320, 365
  DSPs (Digital Signal
    Processors), 319, 366
  machine parameters, 260
  monitors
    bit depth, 117
    color depth, 118
    scan lines, 373
  network access, 259-260
  RCA-type connectors, 372
  S-video cables, 372
  video capture boards, 347
helper applications, 288,
  351-352, 367
hertz (Hz), 326, 367
hexadecimal colors, 56-57,
  367
  calculating, 57-58
hierarchical linking, 367
highlight adjustments, 212
Hijaak Pro software, 379
history of animation,
  147-148
HLS (hue, lightness,
  saturation) color model,
  49-51, 368
home pages, 280, 368
  designing, 303-305
horizontal space (fonts), 68,
  368
Hot Dog, 384
hotlinks, *see* **links**
HoTMetaL Pro, 384
<HR> HTML tag, 5, 361

HTML (Hypertext Markup Language), 5, 284-285, 361, 368
hue, 33, 368
    effects of lighting, 34-40
human-computer interfaces, 368
hyperlinks, *see* links
hypermedia, 238-240, 274-276, 368
hypertext, 368
Hypertext Markup Language, *see* HTML
Hz (hertz), 326

I

IBM Web site, 384
IconAuthor, 382
icons, designing, 24-25, 368
Illuminaire, 382
Illustrator, 368, 378
image maps, 300, 368
Image Size command (Image menu), 134
images, *see* graphics
<IMG> HTML tag, 361
Immedia, 383
implementation phase (Web site development), 271
in-betweens, 151, 368
InContext Spider, 383
Indeo, 349
indexed (8-bit) images, 114
Infini-D, 381
infringement (copyrights), 252
ink effects, 177
inline images, 368
integrating animation with Web pages, 150
interactive multimedia, *see* multimedia
interfaces, 295-296, 368
    clarity, 307-309
    designing, 266-268
        consistency, 299-302
        efficiency, 305-306
    practicality, 310
    visual appeal, 310-311
    developing, 296-298
    navigation, 295-296
        button bars, 302
        frames, 300
        image maps, 300
    sample pages, 311-315
    user controls, 307
interlaced GIFs, 137-138, 368
internal file compression, 141, 368
Internet, 368
    dial-up access, 365
    e-mail, 289
    newsgroups, 289-290
    protocols
        FTP, 290-291, 367
        Gopher, 291
        Telnet, 292-293
Internet Explorer Web site, 384
interpolation, 368
interpreters, 368
interpreting colors
    human physiology, 44-45
    psychological associations, 43-44
    warm/cool colors, 41-43
intersection, 368
intrasite links, 282, 369
inverse kinematics, 223-224, 369

J-K

Jamba, 382
JASC, Inc., 378
Java, 287
    applets, 362
joining vector graphic elements, 92
JPEG (Joint Picture Experts Group) format, 117, 136, 369
    progressive JPEG, 137-138, 372

Kai's Power Goo, 379
Kai's Power Tools, 379
keyframes, *see* frames
kilohertz (kHz), 326, 369
kinematics, 170, 223-224, 369
kinesiology, 170, 223-224, 369
Kinetix
    3D Studio, 380
    3D Studio Max, 381
    Animator Studio, 380
    Web site, 380-381
kinetographs, 148
kinetoscopes, 148

L

languages
    HTML, 284-285, 361, 368
    Java, 287
    SGML, 373
    VBScript, 375
    VRML, 358-359, 375
layering (raster images), 127-135, 369
Layers palette, 131
layout
    design issues
        balance, 10-13, 374
        communicative power, 17-19
        consistency, 15-17
        eyeflow, 5-6, 366
        positive space, 6-9
        tone, 9
        visual appeal, 13-14
        white space, 6-9
    viewing, browser differences, 19-23
leading, 69, 369
learning systems, 275
legal issues
    authorship, 250-251
    copyrights, 251-253, 365
    licenses, 253, 369
    non-disclosure statements, 370

public domain information, 372
releases, 253, 372
lens (cameras), 207
Lepel ZivWelch compression (LZW), 369
letter spacing, 68, 369
licenses, 253, 369
light
  in 3D animation, 209-212
  absorbed light, 361
  ambient, 210, 362
  ambient light, 37
  directed, 28-32
  effects on hue, 34-40
  electromagnetic spectrum, 28, 366
  farcles, 366
  fluorescent, 211
  radiant, 211, 372
  reflectivity, 215-216
  relected, 28-31
  sources, 369
    direction, 36-38
    elevation, 36-38
  spotlights, 212, 373
  translucence, 374
  visible spectrum, 29, 375
  see also color
LightWave 3D, 381
line attributes (vector graphics), 90
linearity, 231-232
  impact on society, 232
    communication, 233
    education, 234-235
  linear media, 235-236
  linear thinking, 232
  non-linear thinking, 237
    supporting, 240-241
linking
  hierarchical, 367
  paths of motion, 172-174
links, 280-282
  external, 282, 366
  graphics, 283
  intrasite, 282, 369
  text styles, 64
  text-based, 282

loading images, 284
lossless compression, 141, 369
lossy compression, 140-141, 348, 369
lowercase, design considerations, 63
LZW (Lepel ZivWelch) compression, 369

M

Macintosh
  display colors, 22
  file formats
    QuickTime, 350
    PICT, 138
Macromedia, 369
  Authorware, 382
  Backstage Designer, 384
  Director, 381-383
  FreeHand, 97-98, 379
  Shockwave, 95
  SoundEdit 16, 381
  SoundForge, 381
  Web site, 379-381
maintaining Web sites, 271-272
mapping
  bump mapping, 217
  procedural mapping, 214, 219
  surface mapping, 213-214, 218
measuring colors
  hexadecimal colors, 56-58
  HLS, 34
media
  hypermedia, 238-240, 274-276, 368
  linearity, 231-236
    in communication, 233
    in learning, 234-235
    impact on society, 232
    linear thinking, 232
    non-linear thinking, 237, 370

multimedia, 330 331, 374, 370
  interactive, 368
  knowledge base, 274-276
  non-linear structure, 231-237
  static, 248
MediaForge, 383
MediaPaint, 379
memory (RAM), 372
meshes, 194
  patches, 196-197
  polygonal surface meshes, 195-196
metaphors in Web site design, 264-266, 369
Metatools
  Bryce2, 381
  Kai's Power Goo, 379
  Kai's Power Tools, 379
  Web site, 379-381
MFactory, 383
Microsoft FrontPage, 384
MIDI (Musical Instrument Device Interface), 320-322, 336-340, 370
  advantages, 336-337
  compared to digital audio, 321-322, 339-340
  General MIDI Mode, 337, 367
MIME (Multipurpose Internet Mail Extension), 288, 370
modelers, 187, 369
modeling, 187
  types, 191
    solid, 194
    surface, 192-199
    wireframe, 191-192
  variables, 187
    coordinate space, 188-189
    objects, 188
    viewpoints, 189-191
models (colors), 49
  CYMK, 53-54
  HLS, 49-51

Munsell, 52
RGB, 54
monitors
 bit depth, 117
 color depth, 118
 colors, 32
 resolution, 84
 scan lines, 373
monaural sound, 331, 369
 file sizes, 333
**monochromatic color
 schemes, 45, 369**
monospaced fonts, 69, 369
morphing, 181-183, 369
Mosaic, 370
motion (animation), 167
 acceleration, 169-171
 deceleration, 169-171
 inverse kinematics, 224
 kinematics, 170, 224
 kinesiology, 170, 224
 paths, 167-169, 221
  adjusting, 169
  begin/end points, 167
  defining, 168
  hierarchical linking,
   172-174
 paths of, 167-169
 rotation, 172
**MPEG (Motion Picture
 Experts Group) format,
 350-351, 370**
mTropolis, 383
**multimedia, 229-230, 274,
 370**
 animation, 145-149
  2D techniques, 175-183
  animation files, 149
  attributes, 345
  bit depth, 154-155
  cels, 145, 162-163
  frame rates, 152
  historical perspective,
   147-148
  image sizes, 152-154
  integrating, 150
  keyframes, 150-151,
   163-164
  paths of motion,
   167-175

persistence of vision,
 145
raster-based, 149
software, 155-158
source images, 178-179
sprites, 151, 165-166
traditional techniques,
 150-152
vector-based, 149
viewing, 150
Web limitations,
 157-158
audio, 317-319
 attributes, 345
 compression, 338
 digital, 319-340
 file formats, 337-338
 file sizes, 333
 frequencies, 325-329
 MIDI, 320-340
 monaural, 331
 sampling, 324-335
 stereo, 331
 streaming, 338-339
defined, 230-231
knowledge base, 274-276
non-linear structure,
 231-237
video, 341-342
 attributes, 345
 compression, 348-349
 file sizes, 342-343
 file formats, 349-351
 frames, 343
 generating, 346-347
 helper applications,
  351-352
 image bit depth, 344
 sampling, 344
 streaming, 351-352
Multiple Master fonts, 370
**multiprotocol capabilities,
 370**
**Multipurpose Internet Mail
 Extension (MIME), 288**
**Munsell color model, 52,
 370**
**Musical Instrument Digital
 Interface,** *see* **MIDI**

N

navigation, 295-296
 button bars, 302
 consistency, 15-17
 designing, 299-302
 efficiency, 305-306
 frames, 300
 image maps, 300
 links, 280-282
 practicality, 310
 sample pages, 311-315
 user control, 307
 visual appeal, 310-311
Navigator, 370
negative space, 6-9, 370
Nelson, Ted, 237
NetObjects Fusion, 384
Netscape Web site, 384
networks
 access, planning, 259-260
 direct connections, 366
**networking concerns in
 Web site design, 278**
newsgroups, 289-290, 370
Newtek software, 381
noise, 370
**non-disclosure statements,
 370**
non-linear communication
 media, 370
 supporting, 240-241
**non-transient information,
 370**
**NURBS (Non-Uniform
 Rational B-Splines), 196,
 370**

O

objectives of Web site
 development, 262
objects
 3D animation, 188
 bumpiness, 217-218
 deformations, 174-175
 opacity/transparency, 216

reflectivity, 215-216
textures, 213-218
**onion-skinning (2D anima-
tion), 176, 370**
opacity, 216, 370
operating system displays
colors, 22
fonts, 22-23
operations, Boolean, 363
Oracle Media Objects, 383
**origins (3D coordinate
systems), 370**
**orthographic views, 206,
370**

P

<P> HTML tag, 361
PageMill, 371, 383
Paint Shop Pro, 378
palettes
browser-safe, 125-126
remapping, 123-124
palettized color, 121-124
paradigms, 371
particle systems, 224, 371
**patches (3D modeling),
196-197**
**paths of motion), 167-169,
221, 371**
adjusting, 169
defining
begin/end points, 167
real-time recording, 168
hierarchical linking,
172-174
multiple, 172
PC display colors, 22
**persistence of vision, 145,
371**
perspective, 371
**perspective view render-
ings, 207**
Phong rendering, 371
Phong shading, 202
PhotoPaint, 378
Photoshop, 371, 378

physiology of color perception, 44-45
PICT format, 138, 369
pitch, 371
pixels, 78, 103-104, 371
**pixels per inch (ppi),
104-106**
planning Web sites, 245-247
audience analysis, 254-256
content, 249-250
copyrights, 251-253
goal analysis, 260-262
licenses, 253
media elements, 254
nontransient information,
247-248
releases, 253
transient information, 248
**platforms, cross-platform
issues, 257-258**
plug-ins, 285-286, 371
Shockwave, 373
storing, 286
PMultiple Masters fonts, 72
**PNG (Portable Network
Graphics), 138-139, 371**
point size, 67, 371
points, 371
polygonal meshes, 371
**Portable Network Graphics
format (PNG), 138-139**
positive space, 6-9, 371
PostScript fonts, 71-72, 371
PostScript graphics, *see*
vector graphics
**ppi (pixels per inch),
104-106, 371**
**practicality in Web page
design, 310**
Premiere, 371, 382
primary colors, 371
additive, 32, 361
subtractive, 31, 374
printer resolutions, 84
**printing, four-color
process, 31, 367**
**procedural mapping, 214,
219, 371**

**production phase (Web site
development), 270-271**
**progressive JPEG, 137-138,
372**
**projection, casting shad-
ows, 39-40**
protocols
FTP, 290-291, 367
Gopher, 291
Telnet, 292-293
**psychology of color
associations, 43-44**
public domain, 372

Q-R

QFX software, 379
Quark Web site, 383
Quarterdeck Corp.
Hijaak Pro, 379
WebAuthor, 384
Web site, 379
Quest, 382
QuickTime format, 350, 372

radiant light, 211, 372
radiosity, 203-204, 372
**RAM (Random Access
Memory), 372**
**raster graphics, 78, 101-103,
126-127**
attributes, 345
bit depth, 111-116
palettized color, 121-124
true-color, 11-121
browser-safe palettes,
125-126
device dependency, 104-105
file sizes, 126
flatland environments, 129
layering, 127-135
pixels, 103-104
resolution, 105-109
scaling, 107-110, 115
sizing, 109-110, 127-135
screen displays, 80

sprites, 165
  acceleration, 169-171
  deceleration, 169-171
  linking multiple paths, 172-174
  paths, 167-169
  rotation, 172
  vector graphics, compared, 80-83
raster-based animation, 149
rasterizing vector images, 97-99
Ray Dream Designer, 380
ray-tracing, 203-204, 372
RCA-type cable connectors, 372
reflected light, 28-31, 366
reflectivity, 215-216, 372
releases, 253, 372
remapping palettes, 123-124, 372
renderers, 372
rendering
  engines, 199, 372
    Gouroud, 201-202, 367
    Phong, 202, 371
    radiosity, 372
    ray-tracing, 203-204
    wireframe, 200, 375
  environments, 204-206
    cameras, 206-209
    lighting, 209-212
    object textures, 213-218
resolution, 84-86, 365-368, 372
  monitors, 84
  raster graphics, 105-109
RGB (red, green, blue) color model, 54, 372
  converting to hexadecimal, 57-58
rhodopsin, 372
rods, 372
rotation (animation), 172, 221
rotoscoping, 180
rules, HTML markup, 5

S

S-video cables, 372
sampling, 113-114, 324, 344, 372
  bit depth, 330-331
  file sizes, 333
  monaural, 331
  preparation, 334-335
  rates, 325-330, 373
  stereo, 331
sans serif fonts, 65-66, 373
saturation, 22, 34, 373
Sausage Software, 384
scaling raster images, 107-110, 115
scan lines, 373
scripting, browser support, 286
search engines
  Gopher, 367
  Yahoo!, 375
serif fonts, 65-66, 373
servers (FTP), 290
SGML (Standard Generalized Markup Language), 373
shade, 373
shadows, 373
  behind text, 73-75
  casting
    light source, 36-38
    projection, 39-40
Shockwave, 95, 373
Simple Text editor, 373
SIT files, 373
site maps, 373
sites, 373
  design, 3-5
    balance, 10-13
    browser issues, 19-23
    communicative power, 17-19
    consistency, 15-17
    eyeflow, 5-6
    icons, 24-25
    impact on audience, 4
    negative space, 6-9

    positive space, 6-9
    tone, 9
    visual appeal, 13-14
  development, 243-244, 256
    applications, 256
    audience analysis, 254-256
    authors, 250
    content, 249-250, 277
    copyrights, 251-253
    development teams, 276-277
    implementation phase, 271
    licenses, 253
    maintenance, 271-272
    media elements, 254
    networking concerns, 278
    nontransient information, 247-248
    platforms, 257-258
    production phase, 270-271
    releases, 253
    resources, 258
    supporting materials, 277
    tools, 258
    transient information, 248
  FTP, accessing, 291
  goal analysis, 260-262
  hardware, 258-259
    machine parameters, 260
    network access, 259-260
    platforms, 260
  home pages, 280, 368
  navigating, 15-17, 280-282
  planning, 245-247
  splash pages, 280, 303-305
  WWW, 381
    3*D EYE Software, 380
    Adobe, 378-382
    Aimtech, 382
    Alien Skin Software, 379
    Allen Communication, 382

Caligari, 380
Corel, 378
Deneba Software, 378
Denim Software, 382
Electric Image, 380
Equilibrium Software, 378
formZ, 380
Fractal Design, 378-380
FutureWave, 380
GoldDisk, 380-382
IBM, 384
InContext, 383
Internet Explorer, 384
JASC, Inc., 378
Kinetix, 380-381
Macromedia, 379-381
Metatools, 379-381
mFactory, 383
Netscape, 384
Newtek, 381
Oracle, 383
QFX, 379
Quark, 383
Quarterdeck Corp., 379
RGB-to-hex converters, 58
Specular, 379-381
Spyglass Mosaic, 384
Strata3D, 379, 381
sizing raster images, 107-110, 127-135
SND (System 7 sound file) format, 337, 374
SoftImage, 381
SoftQuad software, 384
software
3D Studio, 380
3D Studio Max, 361, 381
animation packages
2D animation, 155
3D animation, 155-157
choosing, 158
Animator Studio, 362, 380
Astound, 382
Authorware, 363, 382
Backstage, 363
Backstage Designer, 384
Black Box, 379
browsers, 19, 384

applet support, 287
cache, 284-285
functions, 278-284
preference settings, 284
scripting support, 286
Bryce2, 381
Canvas, 378
Collage, 379
CorelDRAW! 6, 378
Debabelizer, 365, 378
Design Painter, 365
Director, 366, 381-383
Electric Image, 380
formZ, 380
Fractal Design Expression, 378
Fractal Design Painter, 378
FreeHand, 367, 379
FrontPage, 367, 384
FutureSplash Animator, 380
helper applications, 288
Hijaak Pro, 379
Hot Dog, 384
HoTMetaL Pro, 384
IconAuthor, 382
Illuminaire, 382
Illustrator, 368, 378
Immedia, 383
InContext Spider, 383
Infini-D, 381
Jamba, 382
Kai's Power Goo, 379
Kai's Power Tools, 379
LightWave 3D, 381
MediaForge, 383
MediaPaint, 379
mTropolis, 383
NetObjects Fusion, 384
Oracle Media Objects, 383
PageMill, 371, 383
Paint Shop Pro, 378
PhotoPaint, 378
Photoshop, 371, 378
plug-ins, 285-286
Premiere, 371, 382
QFX, 379
Quest, 382
Ray Dream Designer, 380
Shockwave, 95

SoftImage, 381
SoundEdit 16, 381
SoundForge, 381
Studio Pro, 381
Stuffit Expander, 373
Topas, 374
TriSpectives, 380
TrueSpace2, 380
VideoShop, 382
WebAuthor, 384
WebMotion, 380
see also applications
solid models, 194, 373
sound, 317-319
attributes, 345
compression, 338
decibels, 365
degradation, 322-323
digital audio, 319-322, 339-340, 366
advantages, 322-324
DAT (Digital Audio Tape), 366
file sizes, 333
monaural, 331
sampling, 324-335
stereo, 331
file formats, 337-338
MIDI, 320-322, 33-340, 370
VOC, 373
frequencies, 325-329, 367
monaural, 369
pitch, 371
streaming, 338-339
SoundBlaster Vocal Files (VOC), 338, 373
SoundEdit 16, 381
SoundForge, 381
source images (animation)
clip-art, 179
cut-outs, 178
Specular
Collage software, 379
Infini-D, 381
Web site, 379-381
splash pages, designing, 280, 303-305
splines, 373

spotlights, 212, 373
sprites, 151, 373
  motion
    acceleration, 169-171
    deceleration, 169-171
    linking multiple paths,
      172-174
    paths, 167-169
    rotation, 172
  raster sprites, 165
  vector sprites, 165-166
Spyglass Mosaic Web site,
  384
Standard Generalized
  Markup Language
  (SGML), 373
static frame animation,
  163-164
static images, 373
static media, 248
stereo sound, 331-333
stereoscopic vision,
  354-355, 373
storing plug-ins, 286
storyboards, 373
Strata3D
  MediaForge, 383
  MediaPaint, 379
  Studio Pro, 381
  VideoShop, 382
  Web site, 379-381
streaming, 373
  audio, 338-339
  video, 351-352
Studio Pro, 381
Stuffit Expander, 373
subtraction, 374
subtractive colors, 28-31,
  374
Sun Audio (AU) format, 337
surface mapping, 213-214,
  374
  limitations, 218
surface models, 192-199,
  374
  Boolean operations,
    197-199
  surface meshes, 195-197
symmetrical balance, 10,
  374

synthesis (MIDI), 336, 374
System 7 sound files, 337
system palettes, 374

T

Tagged Image File Format
  (TIFF), 138, 374
tags (HTML), 5, 361
technical design, 268
  directory structure, 270
  site layout, 269
Telnet, 292-293
text
  ASCII, 362
  hypertext, 368
  styles, 64
  typography, 59-65
    alignment, 69
    case, 63
    choosing, 75
    computer fonts, 70-73
    fonts, 61
    leading, 69, 369
    letter spacing, 68
    point size, 67
    shadows, 73-75
    typefaces, 65-66
    weights, 68
text editors, 374
texture, rendering, 213
  bumpiness, 217-218
  opacity/transparency, 216
  procedural mapping, 214
  surface mapping, 213-214
TIFF (Tagged Image File
  Format), 138, 374
tiles, 374
tiling backgrounds, 74
tinting, 374
tone (Web site design), 9,
  374
tools (development), 258
  animation, 380-381
  authoring, 382-383
  graphics, 378-379
  sound, 381
  video, 382

Topas, 374
transient information, 374
translation (animation),
  167, 374
  motion
    defining over time, 169
    paths, 167-169
    rotation, 172
translucence, 374
transparency, 177, 216, 374
transparent GIFs, 136
triad color schemes, 46, 374
TriSpectives, 380
true-color images, 114-121
TrueSpace2, 380
TrueType fonts, 72, 374
typefaces, 65-66
typefonts, see fonts
typography, 59-65, 374
  case, 63
  fonts, 61
    alignment, 69
    choosing, 75
    computer fonts, 70-73
    horizontal space, 68,
      368
    leading, 69
    letter spacing, 68, 369
    monospaced, 369
    point sizes, 67
    sans serif, 65-66, 373
    serif, 65-66, 373
    vector, 375
    weight, 68, 375
  shadows, 73-75
  styling, 64
  typefaces, 65-66

U-V

ungrouping vector graph-
  ics, 92
Uniform Resource Locators
  (URLs), 278
union operations, 374
uppercase, design consid-
  erations, 63

URLs (Uniform Resource Locators), 278-279, 375
Usenet newsgroups, 289-290, 370
user controls (Web page design), 307
user interfaces, designing, 266-268

values (colors), 33
VBScript, 375
VDOLive format, 375
vector fonts, 70-72, 375
    Multiple Master, 72, 370
    PostScript, 72
    TrueType, 72
vector graphics, 77-80, 375
    advantages, 86-87
    anti-aliasing, 88
    Boolean operations, 93-94
    closed areas, 89-90
    depth, 82
    device independence, 86
    disadvantages, 87-88
    fills, 89-90
    grouping, 91-92
    joining elements, 92
    raster graphics, compared, 80-83
    rasterizing, 97-99
    resolution, 84-86
    screen displays, 80-81
    sprites, 165-166
        acceleration, 169-171
        deceleration, 169-171
        linking multiple paths, 172-174
        paths, 167-169
        rotation, 172
    ungrouping, 92
    Web displays, 95-96
vector-based animation, 149
video, 341-342
    animation, compared, 345-346
    attributes, 345

compression, 348-349
file sizes, 342-343
formats
    AVI, 349-350
    MPEG, 350-351
    QuickTime, 350
frames, 343
generating, 346-347
helper applications, 351-352
image bit depth, 344
sampling, 344
software, 382
streaming, 351-352
video capture boards, 347
VideoShop, 382
viewing animations, plug-ins, 150
viewpoints
    3D animation, 189-191
    virtual reality environments, 357-358
views
    camera, 364
    orthographic, 206, 370
    perspective, 207
virtual reality, 353-358
    costs, 358
    depth perception, 355
    environments, 357
        coordinate systems, 357
        rendering, 359-360
        viewpoints, 357-358
    stereoscopic vision, 355
    VRML, 358-359
Virtual Reality Modeling Language (VRML), 358-359
visible light spectrum, 29, 375
vision, 44-45
    persistence, 145
visual appeal (Web site design), 13-14, 310-311, 375
visual flow, 5-6

VOC (SoundBlaster Vocal) files, 338, 373
VRML (Virtual Reality Modeling Language), 358-359, 375

W-X-Y-Z

warm colors, 41-43, 375
WAV (Windows Waveform) format, 338, 375
Web, see World Wide Web
WebAuthor, 384
WebMotion, 380
welding points, 93
white space, 6-9
Windows Waveform (WAV) format, 338, 375
Windows Bitmap (BMP) format, 138, 375
wireframe models, 191-192, 375
wireframe rendering, 200, 375
WordPad, 375
World Wide Web (WWW), 375
    graphics, 80
    sites, 373
        delivery systems, 258-260
        development, 256-258
        goals, 260-262
        navigating, 280-282
    see also sites

Yahoo!, 375
yaw, 359, 375

ZIP files, 375

Laura Lemay's Guide to Sizzling Web Site Design

—Laura Lemay & Molly Holzschlag

This book is more than just a guide to the hottest Web sites. It's a behind-the-scenes look at how those sites were created. Web surfers and publishers alike will find this book an insightful guide to some of the most detailed pages. The latest Web technologies are discussed in detail, showing readers how the technologies have been applied. Readers also learn how they can implement those features on their own Web pages. The CD-ROM includes source code from the book, images, scripts, and more.

$45.00 USA/$63.95 CDN   *Casual–Accomplished*
1-57521-221-8   *400 pages*   *Internet-Web Publishing*

Web Publishing Unleashed, Professional Reference Edition

—William Stanek, et al.

Web Publishing Unleashed, Professional Reference Edition is a completely new version of *Web Publishing Unleashed*, combining coverage of all Web development technologies in one volume. The book now includes entire sections on JavaScript, Java, VBScript, and ActiveX, plus expanded coverage of multimedia Web development, adding animation, developing intranet sites, Web design, and much more! The book includes a 200-page reference section. The CD-ROM includes a selection of HTML, Java, CGI, and scripting tools for Windows/Mac, plus Sams.net Web Publishing Library and electronic versions of top Web publishing books.

$59.99 USA/$84.95 CDN   *Intermediate–Advanced*
1-57521-198-X   *1,200 pages*   *Internet-Web Publishing*

Web Programming Unleashed

—Bob Breedlove, et al.

This comprehensive tome explores all aspects of the latest technology craze—Internet programming. Programmers can turn to the proven expertise of the *Unleashed* series for accurate, day-and-date information on this hot new programming subject. This book gives timely, expert advice on ways to exploit the full potential of the Internet. The CD-ROM includes complete source code for all applications in the book, additional programs with accompanying source code, and several Internet application resource tools.

$49.99 USA/$70.95 CDN   *Accomplished–Expert*
1-57521-117-3   *1,056 pages*   *Internet-Programming*

HTML 3.2 & CGI Unleashed, Professional Reference Edition

—John December & Mark Ginsburg

Readers will learn the logistics of how to create compelling, information-rich Web pages that grab readers' attention and keep them returning for more. This comprehensive professional instruction and reference guide for the World Wide Web covers all aspects of the development processes, implementation, tools, and programming. The CD-ROM features coverage of planning, analysis, design, HTML implementation, and gateway programming. The book covers the new HTML 3.2 specification, plus new topics such as Java, JavaScript, and ActiveX. It also features coverage of planning, analysis, design, HTML implementation, and gateway programming.

$59.99 USA/$84.95 CDN   *Accomplished–Expert*
1-57521-177-7   *900 pages*   *Internet-Programming*

Java Developer's Reference

—Mike Cohn, et al.

This is the informational, resource-packed development package for professional developers. It explains the components of the Java Development Kit (JDK) and the Java programming language. Everything needed to program Java is included within this comprehensive reference, making it the tool that developers will turn to over and over again for timely and accurate information on Java and the JDK. The CD-ROM contains source code from the book and powerful utilities. The book includes tips and tricks for getting the most from Java and your Java programs. It also contains complete descriptions of all the package classes and their individual methods.

$59.99 USA/$84.95 CDN   *Accomplished–Expert*
1-57521-129-7   *1,200 pages*   *Internet-Programming*

Java Unleashed, Second Edition

—Michael Morrison, et al.

Java Unleashed, Second Edition is an expanded and updated version of the largest, most comprehensive Java book on the market. This book covers Java, Java APIs, JavaOS, just-in-time compilers, and more. The CD-ROM includes sample code, examples from the book, and bonus electronic books.

$49.99 USA/$70.95 CDN   *Intermediate–Advanced*
1-57521-197-1   *1,200 pages*   *Internet-Programming*

JavaScript 1.1 Developer's Guide

—Wes Tatters

JavaScript 1.1 Developer's Guide is the professional reference for enhancing commercial-grade Web sites with JavaScript. Packed with real-world JavaScript examples, the book shows the developer how to use JavaScript to glue together Java applets, multimedia programs, plug-ins, and more on a Web site. The CD-ROM includes source code and powerful utilities.

$49.99 USA/$70.95 CDN   *Accomplished–Expert*
1-57521-084-3   *600 pages*   *Internet-Programming*

Visual Basic for Applications Unleashed

—Paul McFedries

Combining power and ease of use, Visual Basic for Applications (VBA) is the common language for developing macros and applications across all Microsoft Office components. With the format of the best-selling *Unleashed* series, users can master the intricacies of this popular language and exploit the full power of VBA. This book covers user interface design, database programming, networking programming, Internet programming, and stand-alone application creation. The CD-ROM is packed with the author's sample code, sample spreadsheets, databases, projects, templates, utilities, and evaluation copies of third-party tools and applications.

$49.99 USA/$70.95 CDN   *Accomplished–Expert*
0-672-31046-5   *800 pages*   *Programming*

Add to Your Sams.net Library Today
with the Best Books for Internet Technologies

ISBN	Quantity	Description of Item	Unit Cost	Total Cost
1-57521-221-8		Laura Lemay's Guide to Sizzling Web Site Design (Book/CD-ROM)	$45.00	
1-57521-198-X		Web Publishing Unleashed, Professional Reference Edition (Book/CD-ROM)	$59.99	
1-57521-117-3		Web Programming Unleashed (Book/CD-ROM)	$49.99	
1-57521-177-7		HTML 3.2 & CGI Unleashed, Professional Reference Edition (Book/CD-ROM)	$59.99	
1-57521-129-7		Java Developer's Reference (Book/CD-ROM)	$59.99	
1-57521-197-1		Java Unleashed, Second Edition (Book/CD-ROM)	$49.99	
1-57521-084-3		JavaScript 1.1 Developer's Guide (Book/CD-ROM)	$49.99	
0-672-31046-5		Visual Basic for Applications Unleashed (Book/CD-ROM)	$49.99	
		Shipping and Handling: See information below.		
		TOTAL		

Shipping and Handling: $4.00 for the first book, and $1.75 for each additional book. If you need to have it NOW, we can ship product to you in 24 hours for an additional charge of approximately $18.00, and you will receive your item overnight or in two days. Overseas shipping and handling adds $2.00. Prices subject to change. Call between 9:00 a.m. and 5:00 p.m. EST for availability and pricing information on latest editions.

201 W. 103rd Street, Indianapolis, Indiana 46290

1-800-428-5331 — Orders   1-800-835-3202 — FAX   1-800-858-7674 — Customer Service

Book ISBN 1-57521-243-9